G. K. Chesterton, a Criticism

My brother, Cecil Edward Chesterton, was born when I was about five years old; and, after a brief pause, began to argue. He continued to argue to the end; for I am sure that he argued energetically with the soldiers among whom he died, in the last glory of the Great War. It is reported of me that when I was told that I possessed a brother, my first thought went to my interminable taste for reciting verses, and that I said, "That's all right; now I shall always have an audience." If I did say this, I was in error. My brother was by no means disposed to be merely an audience; and frequently forced the function of an audience upon me. More frequently still, perhaps, it was a case of there being simultaneously two orators and no audience. We argued throughout our boyhood and youth until we became the pest of our whole social circle. We shouted at each other across the table, on the subject of Parnell or Puritanism or Charles the First's head, until our nearest and dearest fled at our approach, and we had a desert around us. And though it is not a matter of undiluted pleasure to recall having been so horrible a nuisance, I am rather glad in other ways that we did so early thrash out our own thoughts on almost all the subjects in the world. I am glad to think that through all those years we never stopped arguing; and we never once quarrelled. G.K. CHESTERTON, 1936

G. K. Chesterton
A Criticism

by

Cecil Chesterton

Michael W. Perry, Editor

Foreword by Aidan Mackey
Introduction by Brocard Sewell
"Remembering Cecil" by G.K. Chesterton
"The Secret People" by G.K. Chesterton
"Why I am not a Socialist" by G.K. Chesterton
"About Chesterton and Belloc" by H.G. Wells
"On Wells and a Glass of Beer" by G.K. Chesterton
"Belloc and Chesterton" by G. Bernard Shaw
"The Last of the Rationalists" by G.K. Chesterton
"Gilbert K. Chesterton" by A.G. Gardiner

INKLING BOOKS   SEATTLE   2007

Description
This book contains the full text of *G.K. Chesterton, a Criticism*, which was published under that title in 1908 by Alston Rivers Ltd., London, as well as under the title *Gilbert K. Chesterton, a Criticism* in 1909 by John Lane Co., New York. Neither edition gave the author's name, soon known to be Cecil Chesterton, the only brother of G.K. Chesterton. This Centennial Edition adds new material, including extensive footnotes by the editor. In the front matter it includes a Foreword by Aidan Mackey, a Preface by Brocard Sewell, and a short biography of Cecil by Gilbert. In the appendices it includes a 1908 debate G.K. Chesterton had in *The New Age* with H.G. Wells and G. Bernard Shaw, as well as a description of Chesterton by A.G. Gardiner, his editor at the *Daily News*.

Copyright Notice

Dedication
The first edition bore a dedication to Marie Louise Chesterton, mother of Gilbert and Cecil: "Dedicated to the Cleverest Woman in London, M. L. C."

Publisher's Note
This book contains four graphics digitally created from the four photographs in the first edition, two additional photographs, title pages from the 1908 and 1909 editions, and four magazine banners. The cover photo, which shows Gilbert and Cecil on the far left, is courtesy of Aidan Mackey. The font used throughout is Adobe Arno Pro.

Library Cataloging Data
Title: *G.K. Chesterton, a Criticism* (originally published anonymously)
Author: Cecil [Edward] Chesterton (1879–1918)   Editor: Michael W. Perry (1948–).
Other Authors: G. K. [Gilbert Keith] Chesterton (1874–1936), A.G. [Alfred George] Gardiner (1865–1946), Aidan Mackey (1922–), Brocard Sewell (1912–2000), George Bernard Shaw (1856–1950), and H.G. [Herbert George] Wells (1866–1946).
Publisher: Seattle: Inkling Books, 2007.
Description: 179 pages, 12 graphics, index.
Size: 6 x 9 x 0.4 inches, 229 x 152 x 11 mm. Weight: 0.6 pounds, 274 grams.
Library of Congress Control Number: 2007928890
Call Number: PR4453.C4   958.C525
Subject: G. K. Chesterton (1874–1936), Cecil Chesterton (1879–1918), Great Britain—History—20th century.
BISAC Subject Headings: BIO000000, BIOGRAPHY & AUTOBIOGRAPHY/GENERAL; LIT004120, LITERARY CRITICISM/EUROPEAN/ENGLISH, IRISH, SCOTTISH, WELSH; HIS015000 HISTORY / EUROPE / GREAT BRITAIN
Paperback—ISBN-13: 978-1-58742-059-7   ISBN-10: 1-58742-059-7
Hardback—ISBN-13: 978-1-58742-060-3   ISBN-10: 1-58742-060-0

Publisher Information
Published in the United States of America on acid-free paper by Inkling Books.
Centennial Edition, Second Printing, August 2007.
Internet: http://www.InklingBooks.com/

CONTENTS

EDITORIAL REMARKS *Michael W. Perry,* 6

FOREWORD *Aidan Mackey,* 7

INTRODUCTION *Brocard Sewell* 11

REMEMBERING CECIL *G. K. Chesterton* 19

PREFACE 25

1 ORIGINS 27

2 THE FIRST PHASE 39

3 A CRITIC OF LETTERS 53

4 THE DRIFT TOWARDS ORTHODOXY 63

5 THE ASSAULT ON THE MODERNS 75

6 G.K.C. AS ANTI-LIBERAL 91

7 A TELLER OF TALES 105

8 THE GLADIATOR AS ARTIST 115

9 THE PERSONAL EQUATION............................ 125

A THE SECRET PEOPLE *G. K. Chesterton,* 133

B WHY I AM NOT A SOCIALIST *G. K. Chesterton,* 135

C ABOUT CHESTERTON AND BELLOC *H. G. Wells.* 141

D ON WELLS AND A GLASS OF BEER *G. K. Chesterton* 147

E BELLOC AND CHESTERTON *G. Bernard Shaw* 151

F THE LAST OF THE RATIONALISTS *G.K. Chesterton* 161

G GILBERT K. CHESTERTON *A. G. Gardiner* 167

INDEX...175

Editorial Remarks

Michael W. Perry,

WELCOME to the Centennial Edition of Cecil Chesterton's marvellous biography of his more famous brother, published in time for the one hundredth anniversary its original release in 1908.

This newly typeset Centennial Edition offered an excellent opportunity to give readers much more than a mere duplication of the original. Aidan Mackey, author of books such as *The Wisdom of Chesterton*, graciously provided a Foreword, and Brocard Sewell, who worked with Gilbert at *G.K's Weekly*, provided an Introduction. (Each wrote his contribution a number of years before this edition, probably in the late 1980s, but I've not altered their words to fit the later publication date.)

It's only fair that Cecil should have a biography too, so I've included the moving tribute Gilbert wrote as an introduction to Cecil's posthumously published *A History of the United States* (1919), giving it a new title, "Remembering Cecil." I've also added as an appendix a wonderful description of Gilbert written by his friend A.G. Gardiner and published in his *Prophets, Priests and Kings* the same year as Cecil's biography (1908), along with the articles in the famous 1908 Chesterbelloc debate about Socialism that Gilbert had in the pages of *The New Age* with H.G. Wells and Bernard Shaw.

I've not changed the words in the original, but I have modernized the typography to avoid confusing modern readers. Books and magazines have their titles italicized rather than inside quotation marks. I've also added the explanatory footnotes and, when possible, I traced down the source of quotations. Finally, I've included the pictures from Cecil's book as well as other sources, well aware that, even with digital enhancement, some may not turn out as well as I would like, given the limitations of printing technology. They are there so readers can watch Gilbert grow from a tall and slender boy to a quite substantial man.

Keep in mind that this book really is, as the title says, "a criticism." Almost from the cradle, Gilbert and Cecil debated one another and that flavours this biography. In a few places where I thought Cecil was being unfair, I note that in a footnote. Otherwise, I leave it to you to decide which is right. I also came to suspect that Cecil, like many brothers of a genius, did not fully appreciate Gilbert's brilliance and intellectual independence. In Chapter 6 he argues that, if Gilbert can't remain a liberal, then he must become a Tory. Having the advantage of hindsight, I believe Chesterton always remained his inimitable himself, not fitting into anyone's box—not even that of his well-meaning brother.

FOREWORD

Aidan Mackey,

Aidan Mackey is a bookseller and the author of a number of books on Chesterton and his writings, including *Mr. Chesterton Comes to Tea* (1978), *G.K. Chesterton* (1985), *The Wisdom of G.K. Chesterton* (1986), *A Smaller Chesterton: Being a Selected List of Chestertonian Rarities* (1989), and *A Richness of G.K. Chesterton* (1989)

IT has been for many years a strong wish of mine to see this, the first of the scores of books to be written on G.K. Chesterton, re-issued. Its interest rests much less in its primacy or authorship, although both of these points do add something to its value, than in its quality as a study and piece of literary criticism. It is no mere curiosity for the collector, nor is it by any stretch of the imagination, merely an exercise in brotherly adulation—witness the hammering which Cecil gives to, for instance, the essay on Bryon and to some aspects of *Robert Browning*.

For a study written so early in G.K.C.'s career, Cecil is remarkably percipient and at times almost prophetic, as in his suggestion that Gilbert should create a "philosophical detective story... a sort of transcendental Sherlock Holmes who probes mysteries, not by attention to facts and clues, but by understanding the spiritual atmosphere." He sees Basil Grant, in *The Club of Queer Trades*, as being the forerunner of such a detective. It is probable that, had he lived, Cecil Chesterton would have worked more in the field of politics than of literature, but many passages in this book show us his strength as a critic. Writing of Chesterton's transfer from art to writing, he has this to say, "That Mr. Chesterton has considerable gifts as a draftsman no competent critic who studies the illustrations to Mr. Belloc's *Emmanuel Burden* will be disposed to deny. But it was not in that direction that his deepest impulses led. He proved this by the fact that he shrank from the technical toils of art as he has never shrunk from the technical toils of writing."

When Cecil wrote this assessment and prognosis, Gilbert was becoming a famous figure in the literary world, but the major works of religious and social philosophy—*Orthodoxy, What's Wrong with the World, Eugenics and Other Evils, The Outline of Sanity, The Everlasting Man, The Thing*, and others—had not then emerged to demonstrate that he was so much more than a literary lion. **He knowingly and cheerfully sacrificed a large measure of support from academic and establishment quarters because of his robust (one might almost say, uproarious) espousal of causes which were not then popular.** Had his Catholicism been a little more deferential and unobtrusive, had his attacks on Capitalism, political corruption and public humbug been less insistent and penetrating, all may have been well, but as it was he was largely refused acceptance, as may be gathered from the almost invariably brief, superficial and dismissive entries under his name in reference books and literary surveys until a very few years ago.

This rejection, however, was only on the part of the establishment, and not by any means on the part of the reading and thinking public. Even apart from his novels and the Father Brown stories, many of his books, *Orthodoxy, St. Francis of Assisi, Charles Dickens, A Short History of England, The Everlasting Man,* and the *Collected Poems* were reprinted time after time. Publishers, naturally, print only what they expect will readily sell, and it is significant that at the height of paper rationing in the late 1940s, nearly a score of his books were in print. I can think of no other author of whom that was true—certainly not of George Bernard Shaw, then in his heyday.

P.J. Kavanagh, in his admirable introduction to *The Bodley Head G.K. Chesterton,* put it well:

> He seems always to be addressing a large and friendly audience, past the heads of the 'moderns', the 'professors', the 'scientists' (or, worst of all, the 'modern, scientific professors') and telling a receptive gathering what it half-knew already and would now, after his explanation, agree to be obviously true. Possibly these are "the people of England, that never have spoken yet" and he is speaking for them, as well as to them. Very possibly: 'modernist' Ezra Pound was heard to sigh, despairingly, "Chesterton *is* the mob!"

The enormous revival of interest in and tribute to Chesterton which we are now witnessing may, therefore, be seen as some kind of long overdue reparation from 'official' quarters, and a recognition that ordinary people, who never stopped reading and profiting from his thought, were right. This fresh and very welcome realisation of his stature was well demonstrated in a recent and highly important review in *The Times* of *The Bodley Head G.K. Chesterton.* The reviewer, Alan Massie, wrote:

> Chesterton has suffered from... the English distrust of intellect, and tendency to prefer Teutonic muddiness to Latin lucidity.... Mr. Kavanagh has provided us with all the evidence required.... no one can henceforth pretend that Chesterton was a flashy miniaturist or a whimsical eccentric or a delightful humourist not to be taken seriously. He has got the 'character' out of the way in order to allow us to delight in the strenuous intellect, humane judgment, and noble sense.

The full restoration of G.K. Chesterton to his rightful place in English thought and letters is now well underway. As people turn to the study of his thought and work, this study by his brother will remain among the essential sources even though Cecil was not always entirely accurate, especially on matters of chronology.

A much more important addition is that of the fine introductory essay contributed by Brocard Sewell, O. Carm., of whom Colin Wilson wrote:

> When, sometime in the 21st century, the *Cambridge History of English Literature* gets around to issuing its volumes on the 20th century, I think it highly likely that the name of Father Brocard Sewell will figure in the index. He is, to begin with, the author of a minor classic of autobiography, *My Dear Time's Waste*, beautifully written, and containing an evocative account of the literary scene between the wars, as witnessed at first hand by the young Michael Sewell, who was G.K. Chesterton's assistant on *G.K.'s Weekly*. But he has also, as the editor of *The Aylesford Review*, played his own distinctive part in the history of literature since the mid-1950's. During the thirteen years of its existence, *The Aylesford Review* was, together with Miron Grindea's *Adam*, probably among the best small literary magazines in the whole of Europe; Fr. Sewell became a kind of literary liaison man, bringing together writers as different as Henry Williamson, Ann Quin, Bernadine Bishop, Laura Del Rivo, Michael Hastings, and myself… (his) friends and proteges constituted in themselves an independent literary movement, united by his enormous and disinterested passion for literature.

As well as assisting G.K. Chesterton on *G.K.'s Weekly*, Brocard Sewell worked for several years with H.D.C. Pepler and Eric Gill at St. Dominic's Press, Ditchling, Common. His own works include the book of essay, *Like Black Swans*, in which he considers such people as Baron Corvo, Vincent McNabb, Henry Williamson, Montague Summers, H.D.C. Pepler, the contrast between Thomas Hardy and G.K. Chesterton, etc; *The Slender Tress, a Study of Alice Meynell;* In the *Dorian Mode, a Life of John Gray;* a symposium, under his editorship, on *Henry Williamson, the Man and his Writings;* and the autobiography, *My Dear Time's Waste*, of which an extended version is in preparation; and an excellent life of Cecil Chesterton, of which only a shortened version, now out of print, has yet been published.

Gilbert Chesterton at 13

INTRODUCTION

Brocard Sewell

Brocard Sewell is the religious and pen name of Michael Seymour Sewell (1912–2000), a British Carmelite monk. He authored and edited many books, including *Cecil Chesterton* (1975) and *G.K's Weekly: An Appraisal* (1990). He first began to work with Chesterton in 1926 at *G.K's Weekly*, and later wrote of the experience: "When he appeared in the office our editor was always in genial mood, for he enjoyed being in London, and his conversation was of a rare brilliance and highly entertaining."[1]

WHEN in 1908 Cecil Chesterton published this book, the first critical study of his older brother Gilbert Chesterton's work, his brother had published, apart from a mass of 'occasional' journalism, only *Greybeard's at Play, The Wild Knight and Other Poems, The Napoleon of Notting Hill, Robert Browning, Charles Dickens,* and *Heretics. Orthodoxy* was not published until later in 1908, and *Bernard Shaw* in 1909. However, the religious philosophy sketched out in some detail in *Orthodoxy* had been adumbrated in a more general way in various preceding articles and debates, and his views on Shaw were known in much the same way. So there was a quite sufficient body of work already achieved to make a critical study worth while. Today, nearly eighty years later, the only two of these books that are not now read, except by specialists, are *Greybeards at Play* and *The Wild Knight.*[2] *Heretics* is not much read, I think, but it repays reading; the Browning and Dickens books, *The Napoleon of Notting Hill* and *Orthodoxy* have attained classic status, and unlike many classics, are very widely read.

It has often been said that G.K. Chesterton's writing never again reached the same high level of excellence after his serious illness of 1914; but I doubt if this is true. *The Return of Don Quixote* seems to me a much cleverer and wiser novel than *The Napoleon of Notting Hill,* and *The Everlasting Man* a much more solid work of apologetic than *Orthodoxy.* But these later works Cecil Chesterton never saw. In his Preface to *G.K. Chesterton, a Criticism* he says that much of his brother's best work probably still lies before him, but that he writes this book now because if he waited until his brother was dead, so that he could survey his entire literary output, he might probably be dead himself. As indeed happened, Cecil Chesterton died only ten years later, at the age of thirty-two; his brother lived for almost another thirty years, dying at the age of sixty-two.

In his *Autobiography,* published after his death, but most of it written much earlier, Gilbert Chesterton says that he welcomed his brother's birth because he knew that he would now always have someone to argue with. The argument

1. From his *The Habit of a Lifetime,* quoted in Joseph Pearce, *Wisdom and Innocence* (London: Hodder & Soughton, 1996), 359.

2. These two books were published a month apart in 1900 and are in *G.K. Chesterton's Early Poetry* (Seattle: Inkling, 2004) along with his much better known *The Ballad of the White Horse* (1911).

between the two brothers covered a multitude of topics, and only ceased with Cecil's death. But sometimes the younger brother managed to persuade the elder. Cecil had been a prominent member of the Fabian Society, and was on its executive committee; but somewhere around 1911 he abandoned socialism altogether, in favour of the distributionist economic and social philosophy of Hilaire Belloc, and became an active opponent of socialist ideas.[3] Gilbert followed him into the Distributionist camp soon afterwards. The two brothers were brought up as Unitarians, and later became prominent Anglo-Catholics; which of them was the first to join the Church of England is not clear, but in 1913 Cecil was received into the Roman Catholic church; but another ten years was to elapse before Gilbert made the same move.

A matter on which the brothers differed was what then was spoken and written of as the 'Jewish question.' Their basic attitude to the Jews they acquired at their public school, St. Paul's, as they would have done at any other public school at that time. There is no need to invoke the name of Hilarie Belloc in this connexion; they did not meet Belloc until several years later, and in any case, Belloc's book *The Jews* is a very compassionate and sympathetic document, as is G.K. Chesterton's *The New Jerusalem*. Belloc more than once rebuked Cecil for some of the things about Jews that he allowed to be printed in his paper *The New Witness*, especially the articles written by Frank Hugh O'Donnel, a former Irish nationalist M.P. at Westminister. On this matter, Gilbert Chesterton was a supporter of Zionism; Cecil was not.

In his day Cecil Chesterton was a very well known personality. After working as assistant editor on A.R. Orage's *The New Age*, he made his mark as an acute and polemical political journalist in Hilaire Belloc's weekly paper *The Eye-Witness*, which he took over from Belloc in 1912, changing its name to *The New Witness*. The high point in Cecil Chesterton's too brief career was undoubtedly the part he played in uncovering the Marconi Scandal of 1911–1913. This was a matter of improper behaviour on the part of certain Ministers of the Crown in connexion with certain dealings in Marconi Company shares. Belloc seems to have been the first person to suspect that something crooked was going on, and a number of searching articles were published in *The Eye-Witness*. Even stronger articles then began to appear in *The New Witness*. The ministers accused were Sir Rufus Isaacs, the Attorney General; Mr. Lloyd George, the Chancellor of

---

3. The Fabian Society wanted a gradual evolution into bureaucratically managed Socialism. Building on Catholic ideas, Distributionism wanted to spread the ownership of the means of production as widely as possibly rather than concentrating it in the hands of the State (Socialism) or a wealthy few (Capitalism). And while none of the three systems have become dominant, the increasing educational and training requirements for many jobs have given workers much of the power they would have in owning a business and increasing affluence has lead to a wider ownership of corporations (as stock) and their profits. As Gilbert's debate with Wells and Shaw in the appendices indicates, by 1908 Gilbert was already a powerful critic of Socialism while Cecil remained a supporter. In that area, Gilbert was far ahead of Cecil.

the Exchequer; Mr. Herbert Samuel, Postmaster General; and the Treasurer of the Liberal Party, the Master of Elibank (Lord Murray).

Cecil waited for some action on the part of the Ministers, as, for instance, the issuing of writs for libel. But nothing happened. Eventually a writ for criminal libel was issued by the Crown on behalf of Mr. Godfrey Isaacs, Sir Rufus' brother, who was not a Minister of the Crown but the managing director of the Marconi Company. Godfrey had been strenuously attacked in *The New Witness* for his record as managing director of a whole series of public companies that had never paid their shareholders a dividend, and had eventually gone bankrupt.

In the trial at the Old Bailey in 1913 a great deal of confusion was caused by the mixing up of the accusations against Godfrey Isaacs with the charges Cecil had brought against the Ministers of the Crown. Cecil had meant to conduct his own defence, but, unfortunately, his parents took fright, and prevailed on him to employ as his leading counsel Mr. Ernest Wild, K.C. There can be little doubt that if Cecil had been able to put the Ministers into the witness-box and cross-examine them he would have elicited from them some very dangerous admissions. As it was, Ernest Wild, an able lawyer, did his best, but was far too gentle—as was natural enough in the circumstances—in his cross-examination of the Attorney General.[4]

In the end, the jury returned a verdict in favour of Godfrey Isaacs; but the Judge imposed on Cecil Chesterton, who had fully expected to be sent to prison, a fine of £100, plus costs. The costs were immediately subscribed by his supporters, and he was able, not unreasonably, to claim a moral victory.

In the next issue of *The New Witness* he repeated all the charges he had made against the Ministers, who at this point wisely chose to lie low, rather than initiate any further legal action.

When war with Germany broke out in 1914, Cecil tried to enlist as a private soldier, but was rejected as medically C3.[5] He took himself in hand, and cut down on his drinking, so that towards the end of 1916 he was reclassified as B2, fit for home service only. Determined not to give up, he was later again reclassified, this time as B1, and he then joined the Highland Light Infantry— chosen because of his mother's partly Scots descent—and was sent to France. Soon after Armistice Day 1918 he fell ill with nephritis, brought on by the

---

4. In its June 12, 1933 issue *The New Age* wrote: "If circumstantial evidence were ever sufficient to justify a charge, we do not doubt that in the case of *Mr. Godfrey Isaacs v. Mr. Cecil Chesterton*, the latter and not the former would have won. The case of Mr. Chesterton was admittedly based on circumstances and on such reasonable deductions from them as on the face of the facts any average mind would have felt impelled to draw. Unfortunately, however, for him the circumstances themselves proved insusceptible of any further evidence than their own existence." See also Maisie Ward, *Gilbert Keith Chesterton*, (New York: Sheed & Ward, 1943), 331–362.

5. The Military Service Act of January 1916 classified potential recruits in categories from A1 (the best) to C3 (the worst). Some 40% of recruits were classified C3, so Cecil was far from alone.

hardships of life in the trenches, and died in a military hospital near Boulogne on 6 December 1918.

Marie Louise Chesterton, Cecil's mother—the M.L.C, "the cleverest woman in London"—to whom *G.K. Chesterton, a Criticism* is dedicated—thought that Cecil was the cleverer of her two sons; not quite so bizarre a judgement as it first seems. Cecil was very much his mother's boy. Gilbert hardly mentions his mother at all in his *Autobiography,* where he has a great deal to say about his father. One would guess that Marie Louise actually *ran* the household in Warwick Gardens, in however haphazard a way, while Edward Chesterton pottered about and prosecuted his various hobbies. These different characteristics are clearly to be seen in the children: Gilbert, the ruminative contemplative, Cecil the eager man of action. Of course, Cecil was not a genius, which his brother was; but he was an excellent writer, with a plain, forceful prose style, and he was a first-rate *practical* journalist. Gilbert like to describe himself as a "jolly journalist," but he admitted heartily that he was a bad editor, and of the 'mechanical' side of producing a newspaper he knew nothing. *The New Witness,* of which Gilbert became editor when Cecil joined the Army, was actually *produced* week by week by Mrs. Cecil Chesterton; and when, later, it was revived as *G.K.'s Weekly,* there was an assistant editor who did the donkey work; at first that veteran Fleet Street associate of Cecil's, W.R. Titterton, and then the late Edward Macdonald. If Cecil Chesterton had survived the war, it had been his intention to stand for Parliament, and he would almost certainly have become prominent in our national affairs; and the Distributionist movement, which was not properly organised until 1926, would probably have become as familiar and respected a part of our scene as the Fabian Society.

How are we to estimate Cecil Chesterton as a writer? Certainly he is generally forgotten. His name does not occur in Margaret Drabble's revision of the *Oxford Companion to English Literature,* but he does receive mention in R.C. Churchill's revised edition of *The Concise Cambridge History of English Literature.*

Cecil's first book, *Gladstonian Ghosts,* appeared in 1905. Today it is probably the least readable of his books, because so many of the issues with which it deals are now forgotten.

Party and People: A Criticism of the Recent Elections and their Consequencies (1910) is an interesting book, in which he argues that the House of Lords should be reconstituted as a Second Chamber not based on wealth and privilege, and therefore not prone to mutilate or reject measures of social reform in the interests of the property-owning classes. But, he says, it is the House of Commons that should be the first candidate for reform, and the key to that must be the abolition of the Party System.

In 1911 *Party and People* was followed by *The Party System,* written in collaboration with Hilaire Belloc. This pungent analysis of how we are governed, or misgoverned, made a considerable stir, and the Tory parliamentarian Lord Robert Cecil described it as interesting, picturesque, and exciting, and said that, "The description of the extensive evils of Party Government as we know it is forcible and even brilliant."

The *Party System* is a book of some historical importance, and could well be reprinted; but it would need a sympathetic and knowledgeable editor who could relate it, in his introduction, to parliamentary government today.

Cecil Chesterton's *The Story of Nell Gwyn* also appeared in 1911. This lively and interesting book was attractively produced by its Edinburgh publishers, T.N. Foulis, and has a number of reproductions in colour of portraits of its subject. Cecil was a great admirer of Lord Macaulay's vivid historical writing, though he was far from approving Macaulay's Whig view of history. He had a strong talent for such writing himself, and his subject in this book brings it out. It is full of lively detail that conjuures up scenes at the Drury Lane and Dorset Garden theatres, and at the court of Charles II. An excellent book in every way.

Two wartime books, *The Prussian Hath Said in his Heart* (1914) and *The Perils of Peace* (1916) need not detain us. They are pieces of violent anti-German propaganda, and intemperate exposition of ideas more subtly managed by G.K. Chesterton in his *The Crimes of England.*

Finally in 1919, came the posthumously published *A History of the United States,* which must probably be bracketed with *G.K. Chesterton, a Criticism* as the best thing he wrote. Written when Cecil was in the Army, it certainly contains some errors of fact, which were corrected by Dr. Dennis Brogan in a later edition, published in Everyman's Library in 1940. In his introduction Dr. Brogan says of this book: "It is a deeply personal account of the history of a great political experiment.... There are no dead pages in this book." Unquestionably, it is the most *readable* history of the United States ever written in the English language.

I have left until last the present book, whose new edition we owe to the initiative and good judgment of Mr. Aidan Mackey. It was first published in 1908, with no author's name on the title-page. The knowledgeable would have deduced the authorship from the book's dedication, and I should imagine it was a fairly open secret before long. The book is to some extent a continuation in print of the argument, or arguments, that the two brothers had been conducting almost since Cecil was able to talk. In his sixth chapter, for instance, Cecil, who was at that time a Fabian socialist, shows that his brother was not really what he imagined himself to be, a Liberal, but rather the advocate of a kind of High

Tory democracy, not unlike the ideas put forward by Bolingbroke in *The Idea of a Patriot King.*[6]

Cecil believed that his brother's critical works were not seriously weakened by their lack of academic orthodoxy, but he thought that some of Gilbert's literary habits, such as references to quite ephemeral events or persons, would hinder the books from becoming "durable monuments of a durable fame." The books seem to have survived pretty well, notwithstanding; but there is something in the criticism. Who today would want to waste good time on reading about Joseph McCabe, an ex-Franciscan who was for many years a leading secularist and a supposed expert on matters of science. His claims were thin; but his little book *Twelve Years in a Monastry* is still worth a glance if one comes across it.

In his final chapter Cecil says that his brother's "extraordinary versatility and copiousness of output is beyond question a danger to his position in literature," and that "unless he controls his effervescent desire to write everything that comes into his head, he will never write the best that he might have written." That is shrewd. Possibly Gilbert Chesterton never did write the best things he could have written; all the same, he has not done too badly; fifty years, almost, after his death, he still has a big following and a wide readership; many of his books have recently been reprinted, and in America a project for a collected edition of *all* his works is now getting under way. Critical studies of his work continue to appear; this book of his brother's being still one of the best.

What, then, of Cecil Chesterton's own writing? In the short biographical note that he contributed to *A History of the United States* Gilbert Chesterton wondered whether some of his brother's "pamphlets"—i.e. controversial writings—might not prove to be "permanent pamphlets." Four of his books may yet do so, in my judgement: *G.K. Chesterton, a Criticism, The Story of Nell Gwyn, A History of the United States,* and the collaborated book (with Hilaire Belloc) *The Party System.* Not a bad score for a man who died at the age of thirty-two.

In addition, a splendid anthology could be made from the best of Cecil Chesterton's journalism. From *The New Witness* it would include his essays on Macaulay, Newman, and Stopford Brook, among others; also some of the Open Letters published either in that paper or in *The Eye-Witness* over the signature "Junius." These open letters were a very popular feature. They were addressed to a variety of figures of the day, among them Ramsay MacDonald, Mr. Asquith, C.F.G. Masterman, A South Kensington Property Owner, A Stipendiary Magistrate, and the Reverend F.B. Meyer, a Nonconformist divine whom Cecil regarded as a modern Stiggins.[7] There was even an open letter to His Majesty

---

6. Henry St John, Lord Bolingbroke (1678–1751) championed republicanism over monarchy and his writings influenced the American Revolution.

7. F.B. Meyer (1847–1929) was a well-known Baptist preacher and a friend of the evangelist Dwight Moody. At the time Cecil was writing this book he was pastor of the large Christ Church in Lambeth

the King, the sporting monarch Edward VII. It is to be hoped that he read it, for it is highly appreciative of him. From *The Eye-Witness*, the series of articles on "The Drood Problem," signed "K," would be well worth rescuing. Cecil, like his brother, was a keen Dickensian, and these articles are an important contribution to the continuing discussion of the solution to Dicken's unfinished novel, *The Mystery of Edwin Drood*. Cecil's solution is ingenious, and well argued. But I do not think it is the right solution. Again, Cecil's *New Witness* articles championing the causes of Steinie Morrison, a poor East-End Jew who had been imprisoned for life because there was not enough evidence to hang him, for a murder he had not committed;[8] and Ex-Inspector Syme, who had been wrongfully dismissed, without pension, from the police force; these articles are as interesting today as when they were written.[9]

Cecil's important article on "Israel a Nation," in the *British Review* for May 1913, could well be reprinted, together, perhaps, with the reply from one Paul Goodman that appeared in the next number. And the article on the great scientist and freethinker Thomas Henry Huxley, from the same magazine, is well worth studying. Cecil Chesterton always said that he owed his conversion to Catholicism to having read Huxley's works.

Gilbert Chesterton was too shattered by his brother's death ever to be able to write his biography. "A portrait is impossible;" he wrote, "as a friend he is too near me, and as a hero too far away." But he receives handsome tribute in the many references to him in the *Autobiography*. The matter of a biography of Cecil was ventilated after his death in the correspondence columns of *The New Witness*; but in the end nothing was done. Cecil Chesterton was not entirely the lovable figure that his brother was; in fact, not to put too fine a point upon it, as Mr. Snagsby would say, there was quite a lot about him that was not particularly

---

(central London). Meyer denounced drinking and shut down bars, which would not endear him to Cecil. The fictional Rev. Stiggins is a comical, alcoholic preacher in Charles Dicken's *Pickwick Papers*.

8. In early 1911, Steinie Morrison, a Russian Jew and a thief with five prison sentences for burglary, was arrested for the murder of Leon Beron, an impoverished slum landlord. In a trial that attracted much press attention, all the evidence against him was circumstantial and witnesses on both sides lacked credibility. Yet after only 35 minutes of deliberation, the jury found him guilty and the judge sentenced him to death, a sentence commuted to life by then Home Secretary Winston Churchill.

9. A summary of the 1924 "Report of the Commission appointed to enquire into the case of ex-inspector John Syme (of the Metropolitan Police)" said: "In the early morning of 17th August, 1909, two men were brought into Gerald Road Police Station by two Constables on a charge of willfully and wantonly disturbing a Mrs. Costa of 134 Warwick Street, by pulling the door bell and knocking at the door without lawful excuse. Differences of opinion between Inspector Syme and his superior officers over the nature of the arrest and the responsibility of the Constables concerned with the arrests, led to accusations and recriminations, and the transference of Inspector Syme to North Fulham Station. His further protests and the rehearsing of his case led finally to his challenging the decision of the Home Secretary by threatening to lay his case before Parliament. This was interpreted as insubordination and led to his dismissal on January 10th, 1910. Sitting 14 years later the Commission concluded that though the transfer of Mr. Syme was handled far from judiciously, it was not a wrong for which compensation could be claimed; and wrong was not done to Mr. Syme in dismissing him."

endearing. Many of the references to him in memoirs and biographies of the time are not especially favourable; but usually the writers are members or supporters of the 'Establishment.' It goes without saying that the Marconi Ministers and their biographers either write of him pejoratively or else make no mention of him at all. All the same, he was much loved by his friends, and by many others; and we can admire him for both his moral and physical courage, which never failed. The best appreciations of him are those written by Sir Thomas Beecham—who was one of the directors of *The New Witness*, in his autobiography *A Mingled Chime*—and Bernard Shaw. Shaw's witness will be found in the *Autobiography of Bernard Shaw* assembled by Stanley Weintraub from that sage's miscellaneous writings. Shaw thought Cecil's decision to join the Army absolutely mistaken, and told him so; but Cecil, like Oscar Wilde on another critical occasion, ignored Shaw's advice altogether.[10] Father Vincent McNabb, the great Dominican, loved Cecil almost as a brother. His moving "Open Letter to Private Cecil Chesterton," in *The New Witness* of 26 October 1916, is reprinted in *Francis Thompson and Other Essays* by Father McNabb, published in 1935. Hilaire Belloc said that Father McNabb's sermon at the requiem mass for Cecil Chesterton in a London church on 14 December 1918 was the finest sermon he had ever heard. Sadly, this sermon was not reported, and the text is not extant.

In 1975 the present writer's short biography, *Cecil Chesterton,* was published by St. Albert's Press. This book, now out of print, is a condensation of a much fuller study, of the same title, which remains unpublished. Its corrected typescript is now in the Marion E. Wade Collection (of books and papers of G.K. Chesterton) at Wheaton College, Illinois, where it may be consulted by bona fide students.

---

10. In his *What I Really Wrote about the War* (1930), Shaw had this to say:

Cecil Chesterton, then one of the brightest and cleverest of our young author-journalists.... was on the most cordial personal terms with me, and remained so until his death from trench fever, one of those events which so often brought home with a personal stab the fundamental waste and folly of the whole miserable business....

.... When he visited me for the last time he was in khaki, a sturdy, jolly, deeply sunburnt, hopelessly unsoldierlike figure. Military discipline insists on smartness of dress and elegance of carriage; but Cecil, void of vanity, was incorrigibly careless as to what he wore or how he wore it; and his easy personality defied the sumptuary laws of the British barracks.... It is impossible to describe what I used to feel on such occasions. It was hard enough to see any young man thrown into the common heap of cannon fodder with only the inhuman military excuse that there were plenty of the same sort to replace him; but when the young man, possessing a rare and highly valuable talent, was not replaceable, one's hatred for the war bit fiercely in. However, there was nothing to be done but to keep his spirits up and my own wrath down, and to console myself with his statistical chances of coming back safe and sound. I wished he'd left the job of being a military hero to the poor fellows who were not clever enough to be heroic at anything else; but it was not a point on which I could interfere with another man's conscience. So we parted gaily; and the next I heard of him was that he was dead of the war pestilence against which he was so ill fortified by his anti-Prussian contempt for my vegetarian diet. *Shaw: An Autobiography, 1898–1950,* Stanley Weintraub, ed. (New York: Weybright and Talley, 1970), 101–102.

REMEMBERING CECIL

G.K. Chesterton

THE author of this book, my brother, died in a French military hospital of the effects of exposure in the last fierce fighting that broke the Prussian power over Christendom; fighting for which he had volunteered after being invalided home. Any notes I can jot down about him must necessarily seem jerky and incongruous; for in such a relation memory is a medley of generalisation and detail, not to be uttered in words. One thing at least may fitly be said here. Before he died he did at least two things that he desired. One may seem much greater than the other; but he would not have shrunk from naming them together. He saw the end of an empire that was the nightmare of the nations; but I believe it pleased him almost as much that he had been able, often in the intervals of bitter warfare and by the aid of a brilliant memory, to put together these pages on the history, so necessary and so strangely neglected, of the great democracy which he never patronised, which he not only loved but honoured.[11]

Cecil Edward Chesterton was born on November 12, 1879; and there is a special if a secondary sense in which we may use the phrase that he was born a fighter. It may seem in some sad fashion a flippancy to say that he argued from his very cradle. It is certainly, in the same sad fashion, a comfort, to remember one truth about our relations: that we perpetually argued and that we never quarrelled. In a sense it was the psychological truth, I fancy, that we never quarrelled because we always argued. His lucidity and love of truth kept things so much on the level of logic, that the rest of our relations remained, thank God, in solid sympathy; long before that later time when, in substance, our argument had become an agreement. Nor, I think, was the process valueless; for at least we learnt how to argue in defence of our agreement. But the retrospect is only worth a thought now, because it illustrates a duality which seemed to him, and is, very simple; but to many is baffling in its very simplicity. When I say his weapon was logic, it will be currently confused with formality or even frigidity: a silly superstition always pictures the logician as a pale-faced prig. He was a living proof, a very living proof, that the precise contrary is the case. In fact it is generally the warmer and more sanguine sort of man who has an appetite for abstract definitions and even abstract distinctions. He had all the debating dexterity of a genial and generous man like Charles Fox.[12] He could command that more than legal clarity and closeness which really marked the legal arguments of a genial and generous man like Danton. In his wonderfully courageous public

---

11. This is the introduction to Cecil's *A History of the United States* (New York, George H. Doran, 1919).

12. Charles Fox (1749–1806), Britain's first Foreign Secretary, supported American independence. Georges Jacques Danton (1759–1794) was a leader in the early part of the French Revolution.

speaking, he rather preferred being a debater to being an orator; in a sense he maintained that no man had a right to be an orator without first being a debater. Eloquence, he said, had its proper place when reason had proved a thing to be right, and it was necessary to give men the courage to do what was right. I think he never needed any man's eloquence to give him that. But the substitution of sentiment for reason, in the proper place for reason, affected him "as musicians are affected by a false note." It was the combination of this intellectual integrity with extraordinary warmth and simplicity in the affections that made the point of his personality. The snobs and servile apologists of the *régime* he resisted seem to think they can atone for being hard-hearted by being soft-headed, He reversed, if ever a man did, that relation in the organs. The opposite condition really covers all that can be said of him in this brief study; it is the clue not only to his character but to his career.

If rationalism meant being rational (which it hardly ever does) he might at every stage of his life be called a red-hot rationalist. Thus, for instance, he very early became a Socialist and joined the Fabian Society, on the executive of which he played a prominent part for some years. But he afterwards gave the explanation, very characteristic for those who could understand it, that what he liked about the Fabian sort of Socialism was its hardness. He meant intellectual hardness; the fact that the society avoided sentimentalism, and dealt in affirmations and not mere associations. He meant that upon the Fabian basis a Socialist was bound to believe in Socialism, but not in sandals, free love, bookbinding, and immediate disarmament. But he also added that, while he liked their hardness, he disliked their moderation. In other words, when he discovered, or believed that he discovered, that their intellectual hardness was combined with moral hardness, or rather moral deadness, he felt all the intellectual ice melted by a moral flame. **He had, so to speak, a reaction of emotional realism, in which he saw, as suddenly as simple men can see simple truth, the potterers of Social Reform, as the plotters of the Servile State.**[13] He was himself, above all things, a democrat as well as a Socialist; and in that intellectual sect he began to feel as if he were the only Socialist who was also a democrat. His dogmatic, democratic conviction would alone illustrate the falsity of the contrast between logic and life. The idea of human equality existed with extraordinary clarity in his brain, precisely because it existed with extraordinary simplicity in his character. His popular sympathies, unlike so many popular sentiments, could really survive any intimacy with the populace; they followed the poor not only at public meetings but to public houses. He was literally the only man I ever knew who was not only never a snob, but apparently never tempted to be a snob. The fact is almost more important than his wonderful lack of fear; for such good causes, when they cannot be lost by fear, are often lost by favour.

---

13. An allusion to Hilaire Belloc's *The Servile State* (1912).

Thus he came to suspect that Socialism was merely social reform, and that social reform was merely slavery. But the point still is that though his attitude to it was now one of revolt, it was anything but a mere revulsion of feeling. He did, indeed, fall back on fundamental things, on a fury at the oppression of the poor, on a pity for slaves, and especially for contented slaves. But it is the mark of his type of mind that he did not abandon Socialism without a rational case against it, and a rational system to oppose to it. The theory he substituted for Socialism is that which may for convenience be called Distributivism;[14] the theory that private property is proper to every private citizen. This is no place for its exposition; but it will be evident that such a conversion brings the convert into touch with much older traditions of human freedom, as expressed in the family or the guild. And it was about the same time that, having for some time held an Anglo-Catholic position, he joined the Roman Catholic Church. It is notable, in connection with the general argument, that while the deeper reasons for such a change do not concern such a sketch as this, he was again characteristically amused and annoyed with the sentimentalists sympathetic or hostile, who supposed he was attracted by ritual, music, and emotional mysticism. He told such people, somewhat to their bewilderment, that he had been converted because Rome alone could satisfy the reason. In his case, of course, as in Newman's[15] and numberless others, well-meaning people conceived a thousand crooked or complicated explanations, rather than suppose that an obviously honest man believed a thing because he thought it was true. He was soon to give a more dramatic manifestation of his strange taste for the truth.

The attack on political corruption, the next and perhaps the most important passage in his life, still illustrates the same point, touching reason and enthusiasm. Precisely because he did know what Socialism is and what it is not, precisely because he had at least learned that from the intellectual hardness of the Fabians, he saw the spot where Fabian Socialism is not hard but soft. Socialism means the assumption by the State of all the means of production, distribution, and exchange. To quote (as he often quoted with a rational relish) the words of Mr. Balfour, that is Socialism and nothing else is Socialism.[16] To such clear thinking, it is at once apparent that trusting a thing to the State must always mean trusting it to the statesmen. He could defend Socialism because he could define Socialism; and he was not helped or hindered by the hazy associations of the sort of Socialists who perpetually defended what they never defined. Such men might

---

14. Also called Distributionism and Distributivism. Building on Catholic teachings, it believes that the ownership of property should be as wide as possible.

15. John H. Newman (1801–1890) was a famous English convert to Catholicism and a gifted writer.

16. In 1907 Arthur J. Balfour (1848-1930) said: "Socialism has one meaning only. Socialism means and can mean nothing else than that the community or the State is to take all the means of production into its own hands, that private property and private enterprise are to come to an end, and all that private property and private enterprise carry with them. That is Socialism and nothing else is Socialism."

have a vague vision of red flags and red ties waving in an everlasting riot above the fall of top-hats and Union jacks; but he knew that Socialism established meant Socialism official, and conducted by some sort of officials. All the primary forms of private property were to be given to the government; and it occurred to him, as a natural precaution, to give a glance at the government. He gave some attention to the actual types and methods of that governing and official class, into whose power trams and trades and shops and houses were already passing, amid loud Fabian cheers for the progress of Socialism. He looked at modern parliamentary government; he looked at it rationally and steadily and not without reflection. And the consequence was that he was put in the dock, and very nearly put in the lock-up, for calling it what it is.

In collaboration with Mr. Belloc he had written *The Party System*, in which the plutocratic and corrupt nature of our present polity is set forth. And when Mr. Belloc founded the *Eye-Witness*, as a bold and independent organ of the same sort of criticism, he served as the energetic second in command. He subsequently became editor of the *Eye-Witness*, which was renamed as the *New Witness*. It was during the latter period that the great test case of political corruption occurred; pretty well known in England, and unfortunately much better known in Europe, as the Marconi scandal.[17] To narrate its alternate secrecies and sensations would be impossible here; but one fashionable fallacy about it may be exploded with advantage. An extraordinary notion still exists that the *New Witness* denounced Ministers for gambling on the Stock Exchange. It might be improper for Ministers to gamble; but gambling was certainly not a misdemeanor that would have hardened with any special horror so hearty an Anti-Puritan as the man of whom I write. The Marconi case did not raise the difficult ethics of gambling, but the perfectly plain ethics of secret commissions. The charge against the Ministers was that, while a government contract was being considered, they tried to make money out of a secret tip, given them by the very government contractor with whom their government was supposed to be bargaining. This was what their accuser asserted; but this was not what they attempted to answer by a prosecution. He was prosecuted, not for what he had said of the government, but for some secondary things he had said of the government contractor. The latter, Mr. Godfrey Isaacs, gained a verdict for criminal libel; and the judge inflicted a fine of £100. Readers may have chanced to note the subsequent incidents in the life of Mr. Isaacs, but I am here only concerned with incidents in the life of a more interesting person.

In any suggestion of his personality, indeed, the point does not lie in what was done to him, but rather in what was not done. He was positively assured,

---

17. Maisie Ward described the Marconi Scandal in Chapter 19 of her 1943 *Gilbert Keith Chesterton*. Ministers in the Liberal government were buying stocks in one branch of the Marconi company at the same time they awarded a lucrative government contract to another branch headed by Godfrey Isaacs.

G. K. Chesterton, a Criticism

upon the very strongest and most converging legal authority, that unless he offered certain excuses he would certainly go to prison for several years. He did not offer those excuses; and I believe it never occurred to him to do so. **His freedom from fear of all kinds had about it a sort of solid unconsciousness and even innocence.** This homogeneous quality in it has been admirably seized and summed up by Mr. Belloc in a tribute of great truth and power. "His courage was heroic, native, positive and equal: always at the highest potentiality of courage. He never in his life checked an action or a word from a consideration of personal caution, and that is more than can be said of any other man of his time." After the more or less nominal fine, however, his moral victory was proved in the one way in which a military victory can ever be proved. It is the successful general who continues his own plan of campaign. Whether a battle be ticketed in the history books as lost or won, the test is which side can continue to strike. He continued to strike, and to strike harder than ever, up to the very moment of that yet greater experience which changed all such military symbols into military facts. A man with instincts unspoiled and in that sense almost untouched, he would have always answered quite naturally to the autochthonous appeal of patriotism; but it is again characteristic of him that he desired, in his own phrase, to "rationalize patriotism," which he did upon the principles of Rousseau, that contractual theory which, in these pages, he connects with the great name of Jefferson.[18] But things even deeper than patriotism impelled him against Prussianism. His enemy was the barbarian when he enslaves, as something more hellish even than the barbarian when he slays. His was the spiritual instinct by which Prussian order was worse than Prussian anarchy; and nothing was so inhuman as an inhuman humanitarianism. If you had asked him for what he fought and died amid the wasted fields of France and Flanders, he might very probably have answered that it was to save the world from German social reforms.

This note, necessarily so broken and bemused, must reach its useless end. I have said nothing of numberless things that should be remembered at the mention of his name; of his books, which were great pamphlets and may yet be permanent pamphlets; of his journalistic exposures of other evils besides the Marconi, exposures that have made a new political atmosphere in the very election that is stirring around us; of his visit to America, which initiated him into an international friendship which is the foundation of this book. Least of all can I write of him apart from his work; of that loss nothing can be said by those who do not suffer it, and less still by those who do. **And his experiences in life and death were so much greater even than my experiences of him, that a double incapacity makes me dumb. A portrait is impossible; as a friend he is too near me, and as a hero too far away.**

---

18. A reference to the Social Contract theory of the French Jean-Jacques Rousseau (1712–1778), which was taken up by the American Thomas Jefferson (1743–1826).

G. K. CHESTERTON

A CRITICISM

WITH FOUR PHOTOGRAPHS

LONDON: ALSTON RIVERS, LTD.
BROOKE STREET, HOLBORN BARS, E.C.
1908

PREFACE

IT may be thought by some that this book demands an apology. Mr. G.K. Chesterton is still a young man, not much over thirty. In all reasonable probability much of his best work lies before him. His opinions may undergo a considerable change before he dies; his style may develop; he may attempt all sorts of new artistic experiments. Why, then, it may be asked, try to sum him up at a time when in the nature of things he cannot be summed up? Why not wait till he is dead, perhaps till be has been dead for some twenty years, when the world will have decided whether he is really worth writing a book about at all?

I admit the force of such arguments. But I submit that (waiving the point that if I waited till Mr. Chesterton were dead, I might quite probably be dead myself) there is something to be said on the other side, especially in the case of such a writer as Mr. Chesterton.

If a writer be a pure artist and aims solely at creating beautiful things, or, not to beg the "art for art's sake" controversy, at depicting the eternal things in beautiful forms, we can hardly wait too long before we judge him. But Mr. Chesterton is not and does not profess to be such an artist. **He is primarily a propagandist, the preacher of a definite message to his own time. He is using all the power which his literary capacity gives him to lead the age in a certain direction.** It is surely important to consider, firstly, whether he has the power to lead it at all, and secondly, whether, if he does lead it, he is likely to lead it right or wrong. When dealing with such a man, especially when he has, as Mr. Chesterton undoubtedly has, great influence over many young and developing brains, it is as absurd to say that we ought to postpone discussing him till time has shown how far his fame will be permanent. As well might one suggest that Mr. Balfour should defer replying to a speech by Mr. Asquith till time has shown whether Mr. Asquith will be classed with Fox or with Addington. Discussing Mr. Chesterton is not a question of literary criticism; it is a question of practical politics.

I have in the book itself disclaimed any intention of speculating on the durability of Mr. Chesterton's reputation. What is quite clear is that at the present moment he is profoundly influencing a great number of people. How far he is influencing them for good and how far for evil is surely a matter well worth discussing.

Mr. Kipling was worth discussing in the 'nineties quite apart from the permanence of his position in literature (in which personally I believe profoundly), because Mr. Kipling stood for Imperialism—a force to be reckoned with. **Mr. Chesterton stands for Anti-Imperialism and for much else besides, for Catholicism with its back to the wall, for the hunger of a perplexed age for the more lucid life of the Ages of Faith, for the revolt against Modernity—in a word, for what may legitimately be called "reaction."** That word, which I use because it really conveys my meaning, may be used without the slightest moral bias. You cannot tell whether reaction is good or bad until you know what it is reacting against. To distinguish the good from the evil in Mr. Chesterton's violent reaction against his age is partly the object of this book.

Another object is to estimate Mr. Chesterton's value as a literary artist. This object naturally falls within the scope of the other, for Mr. Chesterton's artistic talents are simply the weapons that he uses in his war against his controversial enemies. No doubt there are great chunks of his work that can be enjoyed frankly for their own sake without reference to his teaching; but those little know G.K.C. who imagine that it was for their own sake that he enjoyed them.

I think that the time has just about arrived when it is important that the modern world should make up its mind just what it does think of G.K. Chesterton. When a man, quite obviously in earnest, planks down a view of life unlike that of most of his contemporaries, it is silly to think you can dispose of him by calling him "paradoxical." He may be right or he may be wrong, or he may be (as he probably will be) partly right and partly wrong. If he is right, let us do all we can to strengthen his hands, and let us welcome his humour and fascination, not merely because they amuse us, but also because they are weapons to be used in the fight against the evil of our world. If he is wrong, let him be denounced, let him be, if you will, burnt as a heretic. But do not let him be praised as a buffoon. If he is partly right and partly wrong, it becomes a matter of urgent importance that we rightly distinguish his truths from his errors. Otherwise the tares may grow up and choke the wheat.

Buck, in dealing with Adam Wayne in *The Napoleon of Notting Hill*, was saner than most of Mr. Chesterton's readers. "He may be God. He may be the Devil. But we think it more likely as a matter of human probability that he is mad."[19] If people said that about G.K.C. I should respect them. It would be better than calling him "paradoxical."

Another point upon which I may say an apologetic word or two is the free use which I have made of Mr. Chesterton's personal characteristics and private life to illustrate my view of his position. I do not think such action needs any excuse to sensible people. There may be men whose art work is a thing utterly separate from their personality. I do not know. I cannot conceive what they can be like; but they may exist. One thing is certain. Mr. Chesterton is not such a man. To him thought and conduct are alike expressions of human personality. Whenever, therefore, circumstances have put me in possession of facts concerning Mr. Chesterton personally which may throw light upon the origin or development of his ideas, I have used them without scruple, so long as I could do so without violation of kindliness or honour. To "good taste," the modern name for snobbery, I hope I am indifferent. Some people will probably blame me for this; but one person will not, I think, blame me, and that person is Gilbert Keith Chesterton.

19. This argument resembles the Trilemma argument about Jesus advanced some forty years later in C.S. Lewis, *Mere Christianity*, Bk. II, Ch. 3, "The Shocking Alternative."

1
ORIGINS

The effect which Whitman's poems produced on him was electric.
They seemed to sum up the aspirations of his own youth. They
gave him a faith to hold to, and a gospel to preach.

"IT is a great deal easier," writes Mr. Chesterton in his study of Browning, "to hunt a family from tombstone to tombstone back to the time of Henry II, than to catch and realize and put upon paper that most nameless and elusive of all things—social tone." In studying Mr. Chesterton himself in his turn, it is as well to keep this very just opinion in mind. There is but little to be learned from what can be known of his ancestry; his heredity is a mixed one, but so probably is that of most middle-class Englishmen. One strand leads back to a burgher family of Aberdeen; it gives G.K.C. his second name of "Keith," and can be traced back further than other lines, because it comes from a country where the bourgeoisie have all the family pride of a noblesse. There is also Swiss blood in his veins, and a legend of a great-great-grandfather buried while still alive in the trenches after the Battle of the Pyramids, dug out in consequence of an accidentally heard groan, and surviving to be a father and an ancestor.[20] The Chestertons themselves seem to have been small landowners in Cambridgeshire until their fortunes were apparently dissipated by an Edward Chesterton, who flourished about the time of the Regency.[21] Students of heredity may find in this gentleman the source of his descendant's literary turn, for his letters, still preserved in the family, and most dated from debtors' prisons, are models of polished eighteenth-century eloquence. His son, reacting to respectability, became a coal-merchant, and subsequently founded an estate-agency business, which in the fourth generation still flourishes. In this business Mr. Edward Chesterton, the father of the subject of this sketch, was a partner.

---

20. This illustrious Swiss ancestor would have been fighting for Napoleon near Cairo, Egypt on July 21, 1798. The French victory ended some 700 years of Mamluk rule, but a British naval victory soon after in the Battle of the Nile on August 1–2 kept Napoleon from dominating the Middle East.

21. Narrowly, the Regency was the 1811–1820 period when George III was deemed unfit to rule and others ruled in his place. Broadly, it applies to a culture between 1800–1837 that included wasteful extravagance by the nobility, an extravagance apparently shared by this Edward Chesterton. His successful merchant son would reflect the more proper behavior of the Victorian Era (1837–1901) that followed.

But all this tells us little. It is not important to know who Gilbert Chesterton's great-grandfather was. It is important to know in what sort of a home he grew up. It is important to understand the particular kind of educated middle-class household in which he passed his most impressionable years; and you can only understand this by understanding the nineteenth century. I propose to approach G.K.C. after his own fashion, by means of a stupendous digression.

The Socialist writers and orators of the 'eighties (themselves almost exclusively drawn from the middle classes) were very fond of denouncing the middle class, or, as they generally called it, the bourgeoisie, for its stupidity, narrowness, and inaccessibility to ideas. Never was a charge more undiscerning. As a matter of fact, all the ideas, including Socialism, which were then fermenting in the minds of men came from the middle class. It was, indeed, the only section of the community in which ideas as such had any chance of taking root.

"Geist," as Matthew Arnold said long ago, "is forbidden by its nature to flourish in an aristocracy"; nor did our aristocracy, when it was vigorous and sincere, ever pretend to possess it.[22] Of late years, it is true, an attempt has been made to defend our oligarchical system on the ground that it gives us a leisured class, able to devote itself wholly to the cultivation of the intellect. But, as a matter of fact, our European aristocracies never did so devote themselves, and, for my part, I am glad they did not. **An intellectual aristocracy is the most horrible tyranny under which mankind can groan; I would rather, any day, be ruled by barons than by Brahmins.**[23] But whether it would be well to have such an aristocracy or not, it is quite certain that we have not got it and never have had it.

Our aristocrats were proud of being strong, of being brave, of being handsome, of being chivalrous, of being honourable, of being happy, but never of being clever. The idea that brains were any part of the make-up of a gentleman was never dreamed of in Europe until our rulers fell into the hands of Hebrew moneylenders, who, having brains and not being gentlemen, read into the European idea of aristocracy an intellectualism quite alien to its traditions.[24]

Nor have ideas ever had any better chance with the working classes. Even such ideas as they have borrowed from the middle class, because they suited their immediate class interests, have been de-intellectualized in the process.

22. This may be Arnold's concept of the *Zeitgeist*—"spirit of the times" One scholar said: "At least since Matthew Arnold exploited the term *Zeitgeist* in *Literature and Dogma*, the expression has been variously a source of irritation and confusion in a number of his critics. Identifying it with a tendency to disparage the past, an exasperated contemporary reviewer of his work in *Blackwood's Edinburgh Magazine* cried, 'Can anything be more unscientific than such a spirit? It is the very apotheosis of self-opinion intoxicated by its own pride, and flaunting its own dogmatisms with a crude audacity in the faced of preceding dogmas.'" Fraser Neiman "The Zeigeist of Matthew Arnold, *Proceedings of the Modern Language Association* 72:5 (December 1957), 977.

23. This remark demonstrates that Cecil could coin a pithy phrase like his brother.

24. This illustrates what Brocard Sewell meant in his "Introduction" when he referred to the snobbish anti-Semitism being taught at St. Paul's school during the time when Gilbert and Cecil were attending.

Socialism is a case in point. Socialism, as preached by its middle-class inventors, was an idea. In the form in which it has been adopted by a section of the labouring classes it is half sentiment, half eye-to-business. Its popularity is due partly to the trade unionist's desire for better wages and conditions of labour, partly to that ready sympathy and compassion for suffering which is the most beautiful of all the virtues of the English poor.

All this is, doubtless, both honourable and salutory. But if we wish to hear Socialism preached as an idea, we still have to go to Hyndman, to Belfort Bax, to Bernard Shaw, to H.G. Wells—in a word, to middle-class men.[25]

Now, during the second half of the nineteenth century the middle class was absolutely bubbling over with ideas. It had just broken down the iron doors which since the seventeenth century had barred its escape from the prison of Calvinism. It was rioting in its new-found intellectual liberty as heartily as the men of the Restoration rioted in their new-found moral liberty.[26] Everywhere you found households where new theories of politics, philosophy, religion, or science were eagerly welcomed, debated, and assimilated. Most of us have come across dozens of such households. Into such a household, on 29 May, 1874, G.K.C. was born.

His father was by profession a surveyor; by temperament something of a craftsman and something of a philosopher. Of his mother I need only say that, though, so far as I know, she has never written a line for publication, anyone who wishes to know from whence G.K.C. gets his wit need only listen for a few minutes to her conversation.

The politics and religion of his parents were emphatically Liberal. That intellectual activity, that voracious curiosity of the mind, which I have endeavoured to suggest, was itself the product of the great Liberal movement. We, its children, have revolted against it—and often rightly—but still we are its children. No one, as I shall endeavour to show, is more typical of the revolt against it than Mr. Chesterton, but no one is more typically its child. It was a movement of destruction rather than of construction, of doubt rather than of faith. But a faith it had; for no movement can live without a faith. It believed, without question, in the right and power of the human mind, if left free, to judge the world. It proved all things, but because it felt assured that men would hold fast to that which was good.

In this atmosphere of free inquiry was developed a theology which was called undogmatic, because its dogmas were so simple and humane that they seemed

25. The son of a wealthy businessman, in 1881 Henry M. Hyndman (1842–1921) founded Britain's first socialist party, the Social Democratic Federation. The well-educated E. Belfort Bax (1854–1926) helped form the Socialist League in 1885. The much better known Bernard Shaw and H.G. Wells were active (with Cecil) in the socialist Fabian Society. Keep in mind that in Britain (and particularly at this time) the middle-class was very different from the working class and regarded itself as such.
26. The English Restoration came in 1660 when Charles II took the throne, ending Puritan rule.

to their exponents to be self-evident. The Fatherhood of God, the Brotherhood of Man, the non-eternity of evil, the final salvation of all souls—these seemed to many in that era to form a faith at once sufficient and unassailable. Since then that free method of thought which created this system has largely destroyed it, forcing some of its children back to a more orthodox creed, others onward to a completer denial. But at that time thousands found rest in a vague but noble theo-philanthropy, such as G.K.C. absorbed in his youth. He was never made to read the Bible, and therefore read it—much to the advantage of his literary style. No one in the family was ever pressed to go to church, but, when they did go, it was to Bedford Chapel to hear the sermons of the Rev. Stopford Brooke.[27] There, more than fifteen years ago, the young Chesterton learned from the lips of a genuine poet and orator the whole of that system of religious thought which has been discovered by certain Nonconformist ministers within the last eighteen months, and is now emphatically called "The New Theology."[28]

The politics of the family bore some resemblance to its religious atmosphere. They were not Jacobin, but they were decidedly Liberal. The childhood of G.K.C. coincided more or less with the St. Martin's Summer of Liberalism, from 1880 to 1885.[29] Political controversy was so much in the air of the household that even as an infant he must have heard echoes of that last stand of Gladstonian Liberalism; he was certainly beginning to be politically conscious when the "flowing tide" in which Gladstone had trusted suddenly turned and overwhelmed him.

But though Mr. Chesterton must have been tolerably familiar with religious and political controversies almost before he could speak, it can hardly be supposed that he had developed ideas of his own on these subjects until well on in his school days. He went to St. Paul's School when he was about twelve and stayed there some five years, interesting the more intelligent masters by his mental originality, and irritating the stupider ones by his refusal to take the routine of the place seriously.[30] The records that one has of him during this period supply a picture of a tall, thin, rather good-looking boy, incredibly absent-minded (almost all the anecdotes of his boyhood turn on this trait), passionately fond of reading, covering all his school-books with drawings till the printing was unrecognizable, delightfully indifferent to ordinary school work, and quite equally indifferent to athletics.

---

27. Stopford A. Brooke (1832–1916) was a distinguished clergyman. In 1880 he left the Anglican church to become a Unitarian, preaching at Bedford Chapel in Bloomsbury (central London) until 1894.

28. The New Theology denied miracles and treated much of the Bible with skepticism.

29. Jacobins wanted social and political change to come through revolution, while liberals wanted change to develop gradually. "Summer of Liberalism" refers to the second of William E. Gladstone's four terms as Prime Minister. He resigned, in part, because English reforms had begun to move in directions he did not like, driven, in part, by the "flowing tide" of new voters he helped to enfranchise.

30. This was the Colet Court prep school and St. Paul's itself, located on Hammersmith Road in West London. In British terminology, a "public school" was a *private* school (with paid tuition) intended to train for *public* service. Maisie Ward, *Gilbert Keith Chesterton* (New York: Sheed & Ward, 1943), 19.

The High Master of St. Paul's School at that time was Mr. F.W. Walker, a man who left a deep impress of his personality, not only on the school over which he presided, but also on the characters of all those who came in contact with him. He was one of those forceful characters that instinctively suggest greatness. He was, I believe, a very fine scholar; he was certainly a remarkable organizer, and the school, moulded by his hands, won triumph after triumph. But it was neither scholarship nor organizing capacity that one thought of in connection with him; it was mere bigness and irresistible natural power. His head was leonine, and his voice, when raised in anger, was not unlike the roar of a lion. His geniality was scarcely less deafening than his wrath. His laughter, in particular, used to make the corridors rock, and it was currently believed that it could be heard at Hammersmith Broadway. I have sometimes wondered whether some reminiscence of his old High Master may be traced in Mr. Chesterton's description of the huge personality of the terrible "Sunday," just as old Paulines of his epoch will certainly recognize memories of one of the assistant masters in some of the humours of Auberon Quin.[31]

Mr. Walker could be a sufficiently stern and even terrible disciplinarian when he liked, but he had in his nature vast reserves of good humour and tolerance. Also there was in him a touch of unconventionality; he lived the kind of life he liked, and not the kind of life a schoolmaster was expected to live. With a little change in his circumstances he might almost have been a Bohemian. He had a shrewd sense of human character and a keen eye to types of talent alien from his own. He always liked G.K.C. and prophesied great things of him, though the latter was, I fear, by no means a model pupil.

While at school he gained what was known as the "Milton" prize for English verse. It was considered a remarkable achievement, because that prize had been regarded hitherto as a monopoly of the "eighth," and G.K.C. was still in one of the lower forms. The subject of the poem (selected, of course, by the examiners) was "St. Francis Xavier."[32] What G.K.C. made of that singularly unpromising theme I have forgotten—if I ever knew. But it served to direct attention to him as one who might do honour to the school, in spite of his somewhat casual treatment of his official studies.

But the most important event of his school career, so far as its influence on his own future is concerned, was undoubtedly the formation of the Junior Debating Club (or J.D.C.), of which he became chairman.

This remarkable institution, which has already given three journalists to the Liberal press, one excellent short story writer to the magazines, one parliamentary candidate to the Liberal Party, one professor to University College, and

---

31. Sunday is a mysterious, powerful character in *The Man Who Was Thursday* (1907). Auberon Quin is the idiosyncratic king in *The Napoleon of Notting Hill* (1904).

32. Maisie Ward has the poem in *Gilbert Keith Chesterton* (New York: Sheed & Ward, 1943), 660–661.

another to an educational institution in the Midlands, was founded, I believe, for the purpose of reading Shakespeare, but this intention was abandoned by general consent after the first meeting. It subsequently turned itself into a general debating society, and prospered so far as to be able to produce a monthly magazine called *The Debater*, in which will be found numerous essays and poems, signed with the familiar initials "G.K.C."

Some of these contributions are extremely interesting. From the point of view of literary merit the verse is certainly much better and maturer than the prose. Some of the poems are quite startlingly vigorous for a boy of sixteen, the best, I think, being the first ever printed—a soliloquy of Danton on the scaffold. Others are somewhat crude, and many of them frankly imitative. When one comes across a line like

As wholly a hideous dream from the gloom of the gateway of Hell

one does not need to ask what poet the writer has just been reading.[33] But the especial interest of these boyish verses lies in the light they throw upon their author's point of view at the time. Most of them deal with religious and moral problems with all the sumptuous responsibility of extreme youth; indeed, there is hardly a touch anywhere of the humour and fantasy of the later G.K.C. The old atmosphere of the faith of his childhood still remains, but the grip of its positive dogmas is weakening—he is leaning towards Agnosticism; while, on the other hand, a note of pugnacity personal to himself has been added to it. This note is struck with a certain force in a poem called "Ave Maria," written very obviously under the influence of Swinburne's style, and as obviously in a mood of revolt against Swinburne's teaching.[34] It begins

Hail Mary! Thou blest among women; generations shall rise up to greet,
After ages of wrangle and dogma, I come with a prayer to thy feet.
Where Gabriel's red plumes are a wind in the lanes of thy lilies at eve,
We pray, who have done with the churches; we worship, who may not believe!

The human origin of all religions is admitted, but the argument is turned against the Neo-Pagans effectively enough:

We know that men prayed to their image, and crowned their own passions as Powers;
We know that their Gods were as shadows, nor are shamed of this Queen, that was ours!
We know as the people the priest is, as men are, the Goddess shall be—
All harlots were worshipped in Cypris: all maidens and mothers in thee!

He left school when about seventeen. His father, whose own tastes were far more literary and artistic than commercial, and whose judgment was sane

33. Canto III of Dante Alighieri's *Inferno* has the lines, "Abandon all hope, you who enter here."
34. Algernon C. Swinburne (1837–1909) wrote poetry hostile to religion.

and just to a most unusual degree, wisely refrained from attempting to force him into business. During his boyhood Gilbert Chesterton had been at least as fond of scribbling drawings as of scribbling verses. Some of these were thought by good judges to show great promise, and it was decided that he should study art. The experiment was not wholly a success. That Mr. Chesterton has considerable gift as a draftsman no competent critic who studies the illustrations to Mr. Belloc's *Immanuel Burden* will be disposed to deny.[35] But it was not in that direction that his deepest impulses led. **He proved this by the fact that he shrank from the technical toils of art as he has never shrunk from the technical toils of writing.**

But the years during which this experiment was being made were certainly not wasted. During the whole time he was writing incessantly and publishing practically nothing. He entered it crude and unformed; he left it almost mature. These silent years were full of reading and of thinking. He was brought face to face with the modern world, the creation of that liberal philosophy in which he had been trained, and it failed to satisfy him. The disappointment, aggravated by his loathing for the decadent school which then dominated "advanced" literature, must have set him thinking. Perhaps it touched the nerve of humour in him, for we find little humour in what he wrote before this time, while in all that he wrote after it is dominant and clamorous. The change that came over his temperament was, perhaps, mirrored in his changed appearance. The tall, slender idealist became the full-girthed giant, shaking with Gargantuan laughter.

One reminiscence of his art-school days he gave to the world not long ago in a *Daily News* article.[36] It may be worth recalling, firstly because it gives a glimpse of his impressions of the world he was then living in, secondly because it marks the beginning of that change of view which we shall follow in future chapters, thirdly because Mr. Chesterton himself says that it was "by far the most terrible thing that ever happened to him in his life":

> An art school is different from almost all other schools or colleges in this respect that, being of new and crude creation and of lax discipline, it presents a specially strong contrast between the industrious and the idle. People at an art school either do an atrocious amount of work or do no work at all. I belonged, along with other charming people, to the latter class; and this threw me often into the society of men who were very different from myself, and who were idle for reasons very different from mine. I was idle because I was very much occupied; I was engaged about that time in discovering, to my own extreme and lasting astonishment, that I was not an atheist. But

35. This is Belloc's 1904 novel *Emmanuel Burden* with 34 sketches by G.K.C. The book is a parody of the adulatory biographies of prominent people common in that era. In the first chapter, for instance, Belloc notes that Mr. Burden "never attempted to enter the House of Commons" although it was a "career which Englishmen justly regard as among the most honourable, *lucrative* and eminent." (Italics added.)

36. What is quoted below was republished as "The Diabolist" in *Tremendous Trifles* (1909).

there were others also at loose ends who were engaged in discovering what Carlyle called (I think with needless delicacy) the fact that ginger is hot in the mouth.[37]

I value that time, in short, because it made me acquainted with a good representative number of blackguards. In this connection there are two very curious things which the critic of human life may observe. The first is the fact that there is one real difference between men and women; that women prefer to talk in twos, while men prefer to talk in threes. The second is that when you find (as you often do) three young cads and idiots going about together and getting drunk together every day you generally find that one of the three cads and idiots is (for some extraordinary reason) not a cad and not an idiot. In those small groups devoted to a drivelling dissipation there is almost always one man who seems to have condescended to his company; one man who, while he can talk a foul triviality with his fellows, can also talk politics with a Socialist, or philosophy with a Catholic.

It was just such a man whom I came to know well. It was strange, perhaps, that he liked his dirty, drunken society; it was stranger still, perhaps, that he liked my society. For hours of the day he would talk with me about Milton or Gothic architecture; for hours of the night he would go where I have no wish to follow him, even in speculation. He was a man with a long, ironical face, and close and red hair; he was by class a gentleman, and could walk like one, but preferred, for some reason, to walk like a groom carrying two pails. He looked like a sort of super-jockey; as if some archangel had gone on the Turf. And I shall never forget the half-hour in which he and I argued about real things for the first and the last time.

The man asked him why he was becoming more orthodox, and was met by the now familiar Chestertonian argument for religion and humility; illustrated by the symbol the sparks from the fire that was burning in front of them: "Seduce a woman, and that spark will be less bright. Shed blood, and that spark will be less red":

He had a horrible fairness of the intellect that made me despair of his soul. A common, harmless atheist would have denied that religion produced humility or humility a simple joy; but he admitted both. He only said, "But shall I not find in evil a life of its own ? Granted that for every woman I ruin one of those red sparks will go out; will not the expanding pleasure of ruin..."

"Do you see that fire ?" I asked. '"If we had a real fighting democracy, some one would burn you in it; like the devil-worshipper that you are."

---

37. In his *Critical and Miscellaneous Essays*, Thomas Carlyle asked whether a "creed and world-theory" such as Atheism would be adequate: "Alas, no; not even Atheism: only Machiavelism; and the indestructible faith that 'ginger is hot in the mouth.' Get ever and newer ginger, therefore; chew it ever the more diligently; 'tis all thou hast to look to, and that only for a day." Thus an atheist's "creed" must be crass expediency (for results) and a faddish pursuit of passing sensations (for an illusion of meaning).

"Perhaps," he said, in his tired, fair way. "Only what you call evil I call good."

He went down the great steps alone, and I felt as if I wanted the steps swept and cleaned. I followed later, and as I went to find my hat in the low, dark passage where it hung, I suddenly heard his voice again, but the words were inaudible. I stopped, startled; then I heard the voice of one of the vilest of his associates saying, "Nobody can possibly know." And then I heard those two or three words which I remember in every syllable and cannot forget. I heard the Diabolist say, "I tell you I have done everything else. If I do that I shan't know the difference between right and wrong." I rushed out without daring to pause; and as I passed the fire I did not know whether it was hell or the furious love of God.

I have since heard that he died; it may be said, I think, that he committed suicide; though he did it with tools of pleasure, not with tools of pain. God help him, I know the road he went; but I have never known or even dared to think what was that place at which he stopped and refrained.

A few of his writings found their way into print. While he was still at school, a poem of his called "A Song of Labour" was published in *The Speaker*. To one of the fugitive artistic periodicals of the 'nineties, *The Quarto*, he contributed a tale called "A Picture of Tuesday," which has a certain interest in that it anticipates one of the minor ideas of his latest novel. Then, while still an art student, he began to do a certain amount of art criticism for *The Bookman*, and later attempted some reviewing for the same paper. Meanwhile, having abandoned art, he passed through the offices of two publishers, who probably found him something lacking on the commercial side of his duties. Finally, in 1900, he took the plunge into journalism.

But I am anticipating. Before I record Mr. Chesterton's entrance into the fields of journalism and literature I must say a word of the forces which had helped to mould him. Reading, no less than discussion, was in the air of his home, and from his childhood he was a voracious reader.

His memory was and is almost as astounding as Macaulay's, and he always had pages of his favourite authors stored in his head. His taste, then as now, was always for the romantic school. Shakespeare, Dickens, Scott (both prose and verse), Macaulay, were the writers he devoured, I think, most eagerly in his boyhood. I do not think that he gave much attention to contemporary or even to later Victorian writers. Swinburne caught him in his later schooldays; Browning, I believe, later still; Tennyson I do not fancy he ever fully appreciated. But just about the time that he was leaving school he met with a book which had a profound and decisive influence on the growth of his mind. That book was Walt Whitman's *Leaves of Grass*.

The effect which Whitman's poems produced on him was electric. They seemed to sum up the aspirations of his own youth. They gave him a faith to hold to, and a gospel to preach. He set himself to proclaim "the whole divine democracy of things," as he calls it in *The Wild Knight*.[38] He idealized the remnant of the J.D.C. into the Mystical City of Friends. He embraced passionately the three great articles of Whitman's faith, the ultimate goodness of all things implying the acceptance of the basest and meanest no less than the noblest in life, the equality and solidarity of men, and the redemption of the world by comradeship. You will find Whitman's influence everywhere present in his earlier work, especially in *The Wild Knight* and *The Defendant*. The preface to *The Defendant* is instinct with his spirit. "The Wild Knight" itself is a Whitmanite poem; so is "Ecclesiastes"; so is "World Lover"; so is "The Earth's Shame."[39] Other forces have since compelled him to modify the Whitmanite faith, and even to emphasize doctrines antagonistic to it—the existence of positive evil and the need of authority and definition. But the robust faith in life which Whitman drove into him he has never abandoned, and in the dedication of his latest book, *The Man who was Thursday*, he pays a fine tribute to Whitman's influence on his youth.

In another respect his opinions changed about this time, and the change is worth mentioning, although it was not permanent, and probably throws more light on the mental atmosphere of the time than on Mr. Chesterton's personal feelings and opinions. Hitherto, unlike his brother Cecil, who early rebelled against Liberalism, learned to hate the name of Gladstone before his own views were at all defined, and finally formulated his revolt in that particular brand of Tory-Socialism which he still, I believe, professes, Gilbert Chesterton had remained faithful to the family traditions in politics as in religion. The only point of departure was Home Rule, about which his father had doubts, but of which he was always a warm advocate. We shall see, I think, later how insignificant it was that he should have chosen this doubtful article of the Liberal creed for special championship. But for the present we are concerned with his temporary conversion to Socialism. I do not think his grip on economic Socialism was ever very firm. I should be disposed to attribute his adoption of its tenets partly to the example of some of his J.D.C. friends who had gone to the University and joined the Oxford Fabian Society, partly to the indirect influence of Whitman, which coloured so much of his life during this period. For, though Whitman himself was an Anarchist rather than a Socialist, his influence on the Socialist movement was immense, and young Socialists talked continually the language of

---

38. Gilbert wrote his wife-to-be a letter describing his estate including, "A number of letters from a young lady, containing everything good and generous and loyal and holy and wise that isn't in Walt Whitman's poems." Maisie Ward, *Gilbert Keith Chesterton* (New York: Sheed & Ward, 1943),95.

39. *The Wild Knight and Other Poems* was published in 1900 and *The Defendant* in 1901. The poems are republished in *G.K. Chesterton's Early Poetry* (2004). In this context (below), Home Rule refers to independence for Ireland from British rule.

Whitmanism, preaching comradeship, equality, and good will among men—in a word, the very things which G.K. Chesterton was then intent on proclaiming.

However that may be, it is certain his Socialism left very little impression upon his mind. For some years he continued to call himself a Socialist. His first published poem was, in its general tendency, at least, a Socialist poem. He also wrote one or two poems and sketches for *The Clarion*. But he took no active part in the Socialist movement, and soon drifted out of it, silently but completely.

He was once more a Liberal. Indeed, even during his Socialist period, he had always believed in working with the Liberals. That fundamental Conservatism, which, as I shall endeavour to show, is the key to his maturer opinions, was even then strong with him, and, by a paradox as wild as any that he has propounded, it kept him and keeps him faithful to the Liberal party. From the time when he practically abandoned Socialism to the time when he emerged from obscurity into public fame, his political views may best be described as vaguely progressive. He believed in the ultimate amelioration of the human lot; he believed (as he no longer believes) in Progress with a capital P; he believed in liberty and democracy. But his views on many current issues were undefined. He was something of an Imperialist, as his poem, "An Alliance," in *The Wild Knight* proves. He was decidedly a patriot. He always, as I say, called himself a Liberal. But his convictions had not been hammered into coherence by the necessities of battle.

Suddenly there came a change. Forces, moral and material, which had been gathering strength for years, appealed to the supreme arbitrament of the sword. Far to the South half a continent sprang to arms, and the heavy sleep of English politics was broken by a sound as of the Trumpets of Armageddon.

Gilbert Chesterton at age 17

2

THE FIRST PHASE

He writes, not like an essayist weaving a fascinating theory, but like a political leader with his eye on the division lobby. He sees his adversary; he sees his audience. He fights like a man fighting to win.

IN the autumn of the year 1899 no one outside his own circle had ever heard of G.K. Chesterton. In the spring of 1900 every one was asking every one else, "Who is 'G.K.C.'?" Before the year was over his name and writings were better known than those of men who had made reputations while he was still an infant. I do not know any example in the last fifty years of so dizzy a rise from obscurity to fame as that which I shall try to describe and analyze in this chapter.

His first serious publication (excluding a volume of nonsense verses called *Greybeards at Play*) was *The Wild Knight*, published at the beginning of 1900.[40] How absolutely unknown was its author at that time may be gathered from one rather amusing incident. Mr. James Douglas, in the *Star*, concluded an enthusiastic review with the declaration that the new poet could be none other than Mr. John Davidson, writing under a pseudonym.[41] Mr. Davidson promptly repudiated the suggestion, not without symptoms of considerable annoyance, and a denial not less emphatic, though somewhat more urbane, appeared over the signature of "Gilbert Chesterton."

But, though Mr. Chesterton thus claimed proprietary rights in his own name, that name remained comparatively unknown. *The Wild Knight* was, on the whole, well reviewed, and it drew warm praise from many competent judges—among others, from Mr. George Meredith.[42] But commercially it was a failure, and it attracted comparatively little attention even from the minority who habitually read current poetry.

Nevertheless these early poems are particularly well worth studying. It is extraordinary that so able a critic as Mr. James Douglas should have thought that they could be the work of Mr. John Davidson. It is true that there are some technical resemblances in the styles of the two poets. Both are daringly indifferent to

---

40. Cecil's dating goes astray. *Greybeards* was published in October 1900 and *Wild Knight* in November.
41. John Davidson (1857–1909) was a Scottish poet and playwright best known for his ballads.
42. George Meredith (1828–1909) was a popular English novelist and poet.

poetic conventions; both use words and imagery shocking to critics of the classical school; both boldly introduce references to modern things—trains and lampposts. Both aim at vigour and strength rather than at beauty. But when we turn from the manner to the substance we find a philosophy farther removed from Mr. Davidson's than Mr. Davidson's is from Tennyson's or Wordsworth's.

The gospel of "The Wild Knight" and of nearly all the poems bound up with it is in essentials the gospel of Whitman. What, for instance, could be more in the spirit of *Leaves of Grass* than the poem called "Ecclesiastes"? I will quote it in full, not because I think it a good specimen from the literary point of view, but because it summarizes so succinctly the poet's early creed:

> There is one sin: to call a green leaf grey,
> Whereat the sun in heaven shuddereth.
> There is one blasphemy: for death to pray,
> For God alone knoweth the praise of death.
> There is one creed: 'neath no world-terror's wing
> Apples forget to grow on apple trees.
> There is one thing is needful—everything—
> The rest is vanity of vanities.

A much finer poem, "The Earth's Shame," I will also quote, because it emphasizes the Whitmanite idea of the ultimate acceptance of all things, however apparently evil:

> Name not his deed: in shuddering and in haste
> We dragged him darkly o'er the windy fells;
> That night there was a gibbet in the waste,
> And a new sin in hell.
>
> Be his deed hid from Commonwealths and Kings;
> By all men born be one true tale forgot;
> But three things, braver than all earthly things,
> Faced him and feared him not.
>
> Above his head and sunken secret face
> Nestled the sparrow's young, and dropped not dead.
> From the red blood and slime of that lost place
> Grew daisies white, not red.
>
> And from high heaven looking upon him,
> Slowly upon the face of God did come
> A smile that Cherubim and Seraphim
> Hid all their faces from.

The religion of the poems, too, is Whitmanite. That is to say, it combines the almost contemptuous rejection of conscious dogmas with the assertion of unconscious dogmas of vast extent—dogmas quite unprovable, but so deeply impressed upon the soul of the believer that they seem to him self-evident. That the whole universe is the expression of a Supreme Will, that that Will is benign and full of love for its creatures, that all things are making for good—these doctrines are written on every page. But there is no trace of the writer's later sympathy for religious orthodoxy. The word "priest" is never used, save in the spirit of Whitman's—"Allons, from all formules! From your formules, O bat-eyed and materialistic priests!" The Founder of Christianity is praised to the point of worship as Whitman praised him, but historic Christianity is almost everywhere represented as a ghastly parody of His teaching. In what is, perhaps, the most powerful poem in the book, "The Ballad of God-Makers," we are shown "the kings of the Earth" planning Christianity as a defence against Christ:

> Said the King of the East to the King of the West
> (I wot his frown was set),
> 'Lo, let us slay him—and make him as dung, It is well that the world forget.'
>
> Said the King of the West to the King of the East
> (I wot his smile was dread),
> 'Nay, let us slay him—and make him a god,
> It is well that our god be dead.'
>
> They set the young man on a hill,
> They nailed him to a rod;
> And there in darkness and in blood
> They made themselves a god.

Here, then, we have a fairly coherent philosophy, which is practically the humane optimistic Modernism of Mr. Chesterton's up-bringing modified by the influence of Whitman, but retaining its main outlines undisturbed. In the articles contributed to *The Speaker*, some of the most characteristic of which were shortly afterwards published under the title of *The Defendant*, much of that philosophy subsists. But there is a marked change—the first step in the transformation which was to turn the author of "The Ballad of God-Makers" into the author of *Heretics*. To what was this change due? In order to answer that question, we must turn for a moment from private to public affairs. **For it is a most significant fact, and one which had a profound effect upon his subsequent development, that it was a public crisis which first forced G.K.C. to the front.**

The history of England during the last quarter of the nineteenth century is the history of the growth of Imperialism. That great movement, foreseen more than thirty years ago by the genius of Disraeli, was not to reach fruition in his time.[43] The Manchester tradition in the middle class, the Radical-Chartist tradition in the most intelligent section of the working class, were still too strong. It was not till the great Gladstonian age was over, till the Socialists had cut much ground from under the feet of the Radicals, and till Churchill and his Tory Democracy had created that alliance between the aristocracy and a large section of the proletariat which Disraeli had desired but had never been quite able to accomplish, that the ground was cleared for the new force.

It is not my business to discuss the merits or demerits of Imperialism. That it was often exploited by faithless politicians for frivolous, and by unscrupulous traders and financiers for sordid purposes, would be admitted by all its intelligent advocates. But whether it was wholly a gross materialistic and immoral movement is quite another matter. It showed that it had some roots in that part of the soul which is noble and aspirant by the one unfailing test—the fact that it produced literature which had the note of greatness. The stories and poems of Mr. Rudyard Kipling gave to the silent movement of public sentiment and opinion an articulate voice, a voice at which the petty critics of the academies might carp, but to which no man with blood in his veins could refuse to listen. They summed up a movement; they roused an Empire. They did more than all the speeches of Mr. Chamberlain to raise the spirit of Imperialism to acting point.[44] For good or evil, they made possible the South African War.

I am only concerned with these things in so far as they help to make clear the position of Mr. Chesterton, who was to do for the Anti-Imperialist reaction much of what Mr. Kipling had done for the Imperialist movement. First, then, let us see what it was that drove him into the camp of those who were called "Pro-Boers."

The young Chesterton had caught Imperialism as he had caught Socialism. Under its influence he wrote at least one poem, included in *The Wild Knight*, which contains four lines such as even Mr. Kipling might have thought a trifle extravagant:

That all our seed be gathered,
That all our race take hands,
And the sea be a Saxon river,
That flows through Saxon lands.

Moreover, he was a disciple of Stevenson; Stevenson was the only writer who could be said to compete with Whitman in forming the philosophy of his adolescence. Stevenson may not have been an Imperialist, but he had taught the gospel of the sword which was being vigorously invoked on behalf of Imperialism by

---

43. Benjamin Disraeli (1804–1881), twice Prime Minister, wanted a larger British empire.
44. Joseph Chamberlain (1836–1914) helped to begin the Second Anglo-Boer War (1899–1902).

his old friend and collaborator, Henley,[45] and by a host of younger men who had learned it from him. Never at any time had the doctrine of Tolstoi, which has so powerfully influenced other British democrats, obtained the faintest hold on Mr. Chesterton. He was not in the least averse either to violence or to bloodshed in themselves. He was passionately patriotic, and detested all that modern theory which condemns flags and frontiers as inherently immoral. Everything seemed to point to the probability that he would be found on the Imperialist side in that fierce controversy in regard to which hardly anyone found it possible to be impartial. How came it that he finally chose the other?

Many minor causes might be suggested; his traditional Liberalism, his sympathy with Irish Nationalism (which had remained unabated even when he half yielded to the Imperial idea), the example of most of his intimate personal friends. But I think the real cause lay deeper.

He interpreted the Stevensonian gospel of fighting in a manner altogether different from that of Mr. Henley and his school. Fighting was noble and romantic, but only if you fought against odds. Alan Breck at the round-house door was a figure to be admired, because he was one man against a ship's crew. But who thought Captain Hoseason romantic?[46] Yet the British Empire appeared to be rather in Hoseason's position than in Alan's. It was a fine thing that the weak should take the sword and conquer the strong. But here we were the strong, and we were endeavouring, without much success, to conquer the weak. As he put it in a striking Christmas poem, written while the war was still raging:

Hard out of English bone my curse falls on an idle war,
That men of other blood have found the secret of the Star.

So, too, he interpreted differently the doctrine of Nationalism. Mr. Chesterton is, as I shall suggest, not always an entirely coherent thinker; but he could think. And thinking was at a discount in the hot days of the war, when men snatched up the first fragment of doctrine they could lay their hands on if it seemed for the moment to tell in their favour. Thus Pro-Boers would denounce patriotism as an obsolete superstition, and then go on to praise the Boers for defending their country! Similarly the Imperialists would alternately acclaim and decry national sentiment as it suited their turn. **Now, Mr. Chesterton was one of the comparatively few people who had on the subject a clear and definable doctrine. He erected the sanctity of nationality into a religious dogma, and he denied the right of any nation or Empire, on the pretence of being more civilized, more progressive, more democratic, or more efficient, to take**

---

45. In 1892 William E. Henley (1849–1903) published three plays he had written with Stevenson.

46. Alan Breck Stewart fights for Scottish independence in Robert L. Stevenson's *Kidnapped* (1886). Hoseason is the ship's captain who kidnaps David Balfour in that tale.

away from another nation its birthright of independence. This creed he was prepared to defend alike against Imperialist and Cosmopolitan critics.

His conviction was probably defined and intensified by the appearance of a school of political thinkers who were prepared to defend Imperialism on the specific ground that it was opposed to Nationalism. This was the position taken up by Mr. Bernard Shaw and other Fabian leaders, and Mr. Chesterton has always maintained that it is the only logical ground upon which Imperialism can be defended. And so, no doubt, it would be if human institutions and the sentiments which gather round them were as immutable and as strictly definable as the lines and angles of Euclid. It is not, however, my business here to debate the issue, but merely to point out that the Fabian defence of Imperialism tended to confirm Mr. Chesterton in his growing conviction that Imperialism was the mortal enemy of patriotism. On that paradox most of his political philosophy is built.

This thesis is the subject of the last essay in *The Defendant*—"A Defence of Patriotism." It is still further developed in the first essay in a volume called *England a Nation*, which was produced by an institution calling itself "The Patriots' Club." The Patriots' Club was Mr. Chesterton's own idea; its aim was to provide a rallying point for those who disapproved alike of the Cosmopolitan and the Imperialist ideals. It never did anything as far as I know except to produce the aforesaid volume, which contained contributions from persons as diverse and typical as Mr. Masterman, Mr. Ensor, Mr. Hugh Law, M.P., Mr. Nevinson, Mr. Hammond, Mr. Reginald Bray, and the Rev. Conrad Noel on various aspects of the Nationalist doctrine. Mr. Chesterton himself wrote the introductory essay on "The Patriotic Idea," which contains perhaps the most lucid expression of the political dogma which has exercised so dominant an influence over his opinions. It opens with an attack upon the Cosmopolitan ideals, based upon the refusal of their humanitarianism to recognize the common needs of humanity:

> Because the modern intellectuals who disapprove of patriotism do not do this, a strange coldness and unreality hangs about their love for men. If you ask them whether they love humanity, they will say, doubtless sincerely, that they do. But if you ask them touching any of the classes that go to make up humanity, you will find that they hate them all. They hate kings, they hate priests, they hate soldiers, they hate sailors, they distrust men of science, they denounce the middle classes, they despair of working men, but they adore humanity. Only they always speak of humanity as if it were a curious foreign nation. They are dividing themselves more and more from men to exalt the strange race of mankind. They are ceasing to be human in the effort to be humane.

Then comes the turn of the Imperialists. The attack is directed mainly against the contention that "a great conglomeration of peoples like the British Empire may be a unification of varied merits." Mr. Chesterton meets this with a denial: empires do not absorb the great qualities of the races they subdue:

> Why did we know so much about German mythology and nothing about Irish mythology? Any person with even the simplest knowledge of the world as it is must realize that the reason lies in the fact that our material conquest of Ireland put us in an utterly artificial position towards everything Irish. The Irish would not sing to us any more than the Jews, as described in their stern and splendid psalm, would sing to the Babylonians.[47] I find it difficult to believe that there can be anyone so ignorant of practical existence as not to know that any attempt on the part of the Irish for centuries after their conquest to say to us what they had to say about their history and legends would have been met with nothing except jokes about Brian Baroo.[48] We all know in reality that England would never have consented to learn from Ireland. It has learnt from France because it failed to conquer her. If Edward III or Henry V had succeeded in adding France to the Empire, we may be absolutely certain that we should have learnt as little from the song of Roland as we have from the legend of Maive, and that we should have profited as little from the genius of Mirabeau as we did from the genius of Parnell.[49]

Perhaps the best passage in the essay, is that which deals with the fugitive native character of empires and the permanence of nations:

> Spain had once a colonial empire, far more brilliant and original than ours. Its empire has vanished, but there are still men who will die for Spain; there are still men who will strike you in the face if you say that they are not Spaniards.

> France had an empire covering all Europe after the great ecstasy of the Revolution. It vanished utterly, and all its ideas are at a low ebb in Europe. But there are still men who will die for France. And when from our mortal nation also this immortal fallacy is passed, when all the colonies of England have gone the wild way of the colonies of Spain, when some strange and sudden Waterloo has made the little dream of Beaconsfield as mad as the great dream of Napoleon, something will remain, I am very certain, which matters more than all these levities. There will still be men who will die for England.[50]

---

47. Psalm 137: 1-4: "By the rivers of Babylon, There we sat down and wept, When we remembered Zion.... For there our captors demanded of us songs.... How can we sing the Lord's song in a foreign land?"

48. Brian Baroo or Brian Baru (d. 1014) was the High King of Ireland from 1002–1014. In Irish legends, he united Ireland, freeing it from Viking invaders, much as Alfred the Great did for England.

49. Edward III (1312–1377) and Henry V (1387–1422) were English kings who failed to conquer France. "The Song of Roland" is one of the oldest French poems. In Irish mythology, Maive or Medb is the Queen of Connacht. Mirabeau is Honoré Gabriel Riqueti (1749-1791), a political moderate who tried to get the French Revolution to adopt an constitutional monarchy. The gifted Charles Parnell (1846–1891) was nineteenth century Ireland's most important political leader and a great champion of Home Rule.

50. Chesterton did not move to Beaconsfield until 1909. The "little dream" refers to Prime Minister Benjamin Disraeli, the First Earl of Beaconsfield and a champion of British Imperialism.

Mr. Chesterton is by no means on such strong ground when he appeals to the common sense of humanity as distinguishing between Imperialism and Patriotism. Indeed, here I think is the weak point in his case. He is always appealing to us to ask what the great mass of ordinary men want. Now, there can be no manner of doubt what the great mass of ordinary men wanted in the year 1899. They wanted the South African War and the annexation of the Dutch Republics. And they wanted it in the name of Patriotism. If anyone had told them that such a desire was unpatriotic they would have replied, as Mr. Chesterton replies to the imaginary humanitarian in *Heretics*: "What a great deal of trouble you must have taken in order to feel like that." And they would have said so, six years later even, when they were in a mood of reaction against Imperialism. The ordinary man, the balancing elector, who voted Conservative in 1900 because he liked Imperialism, and Liberal in 1906 largely because he had grown to dislike it, would not have said in 1906 any more than in 1900 that Imperialism was unpatriotic. He would have said: "Patriotism is all very well, but I think you can have too much of it." And I think he would have been right. To say that an Imperialist is deficient in patriotism because he does not respect other people's *patria* seems to me like saying that a selfish man is deficient in egoism because he does not respect other people's ego.[51]

On the eve of the war *The Speaker*, then the leading Liberal weekly, passed practically into the hands of a group of young Liberals fresh from the Universities, who were resolved to make it the organ of vigorous opposition to the New Imperialism. Among these were several of Mr. Chesterton's old J.D.C. friends, and to the combination he readily lent the aid of his pen. The now-familiar initials "G.K.C." appeared at the bottom of several articles and reviews. And then, as I have already said, every one began to ask every one else, "Who is 'G.K.C.'?" In a few months he was almost famous.

What was it in these articles which struck the imagination of the reading world and captured its attention as by a cavalry charge? It was not, I think, merely the cleverness of the writing. There are many clever writers who do not find so easy a victory. Nor was it any astonishing originality in the views expressed. The really individual opinions of the author were then only struggling into being. He said little that might not have been said, comparatively little that had not been said, by Whitman or Stevenson or some other hero of his youth. Yet every one felt that he was striking a new note.

That note, I think, was the note of pugnacity. The opinions expressed may have been expressed before, may even be pretty generally accepted, but he throws into each a note of challenge. He writes, not like an essayist weaving a fascinating theory, but like a political leader with his eye on the division

---

51. Cecil's argument assumes patriotism is like egotism. Gilbert could reply that Imperialism is *bad* patriotism much as egotism is *bad* humanism. The error lies in the *moral quality* and not the *quantity*.

lobby. He sees his adversary; he sees his audience. He fights like a man fighting to win.

Let me take a single instance—the "Defence of Penny Dreadfuls," subsequently reprinted in *The Defendant*. The idea that Penny Dreadfuls are defensible is one that might have occurred to any paradoxical essayist. We can imagine Mr. Max Beerbohm producing a very delightful phantasia on such a theme on the lines of his attack on the Fire Brigade. Stevenson might have treated it a little more seriously, as in "The Lantern Bearers."[52] But it is safe to say that neither they nor anyone else would have treated it as it is treated here. Mr. Chesterton defends Penny Dreadfuls—not ironically, not with a half-serious, romantic sympathy, but as if he were the counsel retained to defend a man accused of selling them!

He begins quietly enough, pointing out a perfectly fair logical distinction between the desire of artistic people for artistic fiction and the desire of all normal men for stories. The latter desire is as legitimate as the former, and we ought not to condemn the story-teller merely because he does not produce a good work of art. "Bad story-telling is not a crime. Mr. Hall Caine walks the streets openly and cannot be put in prison for an anti-climax."[53] Later he warms to his work, and begins to distribute powerful forensic blows right and left. "If some grimy urchin runs away with an apple, the magistrate shrewdly points out that the child's knowledge that apples appease hunger is traceable to some curious literary researches." The evidence of the readers of these stories that they have been led into crime is brushed aside just as a clever barrister would brush it aside. "If I had forged a will, and could obtain sympathy by tracing the incident to the influence of Mr. George Moore's novels, I should find the greatest entertainment in the diversion." Another stroke rapidly follows: "At any rate, it is firmly fixed in the minds of most people that gutter-boys, unlike everybody else in the community, find their principal motives for conduct in printed books.

Then, after the introduction of *Rob Roy* and *Ivanhoe* as precedents for the sympathetic treatment of criminals, comes the really sensational effect, for the sake of which one feels the article was written.[54] The tables are turned on the prosecution. The accusers of Penny Dreadfuls are themselves put in the dock:

> If the authors and publishers of *Dick Deadshot* and such remarkable
> works were suddenly to make a raid upon the educated class, were to take

---

52. In "The Voice of Shelley" (*Daily News*, June, 10 1905) Chesterton wrote: "Mr. Max Beerbohm in one of his most delightful and absurd essays has denounced the fire brigade as a band of vandals who destroy a 'fair thing.' He has threatened to start an opposition fire brigade whose pipes shall be filled not with water but with oil." "The Lantern-Bearers" was an 1888 article by Robert Louis Stevenson that compared writers to the bearers of lanterns.

53. Hall Caine (1853–1931) was an extremely popular English novelist. His 1897 *The Christian*, about a woman trying to live independently, was the first British novel to sell over a million copies.

54. *Roy Roy* (1817) and *Ivanhoe* (1819) were popular novels by Walter Scott (1771–1832).

down the names of every man, however distinguished, who was caught at a University Extension Lecture, were to confiscate all our novels and warn us all to correct our lives, we should be seriously annoyed. Yet they have far more right to do so than we; for they, with all their idiocy, are normal and we are abnormal. It is the modern literature of the educated, not of the uneducated, which is avowedly and aggressively criminal. Books recommending profligacy and pessimism, at which the high-souled errand boy would shudder, lie upon all our drawing-room tables. If the dirtiest old owner of the dirtiest old bookstall in Whitechapel dared to display works really recommending polygamy or suicide, his stock would be seized by the police. These things are our luxuries. And with a hypocrisy so ludicrous as to be almost unparalleled in history, we rate the gutter-boys for their immorality at the very time that we are discussing (with equivocal German Professors) whether morality is valid at all. At the very instant that we curse the Penny Dreadful for encouraging thefts upon property, we canvass the proposition that all property is theft. At the very instant we accuse it (quite unjustly) of lubricity and indecency, we are cheerfully reading philosophies which glory in lubricity and indecency. At the very instant that we charge it with encouraging the young to destroy life, we are placidly discussing whether life is worth preserving."

You will find that sense of being at grips with a real or imaginary enemy in nearly everything that Mr. Chesterton has written. It permeates his criticisms and reviews, his poems, and even (in defiance of artistic canons) his stories. In the old *Speaker* articles it is particularly prominent. The very title of *The Defendant* bears witness to it, but it is by no means confined to the articles that were thought worth reprinting. All subjects are alike to him, if only a fight can be extracted from them. Those who think that the South African War was justifiable are not subjected to a fiercer fire than those who think that Bacon wrote Shakespeare's plays. We see him laughing, like the war-horse in Job, at the shaking of the spears, dealing thwacking blows with enormous enjoyment and good humour, keeping a dozen controversies going at once as a juggler keeps billiard balls.

It is the combative spirit which has been from the first apparent in Mr. Chesterton which has led to his being labelled "paradoxical." The term may be suffered to pass, but it must be insisted that there is no affinity between Mr. Chesterton's paradoxes and those polished inversions which Oscar Wilde brought into fashion.

Wilde's paradoxes were purely artistic products fashioned solely for the sake of their own wit, neatness, and humour. "Divorces are made in Heaven," is a typical and very admirable specimen. The phrase is intended to startle and amuse, but certainly not to provoke thought, much less controversy. It is wholly self-sufficient, a perfect work of art, which further elaboration, above all, anything in the nature of argument, would utterly spoil. Finally, it has no reference to the serious philosophy of Wilde or of anybody else. Now, Mr. Chesterton occasionally indulges in inversions of this type— "a good bush needs no wine" and "nothing fails like success." He is not, I think, very successful in inventing these phrases—certainly no one would think of comparing them with Wilde's exquisite inventions. But the difference lies deeper than any question of relative merit. The difference is one of aim. Wilde's paradoxes would, as I say, be spoilt altogether by explanation. But the whole value—indeed, the whole meaning—of the expressions quoted above lies in the explanation which accompanies them. They are not toys fashioned and tossed about at random. They are shots fired in a campaign.

The typical Chestertonian paradox consists not in the inversion of a proverb, but in the deliberate presentation of some unusual and unpopular thesis with all its provocative features displayed, with all the consequences which are likely to startle or anger opponents insisted on to the point of wild exaggeration. It is unnecessary to give instances, for almost every essay that Mr. Chesterton has written is an instance. That on Rudyard Kipling in *Heretics* is perhaps one of the strongest. Mr. Chesterton does not gently suggest, as another writer of his opinions would have done, that Mr. Kipling's patriotism is not of the highest and purest type. He boldly flings down the statement that a complete absence of patriotism is his dominant characteristic. Closely connected with this provocative method of attack is a marked refusal to present his own position in pleasing or soothing colours, a determination that his opponents shall miss nothing in it that they will dislike. This peculiarity perhaps lends some colour to Mr. Shaw's suggestion that Mr. Chesterton is French.[55] For Frenchmen often display that fierce refusal to disguise the ugly parts of their creed. Where, for instance, an English Freethinker would say: "The human reason will give men better and truer illumination than the outworn lamps of theology," the French Freethinker exclaims: "With a superb gesture we have put out in Heaven the lights that shall never be lighted again!" Despite the complete antagonism of doctrine, there is something very Chestertonian about that defiant outburst.

Later an incident occurred which gave him a new opportunity and a wider public. At the beginning of the South African War the *Daily Chronicle*, under the editorship of Mr. Massingham, was the principal Pro-Boer organ; while the *Daily News*, under Mr. Cook, was the organ of the Liberal Imperialists. Later the two papers changed sides. The proprietors of the *Daily Chronicle* supplanted Mr. Massingham by an Imperialist editor, and subsequently a syndicate of wealthy Radicals bought the *Daily News* and ousted Mr. Cook.[56] The new *Daily News*

---

55. For this suggestion by Shaw, see Appendix E.

56. This is Henry W. Massingham (1860–1924). The two papers merged into the *News Chronicle* in 1930, which was absorbed by the *Daily Mail* in 1960.

was naturally anxious to enlist all the talent that was available for opposing the Imperialist war policy, and the eyes of its proprietors and editors naturally turned to G.K.C. Then began that series of Saturday articles which have continued without a break ever since.

Every one, I think, must have been struck by the incongruity of Mr. Chesterton's weekly appearance in the *Daily News*. The insertion of a story by Guy de Maupassant in the *Christian Herald* would hardly seem more fantastic.[57] The fact is that the accident of concurrence on the overmastering issue of the war (and even on that the conclusion was reached by wholly different roads) had thrown G.K.C. into the company of those who had really least in common with him. The strong loyalty of old ties and old associations which is characteristic of him has kept him faithful to the *News*, with the result that he is almost the only writer of the day who has the ear of his adversaries, whose congregation is, indeed, almost wholly composed of his adversaries. Generally speaking, people buy the papers that express their own views, and find therein the articles of people who agree with them. But the odd accident of Mr. Chesterton's connection with the *Daily News* provides a notable exception. **Thousands of peaceful semi-Tolstoian Nonconformists have for six years been compelled to listen every Saturday morning to a fiery apostle preaching consistently the praise of the three things which seem to them most obviously the signs-manual of Hell—War, Drink, and Catholicism.**

Shortly afterwards Mr. Chesterton collected another volume of his articles and published them under the title of *Twelve Types*. The book is interesting, as I shall show in another chapter, as indicating a further movement of his mind away from the philosophy of *The Wild Knight* and towards the philosophy of *Heretics*. It is also interesting as the first publication which exhibits him as a critic. To call it a book of criticism would, however, be a complete misnomer. In most of the essays there is really hardly any criticism properly so called. What Mr. Chesterton does is merely to put forward his own views with immense vigour and pugnacity, using the views of some other man as a foil. It is not criticism; but it is immensely entertaining.

All this time his interest in politics continued unabated. It was not only in prose that he assailed the current political philosophy of the day. Week after week verses, terse and vigorous and charged with the fiercest irony or indignation, appeared in *The Speaker* from his pen.

One of these is a defiance launched at the disturbers of Pro-Boer meetings. Another, in a different vein, is a metrical version of Mr. Chamberlain's election speech.[58] I will quote two verses of it, because it is a good specimen of the kind of *jeu d'esprit* which G.K.C. can do extraordinarily well when he chooses:

57. Guy de Maupassant (1850–1893) was a popular French short story writer who was hostile to religion.
58. Joseph Chamberlain (1836–1914), once the mayor of Birmingham, was a popular politician.

At Birmingham among my own
Dear People I appear.
For I was born at Camberwell,
Not very far from here;
And, if you choose another man,
My public life is closed;
But you will find it difficult,
Since I am unopposed.

Have we not armies at the front
That we can turn to mobs,
Which out of love for me have shown
Some deference to "Bobs"?
They're sensitive, and, if they heard
Their Joseph had been hissed,
They'd have no nerve to meet the foe
That does not now exist

In marked contrast to this charming absurdity is the almost brutal violence
of the poem written on the morrow of the General Election, with its torrent of
bitter taunts:

Never so low as this we blundered.
Dead we have been; but not so dead
As these, that live on the life they squandered,
As these, that drink of the blood they shed.

We never boasted the thing we bungled,
We never flaunted the thing that fails,
We never quailed from the living laughter
To howl to the dead who tell no tales.

'Twas another finger at least that pointed
Our wasted men and our empty bags,
It was not we who sounded the trumpet
In front of the triumph of wrecks and rags!

Altogether, then, the pen of G.K.C. was pretty well occupied during the
three years of the war. He fought hard for his side, and he has left on record only
recently his memories of the contest. In a poem in the *Daily News* on last year's
London County Council election he wrote:

I dream of the days when work was scrappy,
And rare in our pockets the mark of the mint;
When we were angry and poor and happy,

And proud of seeing our names in print.
For so they conquered, and so we scattered,
When the Devil rode, and his dogs smelt gold,
And the peace of a harmless folk was shattered,
When I was twenty and odd years old.
When mongrel men that the market classes,
Had slimy hands upon England's rod;
And sword in hand upon Afric's passes,
Her last Republic cried to God!

The three years of war mark the three years of Mr. Chesterton's journalistic apprenticeship. When it began in 1899 he was still a beginner. Its last embers had not been stamped out when Mr. John Morley asked him to do for the English Men of Letters series a monograph on Browning.

With the publication of that book he definitely passes from journalism to literature.

3

A CRITIC OF LETTERS

Dickens is, I think, Mr. Chesterton's masterpiece in criticism, because Dickens is the author whose way of looking at life was most like his own.

I HAVE taken the publication of his *Robert Browning* as the point at which Mr. Chesterton definitely enters the world of permanent, as distinguished from ephemeral, letters. This entrance was accompanied by much the same buzz of curiosity, excitement, and admiration as greeted his growing reputation as a journalist, but with this difference, that the dissentient voices were now louder and more numerous, so that blame and even violent denunciation were more freely mingled with the enthusiasm of praise.

It was natural that it should be so, nor would it be fair to attribute the attitude of his most hostile critics to personal motives of spite or jealousy. Such motives may have operated in some cases—indeed, they are the inevitable price of so sudden and startling a success. But in the great majority of instances the irritation of his critics was quite natural and intelligible.

Mr. Chesterton had served his apprenticeship in journalism, and even among journalists—at any rate, among what may be called literary journalists—his manner had seemed almost provocatively journalistic. He now entered on a new career as a man of letters. In that there is nothing unusual; many men have graduated in Fleet Street for the salons of literature. But what many thought almost indecent was the extent to which the neophyte seemed to be at ease in the intellectual and artistic Zion which ought to have put him on his best behaviour. He walks into its holy places (metaphorically speaking) with his hat on, and utterly refuses to be impressed with its dignity or his own unworthiness. He does not modify or subdue his riotous journalistic style; what was good enough for the readers of *The Speaker* and the *Daily News* ought to be good enough for the students of literature. At any rate, it is all he has to give them, and if they do not like it they can leave it. They did not like it, but to leave it was no easy matter, for the most hardened academic could not disguise from himself the fact that these extraordinary books of criticism which violated every canon of literary decency were uproariously readable.

The cause of their pre-eminence in this respect is identical with the cause of their irritant effect on the epicures of art—they are the work of a journalist, and a journalist must be readable or perish. Of course, in these books, as, for the matter of that, in his purely journalistic work, Mr. Chesterton is much more than readable—he is often profound, nearly always forcible, generally suggestive. But the fact that struck the world as startling in a solid piece of literary criticism and appreciation was not that it should be profound forcible, or suggestive, but that by some strange portent it should actually be readable.

I have said that in approaching serious criticism Mr. Chesterton made no change in his method of writing. There is, indeed, in the *Browning* ample indication that the author is writing with more care and conscience than he gave to his weekly contributions to the Press. But the only effect of this is that what he has been doing all along he now does better. The brilliance is better sustained, the effects are better prepared, but it is the same kind of brilliance, the same kind of effect.

You can hardly turn to any page of the *Browning* without lighting on a passage which you can no more imagine occurring in any other volume of the "English Men of Letters" series than you can imagine a rowdy, topical song occurring in one of Racine's Tragedies. For instance, Mr. Chesterton wishes to contrast the obscurity of Mr. George Meredith, which arises from the subtilty and complexity of the ideas to be expressed, with the obscurity of Browning, which is due to a sort of swift impatience. The distinction is a sound and a valuable one. But who but Mr. Chesterton would have dared to illustrate it by making up imaginary descriptions of a man being knocked downstairs in the styles of the two great writers? Who, again, would have ventured to translate a passage from Tennyson into Browningese, and a passage from Browning into Tennysonese, to show the suitability of their respective styles to their respective subjects? These are no isolated instances; the same defiance of literary conventions runs through the whole of the *Browning*, and is hardly less marked in the later monograph on Dickens.

Lord Macaulay prided himself on having destroyed "the dignity of history,"[59] and it may be that, when sufficient time has passed to enable men to weigh fairly his merits and defects, that service will remain his greatest and most permanent title to gratitude. In the same way Mr. Chesterton might not unfairly claim to have helped to destroy the equally pernicious "dignity of literary criticism." **Of both Macaulay and Mr. Chesterton it may be said that they never omit an anecdote or a reference which may help to make the impression more vivid because the anecdote or reference is in itself trivial or grotesque.** Macaulay at the most exciting crisis of the Revolution does not forget to remind us that

59. In volume 1 of *History of England* Thomas Babington Macaulay (1800–1859), wrote: "I shall cheerfully bear the reproach of having descended below the dignity of history."

Charles II said of the Prince of Denmark "that he had tried him drunk and he had tried him sober, and that, drunk or sober, there was nothing in him." Similarly Mr. Chesterton introduces into a book of grave criticism such stories as that of the lady who, meeting Robert Browning at dinner and ignorant of his identity, asked: "Who is that too exuberant stockbroker?" He has his reward. Doubts may exist as to the correctness of the judgments passed in the *Browning* and the *Dickens*. But there can be no doubt about the amazing graphic vigour of the portraiture.

In these violations of academic orthodoxy Mr. Chesterton is abundantly justified by the result. But more valid objection may be taken to another habit which he had acquired in journalism and which he continued to use in his books—the habit of illustrating his thesis by references to obviously ephemeral phenomena in life or literature. In the *Browning*, for example, we find the obscurity of the poet illustrated by a reference to Miss Marie Corelli. In the *Dickens* the popularity of the novelist is contrasted with the popularity of Mr. William Le Queux.[60] Now, in a *Daily News* article such references would be perfectly defensible, for such an article is only intended to be ephemeral, and it may fairly be assumed that every one who reads it has heard of the two authors referred to. But a serious study of a great man like Robert Browning or Charles Dickens ought to aim at permanence. It should be written with an eye on that posterity which will certainly read Browning and Dickens, and which is hardly likely to be familiar with Miss Corelli or Mr. Le Queux. If they read Mr. Chesterton, they will necessarily find these passages as unintelligible as we find the obscurest parts of the "Dunciad."[61] The same objection applies to the frequent reference to the transient fashions of politics which meets us on almost every page. These things must tend to hinder the books from being what in many ways they deserve to be—durable monuments of a durable fame.

Another criticism commonly brought against Mr. Chesterton's critical works has reference to the digressions in which they abound. Here, I think, a distinction must be made. Mr. Chesterton's habit of creating before he draws a man's portrait an impression of the forces which have moulded him, and the background against which he is to be relieved, appears to me wholly admirable. To do this intelligently and effectively it may be necessary to go back to very remote origins, and discuss problems apparently far removed from the immediate subject of study. Many of the greatest and most perfect architects of letters—Newman, for example, and Burke—do this constantly, and where Mr. Chesterton does it he is often at his best.[62] We could ill spare the admirable

---

60. Marie Corelli (1855–1924) and William T. LeQueux (1864–1927) are British novelists.

61. "The Dunciad" is a literary satire by Alexander Pope (1688-1744).

62. John Henry Cardinal Newman, (1801–1890) was a Catholic writer and an influential intellectual. The conservative Edmund Burke (1729–1797) wrote on politics and continues to be widely read today.

analysis of the temper of the nineteenth century which introduces the little monograph on Watts, or the presentation of the angry yet optimistic Radicalism of the 'thirties in the *Dickens*. These passages are not only good in themselves; they are good in their places, and they make the whole work better, more intelligible, and more complete.

But Mr. Chesterton does undoubtedly from time to time indulge in a kind of digression which is not so easy to defend. Every now and then some comparatively unimportant incident or remark which he thinks it necessary to chronicle will remind him of an issue quite irrelevant to his subject, but supremely interesting to himself. When this happens he frequently deserts his subject without scruple, and begins what is in effect an entirely independent essay on the issue raised.

Several examples of this tendency will be found in the *Browning*. Mr. Chesterton has to chronicle that Browning was very fond of Italy, and that he and his wife went to live there. But the mention of Italy in the 'forties immediately calls up memories of the struggle for Italian liberty which was then commencing. The subject fires his blood, and he goes ahead for five pages, recalling the French Revolution, the victories of Napoleon, the triumph of the Holy Alliance, and the ultimate break-up of "the frozen continent of non-possumus" which that triumph established. It is very fine writing—perhaps one of the finest passages in the book—but what light does it throw on Robert Browning? Had Mr. Chesterton been writing a study of Elizabeth Barrett Browning I would not have complained; for Mrs. Browning celebrated the struggle for Italian freedom and unity in some of her noblest poems, and a full understanding of her would be impossible without some comprehension of the cause into which she threw so much of her energy. Browning as a private citizen may have shared her sympathies, but so far as his work is concerned, the movement might never have existed. That it influenced the bent of his mind or genius in any way is not obvious, nor does Mr. Chesterton make any attempt to show that it did so. He is writing about the Italian Revolution, not because it affected Robert Browning, but because it affects G.K. Chesterton. The whole passage is in reality a *Daily News* article on "Garibaldi" which has accidentally got into the wrong place.

In order to understand properly the peculiar traits of Mr. Chesterton's books of criticism there is another fact to be borne in mind. Just as he was a journalist before he was an author, so he was a writer on philosophical questions before he was a critic. His early reviews in *The Speaker* and *Daily News* use the particular book under discussion only as a peg on which to hang some general doctrine. This will be seen very clearly in the *Twelve Types*. That volume contains studies of some of the most interesting figures in literary history—Pope, Byron, Carlyle, Scott, Charlotte Brontë, Tolstoy, Stevenson, and William Morris. Yet hardly one of them deals exhaustively with the literary quality or position of the author, and several of them are random essays on some theme suggested by the author's name.

The worst case of this is the essay on Byron—the worst essay, I think, that Mr. Chesterton has ever written. Byron is an almost ideally fruitful subject for serious criticism and appreciation. In that most remarkable artistic insurrection which overthrew the dynasty of Pope, and made possible the whole school of naturalistic poets from Shelley[63] to Kipling, he occupies a unique place—a place analogous to that filled by Erasmus in the Reformation and by Mirabeau in the French Revolution. He saw the need of a change, but he would have made it a constitutional one. He would have relaxed the extreme rigours of the classical school, brought it into closer touch with nature, fulfilled it with new energy and passion. But he would have left its fundamental principles unquestioned, its gods undethroned, its permanent tradition unbroken. Of all this there is not a hint in Mr. Chesterton's essay. As little realization is there of the immense importance of Byron to European thought as the Liberal aristocrat with the Liberal's hatred of despotism and an aristocrat's hatred of authority, whose voice ringing through Europe told the banded kings that the Revolution had been conquered too late. All that Mr. Chesterton has to say about Byron is that he was not a pessimist, but an optimist, because he enjoyed his own poetry! There is just about enough truth and value in this to justify a single epigram. Spread thin over fourteen pages, it produces a sense of intense and quite justifiable irritation.

Nevertheless, *Twelve Types* gives pregnant hints of unused powers as a critic. Two of the essays—those on Charlotte Brontë and Scott—real criticism, so far as they go, and extraordinarily illuminating and convincing, though they are rather sketches of their subjects taken from one particular angle than exhaustive studies of them. In some of the others there are phrases and sentences full of insight. The following description of the literary quality of Tolstoy's stories is almost perfect:

> The curious cold white light of morning that shines over all the tales, the folk-lore simplicity with which "a man or a woman" is spoken of without further identification, the love—one might almost say the lust—for the qualities of brute materials, the hardness of wood and the softness of mud, the ingrained belief in a certain ancient kindliness sitting beside the very cradle of the race of man—these influences are truly moral.

In that there is the quick eye for essentials which is the first quality of a good critic.

And, indeed, when Mr. Chesterton allows himself to be a critic pure and simple, he is always good. If some of his critical efforts have been failures, it has not been from any defect in the critical faculty, but rather from that permanent

---

63. Percy Bysshe Shelley (1792–1822) was a gifted lyric poet.

temptation of his to leave the work of criticism for that of philosophizing which becomes irresistible when the philosophy of the author under consideration is in violent conflict with his own. He is always at his best when he is analyzing a writer with whose root point of view he is sympathetic. No critic ever had a keener sense of Wordsworth's maxim that "style is the sacrament of thought." This sense, which gets in his way when he is discussing a writer whose view of life he does not understand, helps him when he is dealing with a sympathetic mind. For then he can not only give free play to his remarkable power of selecting truly and describing vividly the external qualities of an artist, but he can see these externals in the light of the author's conscious or sub-conscious intention.

I think I can best illustrate this by a quotation from his solitary essay in the criticism of painting, the monograph on Watts.[64] He has been repudiating the suggestion that the mysticism of Watts is "Celtic," and has for this purpose been contrasting him with Burne-Jones:

> It is remarkable that even the technical style of Watts gives a contradiction to this Celtic theory. Watts is strong precisely where the Celt is weak, and weak precisely where the Celt is strong. The only thing that the Celt has lacked in art is that hard mass, that naked outline, that αρχιτεκνον [master builder] which makes Watts a sort of sculptor of draughtsmanship. It is as well for us that the Celt has not had this: if he had, he would rule the world with a rod of iron; for he has everything else. There are no hard black lines in Burke's orations, or Tom Moore's songs, or the plays of Mr. W.B. Yeats. Burke is the greatest of political philosophers, because in him only are there distances and perspectives, as there are on the real earth, with its mists of morning and evening, and its blue horizons and broken skies. Moore's songs have neither a pure style nor deep realization, nor originality of form, nor thought nor wit nor vigour, but they have something else which is none of these things, which is nameless and the one thing needful. In Mr. Yeats' plays there is only one character, the hero who rules and kills all the others, and his name is Atmosphere. Atmosphere and the gleaming distances are the soul of Celtic greatness as they were of Burne-Jones, who was, as I have said, weak precisely where Watts is strong, in the statuesque quality in drawing, in the love of heavy hands like those of *Mammon,* of a strong back like that of *Eve Repentant,* in a single fearless and austere outline like that of the angel in *The Court of Death,* in the frame-filling violence of *Jonah,* in the halfwitted brutality of *The Minotaur.* He is deficient, that is to say, in what can only be called the god-like materialism of art. Watts, on the other hand, is peculiarly strong in it. Idealist as he is, there is nothing frail or phantasmal about the things or the figures he loves. Though not himself a robust man, he loves robustness; he loves a great bulk of shoulder, an abrupt

---

64. Gilbert's 1904 *G.F. Watts* is about the painter and sculptor George Frederic Watts (1817–1904), who is compared to Edward C. Burne-Jones (1833–1898), another artist.

bend of neck, a gigantic stride, a large and swinging limb, a breast bound as with bands of brass. Of course, the deficiency in such a case is very far from being altogether on one side. There are abysses in Burne-Jones which Watts could not understand—the Celtic madness, older than any sanity, the hunger that will remain after the longest feast, the sorrow that is built up of stratified delights. From the point of view of the true Celt, Watts, the Watts who painted the great stoical pictures *Love and Death, Time, Death, and Judgment, The Court of Death, Mammon,* and *Cain,* this pictorial Watts would probably be, must almost certainly be, simply a sad, sane, strong, stupid Englishman. He may or may not be Welsh by extraction or by part of his extraction, but in spirit he is an Englishman, with all the faults and all the disadvantages of an Englishman. He is a great Englishman like Milton or Gladstone, of the type, that is to say, that were too much alive for anything but gravity, and who enjoyed themselves far too much to trouble to enjoy a joke. Matthew Arnold has come near to defining that kind of idealism, so utterly different from the Celtic kind, which is to be found in Milton and again in Watts. He has called it, in one of his finest and most accurate phrases, "the imaginative reason."

No better example than this could be found of the co-relation between the spirit and the form of an artist. But there are several passages in both the *Browning* and the *Dickens* where the same thing is done incomparably well. Let every one turn to the analysis of Browning's taste for the grotesque, and say whether among all the multitudinous commentators on the most discussed of modern poets the truth has ever been put so forcibly or with such unerring insight before.

I think the *Dickens* a better book than the *Browning;* certainly it is a more perfect book. The principal literary fault of the *Browning* was a certain careless-ness of perspective. The character of Mrs. Browning's father, for example, is examined with a minuteness of detail which is quite out of proportion to the importance of that gentleman in the poet's life. Again, as we have seen, any little incident which happened to Browning, and which appeals to Mr. Chesterton's imagination, is enough to set him oft on a side issue and lead him to devote to it pages which might well have been given to matter more germane to the subject. In *Dickens* these defects either disappear or are greatly diminished. The proportions of the book are natural and harmonious. The digressions have nearly always some relation to the essentials; they are not introduced, as they often were in the former book, merely for their own sake. Nor has this advance in technical method been purchased by any sacrifice of the old originality or the old exuberant vigour.

Dickens is, I think, Mr. Chesterton's masterpiece in criticism, because Dickens is the author whose way of looking at life was most like his own.

Dickens had the same pugnacity, the same sense of the extravagant possibilities of life, the same incurable romanticism. Mr. Chesterton can therefore get thoroughly inside Dickens, and some of his appreciations have the note of that finest critical genius—the genius that tells us about an author not what we did not know before, but what we always knew but could never say. I do not know a better example of this than the passage in which he describes the eternal quality of the great Dickens characters:

> Dickens was a mythologist rather than a novelist; he was the last of the mythologists, and perhaps the greatest. He did not always manage to make his characters men, but he always managed, at the least, to make them gods. They are creatures like Punch or Father Christmas. They live statically, in a perpetual summer of being themselves. It was not the aim of Dickens to show the effect of time and circumstance upon a character; it was not even his aim to show the effect of character on time and circumstance. It is worth remark, in passing, that whenever he tried to describe change in a character, he made a mess of it, as in the repentance of Dombey or the apparent deterioration of Boffin.[65] It was his aim to show character hung in a kind of happy void, in a world apart from time—yes, and essentially apart from circumstance, though the phrase may seem odd in connection with the godlike horseplay of *Pickwick*. But all the Pickwickian events, wild as they often are, were only designed to display the greater wildness of souls, or sometimes merely to bring the reader within touch, so to speak, of that wildness. The author would have fired Mr. Pickwick out of a cannon to get him to Wardle's by Christmas; he would have taken the roof off to drop him into Bob Sawyer's party. But once put Pickwick at Wardle's, with his punch and a group of gorgeous personalities, and nothing will move him from his chair. Once he is at Sawyer's party, he forgets how he got there; he forgets Mrs. Bardell and all his story. For the story was but an incantation to call up a god, and the god (Mr. Jack Hopkins) is present in divine power. Once the great characters are face to face, the ladder by which they climbed is forgotten and falls down, the structure of the story drops to pieces, the plot is abandoned, the other characters deserted at every kind of crisis; the whole crowded thoroughfare of the tale is blocked by two or three talkers, who take their immortal ease as if they were already in Paradise. For they do not exist for the story; the story exists for them, and they know it.

It is impossible to deny to anyone who could write this passage the possession of critical power of the highest type. Yet that power is not without its limitations, and the worst limitation is this, that his passion for generalization is liable to seduce him from the true work of criticism and to lead him not only into irrelevance, but sometimes into flat nonsense. If a generalization can be expressed

---

65. The Charles Dickens references are to the self-centered Paul Dombey in *Dombey and Son* (1846–1848) and the miserly Nicodemus Boffin in *Our Mutual Friend* (1865), the last novel he completed.

G. K. Chesterton, a Criticism

with some epigrammatic force, and is in harmony with his own broad philosophy of life, he seems sometimes to care nothing at all whether it is consistent with his own argument or with the facts as he himself has stated them.

I will take a curious and striking instance from the *Browning*. Discussing Mr. Santayana's description of Browning as a poet of barbarism, he says:

> Thus Mr. Santayana is, perhaps, the most valuable of all the Browning critics. He has gone out of his way to endeavour to realize what it is that repels him in Browning, and he has discovered the fault which none of Browning's opponents have discovered. And in this he has discovered the merit which none of Browning's admirers have discovered. Whether the quality be a good or a bad quality, Mr. Santayana is perfectly right. The whole of Browning's poetry does rest upon primitive feeling; *and the only comment to be added is that so does the whole of every one else's poetry.*"

Now, it must surely be obvious to every one—it would have been obvious to Mr. Chesterton if he had stopped to think about it—that the clause which I have italicized makes nonsense of his own argument. If there was a specific quality in Browning which repelled Mr. Santayana, it must have been a quality peculiar to Browning. To say that Mr. Santayana was repelled by Browning (in contradistinction to other poets) on account of a quality which Browning shared with all other poets is palpably absurd. Moreover, if the quality in question was not specially Browningesque, but only generally poetical, where does the extraordinary merit of Mr. Santayana's "discovery" come in? Why is he "the most valuable of all the Browning critics"? It is quite obvious that Mr. Chesterton, when he began to discuss Mr. Santayana's criticism, did intend to maintain that the quality complained of was specially characteristic of Browning. But seeing a chance of scoring effectively off Mr. Santayana, and at the same time of propounding a theory of poetry in general harmony with his own critical leanings, he ruthlessly sacrificed an interesting critical thesis to a casual epigram.

That is an example of Mr. Chesterton's occasional indifference to the inconsistency of his generalizations with his previous argument. I will now take a case of his indifference to their inconsistency with facts. In the course of his book on Dickens he had maintained the thesis that Dickens' humane sense of fun made it impossible for him to feel any very vindictive anger towards his great comic characters even when they were great villains—that, for instance, he loved rather than hated Pecksniff. This appears to me to be generally true. But in the introduction to *Martin Chuzzlewit* (one of a series of very brilliant introductions to the individual novels which he undertook immediately afterwards) he makes on the subject of Dickens' humane mirth a much more startling statement. "This," he says, "may be broadly said and yet with confidence, that Dickens is always at his best when he is laughing at the people whom he really admires." He goes on to give instances—Pickwick and Sam Weller, Dick Swiveller and the Marchioness.

Doubtless many other instances could be given of sympathetic characters who are incomparably entertaining. But what a formidable list could be made on the other side. Stiggins, Bumble, Mantilini, Squeers, Quilp, the Brasses, Pecksniff, Mrs. Gamp, Elijah Pogram and his circle, Major Bagstock, Mrs. Skewton, Skimpole, Chadband, Guppy, Turveydrop, Podsnap, Fascination Fledgeby, Silas Wegg. All these and many more that could be named, considered as we consider our neighbours, are either contemptible or vile, yet all are painted in undying colours, and all are full of an eternal laughter. If I were asked to quote the funniest thing in Dickens (an impossible choice, I admit), I think I should choose the speech of Mr. Chadband referring to his requiring "corn and wine and oil." And this is precisely the place where Chadband's wickedness is at its blackest.[66]

The fact is that evidence never matters much to Mr. Chesterton. He has abundant imagination, sympathy, and insight, and he can reason clearly and correctly in the abstract; indeed, he is one of the most effective controversialists of the day. But of the temper which we call scientific, the power of deducting general principles from a vast mass of facts, he shows little at any time, and none at all when his judgment is warped by a general theory.

One thing must be said, in conclusion, about Mr. Chesterton's critical exploit. He is often a good critic, but he is never a critic for criticism's sake. At heart he is always a pamphleteer, a crusader, almost a swashbuckler. That characteristic which I have already noticed more than once, the tendency to write with his eye on an opponent, is as noticeable in his critical works as elsewhere. Watts is studied worthily as a great painter, but he is also studied because his sense of the seriousness and responsibility of art is a foil to the aesthetic frivolity of the modern world. Browning is praised with discrimination as a great poet, but he is also praised because his robust optimism is a challenge to the doubt and despair of the modern world. Dickens is honoured triumphantly as an incomparable humorist and draughtsman of character, but he is also honoured because his fierce, almost rowdy Radicalism is an offence to the oligarchic decencies of the modern world. These dead men are led out as the dead Cid was led out to rout the Saracens. And at the bridle rein of each rides G.K.C. with drawn sword ready for battle.[67]

---

66. *Bleak House,* Ch. 54: "Thus invited, Mr. Chadband steps forth, and after a little sleek smiling and a little oil-grinding with the palms of his hands, delivers himself as follows, 'My friends, we are now—Rachael, my wife, and I—in the mansions of the rich and great. Why are we now in the mansions of the rich and great, my friends? Is it because we are invited? Because we are bidden to feast with them, because we are bidden to rejoice with them,... because we are bidden to dance with them? No. Then why are we here, my friends? Are we in possession of a sinful secret, and do we require corn, and wine, and oil, or what is much the same thing, money, for the keeping thereof? Probably so, my friends.'"

67. "The Cid" was the name given to Rodrigo Diaz de Bivar, a Spanish knight, by the Saracens (Moors). A legend says that just before he died St. Peter told them that he would lead an army to victory over the Moors. Embalmed and with sword in hand, he was taken into battle and a great victory resulted.

4

THE DRIFT TOWARDS
ORTHODOXY

*This conviction brought him into sharp conflict with one of those
vast dogmas which the nineteenth century had assumed without ever
proving or even distinctly formulating—the dogma of Progress.*

I MUST turn aside for a moment at this point to consider the change which was gradually coming over Mr. Chesterton's opinions, a change which grew more marked year by year till it culminated in the controversy with Mr. Blatchford, when for the first time, I think, he publicly avowed his belief in the central doctrines of orthodox Christianity.[68]

Anyone comparing *The Defendant* with *The Wild Knight* will be struck by a very marked difference, and it is none the less real because so far it is a difference of attitude rather than a cognate difference of doctrine. I do not know of any specific opinion expressed in the poems which is recanted in the essays. But, all the same, the spiritual atmosphere is changed.

I think I can best express my sense of the change something in this fashion. I have already pointed out that it is one of the characteristic notes of G.K.C. that he writes with his eye always on a real or hypothetical opponent. Now, in *The Wild Knight* the foes against whom the attack is directed are principally the orthodox, the contented supporters of the established order in Church and State. In *The Defendant* it is the heretics, the revolutionaries, the impugners of existing things who are primarily assailed. The fundamental sanctities recognized are

---

68. Chesterton explained his 1903–1904 clash with Robert Blatchford, editor of the *Clarion*: "That this stage may be understood, it must be realised what the things I was defending against Blatchford were. It was not a question of some abstract theological thesis.... I was not yet so far gone in orthodoxy as to be so theological as all that. What I was defending seemed to me a plain matter of ordinary human morals. Indeed it seemed to me to raise the question of the very possibility of any morals. It was the question of Responsibility, sometimes called the question of Free Will, which Mr. Blatchford had attacked in a series of vigorous and even violent proclamations of Determinism.... It was not that I began by believing in supernormal things. It was that the unbelievers began by disbelieving even in normal things. It was the secularists who drove me to theological ethics, by themselves destroying any sane or rational possibility of secular ethics." *The Autobiography of G.K. Chesterton* (New York: Sheed & Ward, 1936), 181–182.

much the same in both cases, but in the poems they are preached to a conventional world which has forgotten them; in the essays they are defended against an unconventional world which is bent on destroying them. The "Kings" and "Priests" who receive so formidable a castigation in *The Wild Knight*, escape without censure in *The Defendant*. It is the anarchists, the atheists, the people who want to abolish marriage, the people who deny the validity of patriotism, against whom the defences are set up.

At the same time there is abundant evidence that his feelings were softening towards the old faiths. At the time when he was writing the "Defences" he wrote an article for *The Speaker*, defending the Ritualists. The attitude he took up was that of a fairminded outsider, indifferent to doctrinal differences, but disliking persecution by whomsoever practised. Nevertheless there may be noted in that essay a more sympathetic tone towards Catholicism, which is absent from his earlier utterances. In *Twelve Types* he goes further, and in the essay on "Francis of Assisi" enters upon something like a defence of Monasticism, an institution upon which he would certainly have poured scorn and indignation in his *Wild Knight* period

Before I endeavour to trace the further progress of the change it may be well to suggest some of the causes which, even while he was writing the "Defences" for *The Speaker*, were tending to accelerate it.

In June, 1900, Mr. Chesterton married Miss Frances Blogg. She was a lady of a type of which a generation of "advanced" culture is producing a plentiful crop—the conservative rebel against the conventions of the unconventional. Living amidst the aesthetic anarchism of Bedford Park, she was in a state of seething revolt against it. Her husband was not at all the man to discourage such a revolt, and her influence on him (which has been considerable) was, one may guess, all on the side of his growing orthodoxy.

The other personal influence which made itself felt in his life about this time, and told in the same direction, was his friendship with Mr. Hilaire Belloc. Mr. Belloc would require a whole book to himself if he were to be properly described, and I do not propose to attempt such a task in this place. But to omit all mention of him would be to omit one of the most potent influences in the development of the writer whom we are considering. The two men had not only a temperamental affinity, but from the first many points of intellectual sympathy, notably the fact that they were of the few who disliked the war without disliking war. But there was this difference, that while Mr. Chesterton's views were still in process of formation, those of Mr. Belloc had already, so to speak, solidified and solidified round the iron framework of Catholic dogma. In his own phrase, "they formed a system and were final." Now, it may be taken as an almost invariable rule that if two persons are closely associated, and one of them has unsettled opinions while the opinions of the other are fixed, the former will gravitate towards the philosophy of the latter as a meteor gravitates towards a planet. So, under the probably unconscious influence of Mr. Belloc, Mr. Chesterton was drawn towards the Catholic Faith.

But there were other than personal influences tending to sway him. I have already dwelt upon the importance of the South African War and the controversies to which it gave rise in determining the bent of his mind. Now, there was this peculiarity about the war disputes, that both sides appealed to the same ideals—marched, so to speak, under the same banner. It was not defended, as the great French War, for instance, was defended, as a war for the preservation of authority and tradition.[69] On the contrary, it was defended as a democratic war, a war for the purpose of breaking a narrow, corrupt, and old-fashioned oligarchy which obstructed the progress of the world. Nor could it be denied that there was at least this measure of truth in the claim—that the Boers unmistakably represented the old order, and the Outlanders the new. The Rhodesian party in South Africa called itself "Progressive," and it was perfectly justified in doing so, if a progressive be taken to mean a man who goes the way the world appears to be going. It is not altogether surprising if Mr. Chesterton, who hated the whole spirit and ideal of that party, felt that the way the world appeared to be going was the way to Hell!

This conviction brought him into sharp conflict with one of those vast dogmas which the nineteenth century had assumed without ever proving or even distinctly formulating—the dogma of Progress. All the great writers of that century are full of the idea of Progress—the idea that the world is inevitably getting better and better. Men of opinion and temperaments as diverse as Shelley and Macaulay accepted it without question.[70] It received an additional impetus from the current misinterpretations of Darwin's doctrine of Evolution; that biological speculation, which in its inventor's mind involved nothing more than a hypothesis concerning the causes which led organisms to approximate to their environment, was interpreted by poets and rhetoricians as a promise of the ultimate triumph of good over evil—"good" and "evil" being just the two words that no true man of science ever uses. Thus Tennyson held that man would:

> Move upwards, working out the brute,
> And let the ape and tiger die.[71]

---

69. The Napoleonic wars were fought against French aggression and the French Revolution.

70. Percy Shelley (1792–1822) was one of the most gifted English lyricists. As a historian, Thomas B. Macaulay (1800–1859) made English history into a tale in which the heroic champions of progress defeat the forces of reaction, an approach often called the Whig interpretation of history.

71. Alfred Lord Tennyson, "In Memoriam A.H.H." In that poem there is despair at the archaeological record of species extinction and what that means for humanity: "Man, her last work, who seem'd so fair,/ Such splendid purpose in his eyes,/ Who roll'd the psalm to wintry skies,/ Who built him fanes of fruitless prayer,/ Who trusted God was love indeed/ And love Creation's final law—/ Tho' Nature, red

until, in the slow processes of time, all mankind became gradually more and more like the Prince Consort! In a word, Progressive Evolutionism became a new religion. It is as a conspicuous rebel against the dogmas of this religion that Mr. Chesterton is most notable in his generation.

Of course, he did not achieve his emancipation from a doctrine so inextricably bound up with all the traditions of his youth without hesitation and doubt. In *The Wild Knight* you will find the idea of Progress everywhere. In *The Defendant* and in the articles written for *The Speaker* about the same time it is less prominent—indeed, opinions are advanced fundamentally inconsistent with it; but its truth is still tacitly assumed. The first tentative challenge, so far as I can discover, will be found in the essay on "Carlyle" included in *Twelve Types*, where he says:

> He denied the theory of progress which assumed that we must be better off than the people of the Twelfth Century. Whether we were better than the people of the Twelfth Century according to him depended entirely on whether we chose or deserved to be.

But here he leaves himself a loop-hole for escape. He is summarizing Carlyle's doctrine, not avowedly formulating his own, and he leaves his reader free to suppose that this is one of the opinions of which he speaks in the context where he says that "even where his view was not the highest truth, it was always a refreshing and beneficent heresy." In the controversy with Mr. Blatchford, on the other hand, he expresses similar views *in propria persona*. In *The Napoleon of Notting Hill* the denial of Progress becomes almost the main thesis of the book. In *Heretics* it is assumed as confidently as the assertion of Progress was assumed by the great Victorian Liberals.

Closely related to this change was another—the complete transformation of his views in regard to the existence of positive evil. **The cause of G.K.C.'s return to a dogmatic faith was not, as has been the case with others, his discovery of the need for a personal God. In that he had always believed; it is assumed in *The Wild Knight* as unhesitatingly as in *Heretics*. His epoch-making discovery was his discovery of the need for a personal Devil.**

Now, it was of the essence of the new Evolutionary Religion in all its varying forms that it denied the Devil, even where it confessed God, Mr. Campbell, the typical exponent of what I may call Christian Evolutionism, describes evil as a thing merely negative—"a shadow where light should be."[72] Mr. Chesterton

---

in tooth and claw/ With ravine, shriek'd against his creed—/ Who loved, who suffer'd countless ills,/ Who battled for the True, the Just,/ Be blown about the desert dust,/ Or seal'd within the iron hills?" Tennyson's answered that man would not cease; he would become something better: "Who throve and branch'd from clime to clime,/ The herald of a higher race..../ To shape and use. Arise and fly/ The reeling Faun, the sensual feast;/ Move upward, working out the beast,/ And let the ape and tiger die."

72. Rev. R.J. Campbell (1867–1956) was the author of books such as *The New Theology* (1907). In Cecil's day, he pastored London's City Temple (Congregational). In the second chapter of *Orthodoxy*, which was

himself held the same view, a view obviously incompatible with the belief in any Devil worthy of the name, at the time when he wrote *The Wild Knight,* as the quotations given in a previous chapter pretty clearly prove. He continued to hold it, though with some signs of doubt and reservation, at the time when he was writing his literary articles for *The Speaker,* for in a review of "Mark Rutherford"[73] we find him distinguishing between a belief in the Devil and a belief in Devils, doubting whether "there is an abyss of evil as deep as the tower of holiness is high," and expressing a hope for the final salvation of all souls. But evidently his hold on the confident optimism of his childhood is slipping.

I have called this current modern philosophy "Evolutionary Religion," but the phrase is liable to misinterpretation. There is not, of course, the slightest foundation for its dogmas in the facts of physical science or in the scientific speculations of Darwin and his followers. The men who really understood those speculations saw this clearly. No one insisted on the positive existence of evil more emphatically than Huxley; no man had less belief in the ultimate certainty of human perfection. Indeed, Huxley avowed on more than one occasion his conviction that the old theological systems, with their stern and pitiless judgments, and their hell-fire for wrong-thinkers as well as for wrongdoers, corresponded more closely with the facts of the universe as revealed by science than the amiable visions of the Broad Churchmen.[74] But the truth is that the progenitors of the New Theology owed little to the doctrine of Evolution save few inspiring words and a false analogy, which might seem to justify to the unscientific multitude the optimistic humanitarian fatalism which they believed on altogether different, and for the most part subjective, grounds.

For that doctrine there was undoubtedly much to be said. Considered intellectually as a theory of the universe addressed to the human reason, it must seem to many hopelessly inadequate. But considered morally as a revolt of the human

---

about to be published as Cecil was writing, Gilbert mentions that: "Some followers of the Reverend R.J. Campbell, in their almost too fastidious spirituality, admit divine sinlessness, which they cannot see even in their dreams. But they essentially deny human sin, which they can see in the street. The strongest saints and the strongest skeptics alike took positive evil as the starting-point of their argument."

73. Mark Rutherford was the pen name of William Hale White (1831–1913), who often wrote on religion in books such as *Pages from a Journal, with other Papers* (1900), and *John Bunyan* (1905).

74. In an article entitled "An Apologetic Irenicon" published in *The Fortnightly Review* (November 1892), Thomas H. Huxley, the most prominent champion of Darwinism, wrote: "It is the secret of the superiority of the best theological teachers to the majority of their opponents, that they substantially recognise these realities of things, however strange the forms in which they clothe their conceptions. The doctrines of predestination; of original sin; of the innate depravity of man and the evil fate of the greater part of the race; of the primacy of Satan in this world; of the essential vileness of matter; of a malevolent Demiurgus subordinate to a benevolent Almighty, who has only lately revealed himself, faulty as they are, appear to me to be vastly nearer the truth than the 'liberal' popular illusions that babies are all born good and that the example of a corrupt society is responsible for their failure to remain so; that it is given to everybody to reach the ethical ideal if he will only try; that all partial evil is universal good; and other optimistic figments, such as that which represents 'Providence' under the guise of a paternal philanthropist, and bids us believe that everything will come right (according to our notions) at last."

heart against what Mr. Chesterton has since called "that unique dispensation which theologians call Calvinism and Christians Devil-worship," it is wholly to be admired.[75] It was humane, idealistic, generous, lofty in its thoughts of God and Man. There is only one thing to be said against it; it will not fit the facts.

In order to get over the obvious difficulties presented by the existence of unmistakable evil, the New Theologians once more called pseudoscience to their aid. For the Devil they substituted "the Brute," which, according to Tennyson, was to be "worked out" as Man moved upwards. The evil in human nature was merely the fading trace of its animal origin, which would disappear altogether as the race approached its ultimate perfection.

But during the contests which raged round the South African problem Mr. Chesterton had seen evil face to face, and he felt it to be emphatically not the "shadow where light should be" of Mr. Campbell, but rather the "darkness visible" of Milton.[76] He had seen the dark features of the Asiatic adventurers who had, as he believed, plotted a gigantic crime and set two simpler and braver peoples to kill each other for their profit, and they seemed to him the foul faces of Devils. Could the existence of these men be explained by saying that they were "undeveloped," that the animal was still too strong in them? Surely it was obvious that they were very much further removed from mere animals than the decent British soldiers, the decent Boer farmers, whom they were sending to the slaughter. They were no relics of barbarism; they were the very latest product of an elaborate civilization. The Enemy of Man was not, it seemed, the Brute, a thing ruder and more senseless than Man, but a thing infinitely subtler than Man—in a word, the Devil.

To a combination of these causes may be traced, I think, the growing orthodoxy of Mr. Chesterton's religious convictions. But just as the sharp contests concerning South Africa had forced him to define his political doctrines to himself, so it was a sudden outbreak of theological controversy which forced him to define for himself and for others the position at which he had arrived in religious matters. The immediate cause of this outbreak was the sudden attack made on the Christian religion by Mr. Robert Blatchford, the Editor of the *Clarion*.

Mr. Blatchford was a consummate master of all the weapons of popular controversy. He could put his case, whatever it might be, forcibly, yet in language so simple that the most ignorant workman could understand it. He had also at

---

75. In Ch. 7 of *Charles Dickens* (1906), Chesterton, referring to *Little Dorrit* (1855–1857), wrote: "The dark house of Arthur Clennam's childhood really depresses us; it is a true glimpse into that quiet street in hell, where live the children of that unique dispensation which theologians call Calvinism and Christians devil-worship. But some stranger crime had really been done there, some more monstrous blasphemy or human sacrifice than the suppression of some silly document advantageous to the silly Dorrits."

76. Hell in John Milton's *Paradise Lost*: "A dungeon horrible, on all sides round,/ As one great furnace flamed; yet from those flames/ No light; but rather darkness visible/ Served only to discover sights of woe,/ Regions of sorrow, doleful shades, where peace/ And rest can never dwell, hope never comes."

his command a certain strong colloquial eloquence and could make his plain English ring suddenly like a sword on an anvil. His Socialist tracts and pamphlets were incomparably the best work of their kind that had been done, and have contributed incalculably to the spread of Socialism in this country. He was undoubtedly less well qualified for philosophical than for economic discussion. He did not know his facts so well. He sometimes displayed a quite startling absence of familiarity with older controversies on the subject, as when he seemed to claim that the obvious argument against Free Will that it is inconsistent with the omnipotence of God was his own discovery. His science was rather crude, and there were undoubtedly plenty of weak points which a skilful adversary might find in his case. But a skilful adversary was not so easy to find.

Indeed, the response to Mr. Blatchford did little credit to the intellectual equipment of modern Christianity. Half its defenders called Mr. Blatchford a blasphemer; the other half, with much greater impertinence, called him a Christian. On the question in regard to which Mr. Blatchford was somewhat at sea they showed themselves more at sea, while their replies lacked altogether the lucidity and boldness in which Mr. Blatchford never failed. Their controversial strategy was infantile. They gave up without a struggle strong positions which could easily have been defended. They put forward weak hypotheses, invented by themselves, and then defended them as if they were of the essence of Christianity. Of all those who took a prominent part on the Christian side only two put up an effective fight the Rev. Charles Marson and G.K. Chesterton.[77]

The principal interest for us of the *Clarion* controversy lies in the fact that it led Mr. Chesterton to make his first public declaration of faith in the orthodox system of Christian dogma. Mr. Blatchford had put a series of questions to his Christian antagonists. Here they are, together with Mr. Chesterton's answers:

(1) *Are you a Christian?*—Certainly.

(2) *What do you mean by the word Christianity?*—The belief that a certain human being whom we call Christ stood to a certain superhuman Being whom we call God in a certain unique transcendental relation which we call sonship.

(3) *What do you believe?*—A considerable number of things. That Mr. Blatchford is an honest man, for instance, and (though less firmly) that there is a place called Japan. If he means, what do I believe in religious matters, I believe the above statement (answer No. 2) and a large number of other mystical dogmas ranging from the mystical dogma that man is the image of God to the mystical dogma that all men are equal, and that babies should not be strangled.

(4) *Why do you believe it?*—Because I perceive life to be logical and workable with these beliefs, and illogical and unworkable without them.

---

77. Charles Marson (1859–1914), an outspoken Anglican priest, wrote *God's Co-operative Society* (1914).

These answers are explicit enough, and the fourth is particularly interesting because it supplies the clue to the kind of defence he afterwards set up.

That defence was wholly pragmatic. He makes no adequate attempt to show that the Christian creed is an intellectually coherent and reasonable explanation of the Universe. He almost admits that it is not so. But he contends that it is a philosophy by which men can live, and that more logical philosophies smash themselves against elemental human necessities.

> Some Determinists fancy that Christianity invented a dogma like free will for fun—a mere contradiction. This is absurd. You have the contradiction, whatever you are. Determinists tell me, with a degree of truth, that Determinism makes no difference to daily life. That means that although the Determinist knows men have no free will, yet he goes on treating them as if they had.

> The difference, then, is very simple. The Christian puts the contradiction into his philosophy. The Determinist puts it into his daily habits. The Christian states as an avowed mystery what the Determinist calls nonsense. The Determinist has the same nonsense for breakfast, dinner, tea, and supper every day of his life.

> The Christian, I repeat, puts the mystery into his philosophy. That mystery by its darkness enlightens all things. Once grant him that, and life is life, and bread is bread, and cheese is cheese; he can laugh and fight. The Determinist makes the matter of the will logical and lucid; and in the light of that lucidity all things are darkened, words have no meaning, actions no aim. He has made his philosophy a syllogism and himself a gibbering lunatic.

> It is not a question between mysticism and rationality. It is a question between mysticism and madness. **For mysticism, and mysticism alone, has kept men sane from the beginning of the world. All the straight roads of logic lead to some Bedlam, to Anarchism or to passive obedience, to treating the universe as a clockwork of matter or else as a delusion of mind.** It is only the Mystic, the man who accepts the contradictions, who can laugh and walk easily through the world.

> Are you surprised that the same civilization which believed in the Trinity discovered steam?

The proof of the pudding is in the eating. The proof of the truth of Christianity lies, according to Mr. Chesterton, in the comparative practical success of the Christian civilization.

> Christianity, which is a very mystical religion, has nevertheless been the religion of the most practical section of mankind. It has far more paradoxes than the Eastern philosophies, but it also builds far better roads.

> The Moslem has a pure and logical conception of God, the one Monistic Allah. But he remains a barbarian in Europe, and the grass will not grow

where he sets his foot. The Christian has a Triune God, "a tangled trinity," which seems a mere capricious contradiction in terms.[78] But in action he bestrides the earth, and even the cleverest

Eastern can only fight him by imitating him first. The East has logic and lives on rice. Christendom has mysteries—and motor cars."

When Mr. Chesterton comes to the explicit defence of Christian doctrines he pursues the same line of argument. Man must have some philosophy to live by. "We are all Agnostics until we discover that Agnosticism will not work." "It is all very well to tell a man, as the Agnostics do, to cultivate his garden. But suppose a man ignores everything outside his garden, and among them ignores the sun and the rain?" Man cannot live by a philosophy which denies the existence of anything good behind the Universe. Such a philosophy leads to pessimism and despair. As little can he live by a philosophy which recognizes the visible Universe itself as divinity and exemplar—by Pantheism or Nature Worship. Such a philosophy leads to Anarchism and crime. "The one leads logically to murder and the other to suicide." But "then comes a fantastic thing and says to us: 'You are right to enjoy the birds, but wicked to copy them. There is a good thing behind all these things, yet all these things are lower than you. The Universe is right, but the world is wicked. The thing behind all is not cruel, like a bird; but good, like a man.' And the wholesome thing in us says: 'I have found the high road.'... After an agony of thought the world saw the sane path.... It was the Christian God. He made Nature, but He was Man."

In similar fashion he deals with Mr. Blatchford's Determinism. Mr. Blatchford had made the doctrine of Free Will the main object of his attack, had maintained that, if there were a God who created Man, he must be held responsible for all Man's acts, and that, if supernatural powers were left out of account, Man must be held to be the creature of heredity and environment. Mr. Chesterton again replied by an appeal to human necessity. Everybody, including Determinists, did, as a matter of fact, act on the assumption that Man possessed Free Will. There might be a contradiction in that doctrine, but it was a contradiction in the nature of things. The choice was between introducing the contradiction into your philosophy and introducing it into your practice.

Unfortunately for his own case, Mr. Blatchford played his opponent's game by persistently mixing up his Determinism with a theory about the uselessness of punishment, with which it had really nothing to do. The ablest exponents of a fatalistic philosophy have constantly pointed out that a Determinist can quite logically punish. **It may be true that the burglar whom Society sends to prison is what he is in consequence of his heredity and environment. But the fact**

---

78. In *Tremendous Trifles*, "The End of the World," Chesterton wrote about a visit to France: "I heard simultaneously the three sounds which are the trinity of France. They make what some poet calls 'a tangled trinity,' and I am not going to disentangle it."

that burglars are sent to prison is part of the burglar's environment, and may perfectly well modify his actions. To say that threatening the criminal with punishment cannot change his conduct because that conduct is governed by the laws of human nature is as absurd as it would be to say that a brake cannot check the speed of a train because that speed is regulated by the laws of motion. Mr. Blatchford, however, thought well to reinforce his logical argument by an appeal to the world's sentimental compassion for offenders, and by so doing gave G.K.C. his chance.

How he used it the following typical example will show. Mr. Blatchford had explained that if he found a small boy hitting his sister he would not punish the boy, but would make an appeal to him in these words:

> My dear lad, *you mustn't hit a girl.* It is cowardly. *Men don't hit women.* And you must not allow yourself to get into a passion. If you do, your temper will master you. Come, laddie, be a *gentleman.* Who will love Sis if *you* don't? What if she *did* tease you? Let her. She likes it, bless her. And you are not a *baby.* Pooh! don't be a muff. Go and put your cap on, and we'll have a game of cricket.

The opening was too good a one for Mr. Chesterton to lose. He replied, with considerable humour and really unanswerable logic:

> You say you would talk like this to the little boy. I hope you will forgive me if I say that I think you are wise to choose a little boy: I should recommend a very little boy. But do not talk like that to anyone who has read your philosophical works. If the little boy, instead of confining himself to adventure stories (which may be called the literature of Free Will), were to equip himself largely, from back numbers of the *Clarion*, with your philosophy and phraseology, he would, I think, open his infant lips and deliver a crushing reply as follows
>
> "What meaning am I to attach, my dear father, to your extraordinary statement that I must not hit Zenobia? That I have already done it proves that I must have done it. That blow was the inevitable outcome of heredity and environment. My rather ferocious heredity (derived possibly from yourself) the environment (otherwise Zenobia) produced a result like a result in chemistry. You say it is cowardly. I assure you, with scientific calm, that I was born cowardly. As for your assertion that 'Men don't hit women,' my very slight knowledge of life enables me to meet it with a direct negative. Men do. I am Agnostic upon the question you raise of who is to love Sis if I don't. But I am quite clear that somebody or nobody must do it if I can't. Barring the expression, 'Bless her'—which, as probably an abbreviation of "God bless her," I cannot but regard as a relic of barbarism—I am quite ready to allow you to love the young woman if you can. It is a trick of your inherent temperament to love Zenobia. It is a trick of mine to hit her. Are you answered?"

The weak point in Mr. Chesterton's defence of Christianity was left almost unnoticed throughout the controversy. That weak point was that he made no real attempt to defend the Christian philosophy at all. **He defended the doctrine of Free Will; but the doctrine of Free Will is in practice assumed by all ordinary men. He defended the doctrine of Original Sin; but the doctrine of Original Sin is self-evident to any man with eyes in his head.** Of the more mystical and questionable Christian dogmas he says little or nothing. He leaves it open for an independent Freethinker to reply: "Granted that you have scored off Mr. Blatchford; granted that you have shown his system to be untenable and unworkable—what is that to me? I am not committed to that system. Let us assume, if you will, that Man appears to have in him a power of choice; let us assume that in human nature there is an element of permanent weakness and evil. Now prove your strange story of a Heavenly Father, of a God incarnate in Flesh, of an eternal life beyond the grave—prove that incredible story to be true." Mr. Chesterton has never so far answered that challenge. Whether he will ever answer it I do not know. Possibly his promised book on *Orthodoxy* will prove the answer. Until it appears we must register the fact that Mr. Chesterton has only made out half his case.

Gilbert Chesterton at the time of his engagement in 1898 (24 years old)

5

THE ASSAULT ON
THE MODERNS

What is the essence of Mr. Chesterton's attack on modern thought? Briefly, I think it may be summarized as follows. The scepticism of the cleverest thinkers has made men doubtful about those axioms which cannot safely be the subject of doubt, and has consequently left their minds derelict on a sea of indecision.

BY the time the *Clarion* discussion was over Mr. Chesterton's mental transformation was complete. His old confidence in the destiny of the modern world (of which his early poems and essays are full) had given place to a rooted repugnance and antagonism. He hated it in all its aspects, even in those aspects of which the most conservative thinkers have generally spoken with respect. For, whatever his faults, timidity and irresolution were never among them. Having initiated the campaign, he joined battle all along the line.

One example will illustrate the change. Nothing in our civilization has seemed to most people more unmistakably creditable than our advance in physical science. Of that advance G.K.C. had in his earlier days spoken with respect—even with enthusiasm. In a poem called "King's Cross Station" in *The Wild Knight,* he speaks of—

The vision of Man, shouting and erect,
Whirled by the raging steeds of flood and fire.

But in his later books the words "science" and "scientists" are used only as terms of flippant abuse.[79] "The people has no disbelief in the temples of theology.

---

79. That hardly seems a fair characterization of these careful words from 1905: "Now the basis of Christianity as well as of Democracy is, that **a man is sacred.** Now Science, (or what is called Science, as a matter of fact it is not in that sense Science at all, because Science can take no side at all in any discussion on moral character); Science does, or that mass of emotions, the emotions of certain partisans who happen in our day to be connected with Physical Science—that group of feelings does, as a matter of fact, make a very great and terrible denial, and as I have said before, that denial is not the denial of the existence of God. Science, to do it justice, preserves on the whole, its claim to Agnosticism fairly intact. What Science does deny is the existence of Man, *i.e.,* the thing which the evolutionary attitude of mind in our day does deny is that there is any particular sanctity about this particular two-legged being who has come from the ape by imperceptible gradations, and who may be going back again to the ape with

The people has a very fiery and practical disbelief in the temples of physical science." "Both realists and dynamiters are well-meaning people engaged in the task, so obviously ultimately hopeless, of using science to promote morality."

Heretics, the controversial book which followed close on the *Clarion* episode, is an outspoken attack on Modernity. The form it takes is a series of essays in criticism of typical modern writers. But it would be unjust to judge it, as I have judged the *Browning* and the *Dickens,* by canons of literary criticism. The intention of literary criticism is disclaimed from the start:

> I wish to deal with my most distinguished contemporaries, not personally or in a merely literary manner, but in relation to the real body of doctrine which they teach. I am not concerned with Mr. Rudyard Kipling as a vivid artist or a vigorous personality: I am concerned with him as a heretic—that is to say, a man whose view of things has the hardihood to differ from mine. I am not concerned with Mr. Bernard Shaw as one of the most brilliant and one of the most honest men alive: I am concerned with him as a heretic—that is to say, a man whose philosophy is quite solid, quite coherent, and quite wrong.

The justification of the book in its author's eyes is that it calls attention to the neglected truth of "the importance of Orthodoxy"—that is to say, the importance of having a right view of the meaning of the Universe. In the modern world men seem to think the Universe the one entirely unimportant subject. "A man's opinion on tramcars matters: his opinion on Boticelli matters.... Everything matters—except everything." Men of our day refuse altogether to believe that doctrines will influence conduct. They never think that the man who says in a drawing-room that life is not worth living will really treat life as an evil, will reward murderers for saving men from life, or root out the Royal Humane Society like a horde of assassins. We are convinced that theories do not matter.

Hence: "Never has there been so little discussion about the nature of men as now, when, for the first time, anyone can discuss it. The old restrictions meant that only the orthodox were allowed to discuss religion. Modern liberty means that nobody is allowed to discuss it.... Emancipation has only locked the saint

---

equally imperceptible gradations! In other words, Science attacks that thing which I have called the 'corner stone of Christianity'—the sacredness of the ordinary man, that the ordinary man is a person to be reverenced." G.K. Chesterton, "Vox Populi, Vox Dei," *Preachers from the Pew,* W. Henry Hunt, ed. (London: W.H. Lord, 1905), 5. Notice also that in *Heretics,* Chesterton's chief target were his fellow writers, people with little or no scientific credentials (such as Wells), rather than eminent scientists.

Cecil also contributed an article to that same book entitled "Bread or Stones," which opens with these words: "There is nothing, I think, that strikes us more in the recorded utterances of our Lord, than the emphasis which He was perpetually laying upon the child, and the importance of the child. He is, so to speak, always taking a young child and setting it in the midst. 'He that receiveth them, receiveth Me.' 'He that offendeth one of these little ones, it were better for him that a mill stone were hung about his neck, and that he were drowned in the sea.' It is by the test of the child that our Lord seems to have thought that all civilisation and government, and all human institutions should be judged." (p. 158)

in the same tower of silence as the heresiarch. Then we talk about Lord Anglesey and the weather, and call it the complete liberty of all the creeds."

Against this tendency Mr. Chesterton planks down his own proposition that "the most practical and important thing about a man is still his view of the Universe": and that "the question is not whether the theory of the cosmos affects matters, but whether in the long run anything else affects them."[80]

It appears to me that this proposition is by far the most important in the book. The criticisms directed against individual writers may be sound or unsound, but there can surely be no doubt that we moderns have grossly underrated the practical importance of men's philosophy. How many of our mistakes in Ireland might have been avoided if we had once realized that the most important thing about the Irish is that they are Catholics. Thanks to our neglect of that fact our hands have continually been forced by Orangemen, because the Orangemen, at any rate, understood it and paid to Catholicism at least the tribute of hatred. All this is summed up by Mr. Chesterton in an admirable parable with which the introductory essay ends:

> Suppose that a great commotion arises in the street about something, let us say a lamp-post, which many influential persons desire to pull down. A grey-clad monk, who is the spirit of the Middle Ages, is approached upon the matter, and begins to say, in the arid manner of the Schoolmen, "Let us first of all consider, my brethren, the value of Light. If light be in itself good—" At this point he is somewhat excusably knocked down. All the people make a rush for the lamp-post, the lamp-post is down in ten minutes, and they go about congratulating each other on their unmediaeval practicality. But as things go on they do not work out so easily. Some people have pulled the lamp-post down because they wanted the electric light: some because they wanted old iron: some because they wanted darkness, because their deeds were evil. Some thought it was not enough of a lamp-post, some too much: some acted because they wanted to smash municipal machinery: some because they wanted to smash something. And there is war in the night, no man knowing whom he strikes. So, gradually and inevitably, to-day, to-morrow, or the next day, there comes back the conviction that the monk was right after all, and that all depends on what is the philosophy of Light. Only what we might have discussed under the gas-lamp, we now must discuss in the dark.

---

80. 'Planking down' lay at the heart of the debate Wells and Shaw were having with Chesterton in early 1908, a debate you will find in the appendices of this book. Wells and Shaw want Chesterton to 'plank down' his Utopia, meaning describe how an ideal society should be built—something quite different from the stress Chesterton places on developing a workable "view of the universe." Chesterton responds by stressing that talk of utopias, "assumes that all evils come from outside the citizen and none from inside him." Elsewhere, Chesterton would criticize 'practical' men with a similar problem. They work for well-meaning goals (world peace or the elimination of poverty) without a set of ideas (ideals) that tell them what is possible given the realities of human nature.

The aim of *Heretics*, then, is to show that the philosophy current in the modern world and professed by its leading writers is a bad philosophy, and that to the reactions of this bad philosophy may be traced the worst of the evils with which we are confronted.

Such an aim at once absolves the author from any condemnation which might be passed on the essays for their inadequacy as criticisms. What we have to ask is, firstly, whether Mr. Chesterton has rightly apprehended and fairly summed up the body of doctrine taught by the various writers with whom he deals; and, secondly, whether his criticisms of their body of doctrine are valid.

In regard to the first question, the verdict must, in most cases, I think, be in Mr. Chesterton's favour. Nothing, for instance, could be truer and fairer than his statement of the message of Mr. Rudyard Kipling—the writer to whom, above all others, he seems most hostile:

> And unconsciously Mr. Kipling has proved this, and proved it admirably. For in so far as his work is earnestly understood, the military trade does not by any means emerge as the most important or attractive. He has not written so well about soldiers as he has about railway men or bridge builders, or even journalists. The fact is that what attracts Mr. Kipling to militarism is not the idea of courage, but the idea of discipline. There was far more courage to the square mile in the Middle Ages, when no king had a standing army, but every man had a bow or sword. But the fascination of the standing army upon Mr. Kipling is not courage, which scarcely interests him, but discipline, which is, when all is said and done, his primary theme. The modern army is not a miracle of courage: it has not enough opportunities, owing to the cowardice of everybody else. But it is really a miracle of organization, and that is the truly Kiplingite ideal. Kipling's subject is not that valour which properly belongs to war, but that interdependence and efficiency which belongs quite as much to engineers, or sailors, or mules, or railway engines. And thus it is that when he writes of engineers, or sailors, or mules, or steam-engines, he writes at his best. The real poetry, the "true romance" which Mr. Kipling has taught, is the romance of the division of labour and the discipline of all the trades. He sings the arts of peace much more accurately than the arts of war. And his main contention is vital and valuable. Everything is military in the sense that everything depends upon obedience. There is no perfectly epicurean corner: there is no perfectly irresponsible place. Everywhere men have made the way for us with sweat and submission. We may fling ourselves into a hammock in a fit of divine carelessness. But we are glad that the net-maker did not make the hammock in a fit of divine carelessness. We may jump upon a child's rocking-horse for a joke. But we are glad that the carpenter did not leave the legs of it unglued for a joke. So far from having merely preached that a soldier cleaning his side-arm is to be adored because he is military, Kipling at his best and

clearest has preached that the baker baking loaves and the tailor cutting coats are as military as anybody.[81]

Mr. Bernard Shaw, again, receives full and fair recognition for his great intellectual virtue:

> The whole force and triumph of Mr. Bernard Shaw lie in the fact that he is a thoroughly consistent man. So far from his power consisting in jumping through hoops or standing on his head, his power consists in holding his own fortress night and day. He puts the Shaw test rapidly and rigorously to everything that happens in heaven or earth. His standard never varies. The thing which weak-minded revolutionists and weak-minded Conservatives really hate (and fear) in him is exactly this, that his scales, such as they are, are held even, and that his law, such as it is, is justly enforced. You may attack his principles, as I do: but I do not know of any instance in which you can attack their application. If he dislikes lawlessness, he dislikes the lawlessness of Socialists as much as that of Individualists. If he dislikes the fever of patriotism, he dislikes it in Boers and Irishmen as well as in Englishmen. If he dislikes the vows and bonds of marriage, he dislikes still more the fiercer bonds and wilder vows that are made by lawless love. If he laughs at the authority of priests, he laughs louder at the pomposity of men of science. If he condemns the irresponsibility of faith, he condemns with a sane consistency the equal irresponsibility of art. He has pleased all the Bohemians by saying that women are equal to men: but he has infuriated them by suggesting that men are equal to women. He is almost mechanically just: he has something of the terrible quality of a machine.

These two passages prove pretty conclusively that Mr. Chesterton is not debarred from under standing other men's point of view by the mere fact that that point of view is violently antagonistic to his own. When he does fail to understand, his failure appears to arise from some wayward blast of prejudice against the man himself, which sometimes appears to warp and dwarf his intellect like the spell of a magician. One great man of the nineteenth century has suffered many things from Mr. Chesterton, owing, as it seems to me, solely to Mr. Chesterton's incurable inability (or, it may be, obstinate unwillingness) to comprehend his method and meaning. That great man is Henrik Ibsen.

At first sight one would have thought that no man would be better able to appreciate Ibsen than Mr. Chesterton. His literary method is perhaps the supreme demonstration of Mr. Chesterton's favourite theory—the compatibility of profound truth to the essential things of the soul with extravagant impossibility in externals. Those who call Ibsen a "Realist" in the ordinary sense can surely never have read *The Lady from the Sea*, or *The Master Builder*, or *Little Eyolf*. Can we conceive any true Realist—can we conceive Zola, for instance, or George

---

81. C.S. Lewis offered a similar criticism in a 1948 essay, "Kipling's World." Kipling, he said, was a "slave of the Inner Ring," drawn to shared camaraderie even if the bond served an evil cause.

Gissing —introducing into the middle of a tragedy of modern suburban married life a figure that seems to have stepped straight out of Grimm—a Rat Wife who lures away children and drowns them?[82] We cannot conceive them doing such a thing. We cannot conceive any modern story-teller doing such a thing—except G.K. Chesterton. It is not easy to find in literature anything exactly of a kind with Mr. Chesterton's wild, symbolic farces of modern life—*The Napoleon of Notting Hill, The Club of Queer Trades, The Man who was Thursday.* But, if it can be found anywhere, it will be found in the changing atmosphere and grotesque symbolism of *Peer Gynt.*

Nor would the ideas of Ibsen seem less likely to be acceptable to G.K.C. than his form. In his controversy with Mr. Blatchford, and on many subsequent occasions, Mr. Chesterton has emphasized continually the cardinal importance of the doctrine of Free Will. Now, Ibsen is, above all things, the prophet of Free Will. That the brave man is the man who defies circumstance, that the strong man is the man who conquers circumstance, that the lot even of the man or woman who is beaten and broken in pieces in the fight with circumstance, like Solness, is happier and nobler than that of one who slavishly accepts circumstance, like Hedda Gabler—these are the lessons enforced again and again in every one of Ibsen's plays.[83] Yet, Will-Worshipper as he was, Ibsen carefully guarded himself against the Self-Worship of later thinkers. The Neitszchian Superman is actually introduced by Ibsen, but he is introduced to be satyrized, humiliated, presented as a village waster and coward turned fraudulent stockjobber and sham mystic, and finally to be crowned "Emperor of Himself" by a company of escaped lunatics who are thoroughly convinced (as all lunatics are) that they also are emperors of themselves.[84] The real strong man of Ibsen is quite a different sort of person. He is the man "who stands most alone"—indeed, but the man who stands alone for others. It is curious that Mr. Chesterton should not have seen a Pro-Boer analogy in Dr. Stockman's famous outburst: "I love my native town so well that I would rather ruin it than see it flourishing upon a lie." It is still more curious that he should have failed to realize the force of the Doctor's comparison of himself to "a certain person" who was "more good-natured" than he. In a fine Christmas poem which appeared in the *Commonwealth,* Mr. Chesterton wrote the lines:

---

82. Émile Zola (1840–1902) was a famous realist French novelist. In his chapter on Bernard Shaw in *Heretics,* Chesterton wrote sarcastically of "the glad old days, before the rise of modern morbidities, when genial old Ibsen filled the world with wholesome joy, and the kindly tales of the forgotten Émile Zola kept our firesides merry and pure." George Gissing (1857–1903) played a similar role in English literature. In 1898 Gissing published *Charles Dickens: A Critical Study* and in the first chapter of his 1906 *Charles Dickens,* Chesterton referred to Gissings as, "the soundest of the Dickens critics, a man of genius."

83. Halvard Solness is the leading character in Ibsen's 1892 *The Master Builder* and Hedda Gabler is the leading character in his 1890 *Hedda Gabler.*

84. In *Peter Gynt* (1867), Peter is taken to an Egyptian madhouse, where inmates declare him "Emperor of Himself." Nietzsche's superman is explored in Ibsen's next to last play, *John Gabriel Borkman* (1896).

For we are for all men under the sun
And they are against us every one,

lines which might almost be the motto of *The Enemy of the People*.[85]

It is true that Ibsen must naturally appear to Mr. Chesterton in his later phases as too much of an optimist, as trusting the naked human will too completely, as neglecting—so G.K.C. would probably put it—the doctrine of Original Sin. But all this applies much more strongly to Whitman, of whom Mr. Chesterton always speaks with an admiration amounting almost to devotion, than to Ibsen, of whom he never speaks without a curious note of resentment.

As to Mr. Chesterton's specific criticisms of Ibsen in the essay on "The Negative Spirit" in *Heretics,* they are almost childish enough to have been written by Dr. Max Nordau.[86] Ibsen is accused of "a negative spirit," "a vagueness and a changing attitude towards what is really wisdom and virtue," because "falsehood works ruin in *The Pillars of Society,* but truth works equal ruin in *The Wild Duck.*" As well might Shakespeare be accused of "vagueness and a changing attitude" because feminine influence is a destructive force in *Macbeth* and a beneficent force in *The Merchant of Venice.* Dickens might be reproached in the same way because avarice works the moral ruin of Gradgrind, while profusion works the moral ruin of Harold Skimpole.[87] In his *Dickens* Mr. Chesterton himself quotes this latter case, and quotes it as an example of his hero's honesty. Why should the same thing which in Dickens is a sign of "a kind of uncontrollable honesty" be a sign of "the negative spirit" in Ibsen?

As for the complaint that Ibsen cannot tell us "how virtue and happiness are brought about," of course he cannot. Nobody can. Mr. Chesterton would presumably say that they are brought about by the grace of God; and Ibsen, in different phraseology, would probably have given much the same answer. It is much easier to point out that it is generally desirable to avoid rape and murder than to give people a recipe for becoming saints and heroes. But, though Ibsen could not give a prescription warranted to produce heroism, he could do something else. He could do what Shakespeare could not do, what Dickens could not do, what Thackeray could not do, what no one, save perhaps Bunyan, has done since the intellectualism of the Renaissance destroyed the heroic tradition of Europe—he could draw a hero. And to draw a hero is to make men believe again in the heroic. And to make them believe in the heroic is to make them love it.

---

85. In that play, Dr. Thomas Stockmann tries to warn a Norwegian town that the new tourist baths on which their economy depends are being polluted by a tannery and faces ridicule as a result.

86. Max S. Nordau (1849–1923) was a prominent Zionist leader and social critic. Born in Hungary but culturally German, he spent most of his life in Paris. In *Degeneration* (1892) he attacked the 'degenerate art' of artists such as Oscar Wilde, Henrik Ibsen, Richard Wagner, and Friedrich Nietzsche.

87. Grangrind is a character in Dicken's *Hard Times,* and Harold Skimpole is in *Bleak House.*

In a recent article Mr. Chesterton ventured the suggestion that Mr. Bernard Shaw had never read Shakespeare's *Julius Caesar*. With equal diffidence I venture the suggestion that Mr. Chesterton has never read Ibsen—never, at any rate, read him fairly and with an open-minded desire to get at his meaning. He has read Mr. Shaw's *Quintessence of Ibsenism*, and has disagreed with it.[88] He has met people who liked Ibsen and has disliked them. But Mr. Shaw's book is nothing more than the Quintessence of Shawism, and the Ibsenites have no more claim to represent Ibsen than the readers of the *Daily News* have to represent Mr. Chesterton. Mr. Chesterton, however, appears to have allowed an ineradicable association to grow in his mind between Ibsen and long-haired vegetarians, similar to the association which our ancestors formed between Frenchmen and frog-eating, and to have based upon that association a very similar prejudice.

But this by the way. If we turn from the authors whom Mr. Chesterton does not understand to the authors whom he does, we may take as the four typical heretics Mr. Bernard Shaw, Mr. Kipling, Mr. H.G. Wells, and Mr. Lowes Dickinson.

Let us now turn to these writers to whom Mr. Chesterton does some reasonable justice. The essay on Mr. Kipling may be postponed until we come to deal with the critic's politics. Those on Whistler and on Mr. George Moore are rather criticisms of temperament than of doctrine.[89] That wherein Mr. McCabe is urged to cultivate "a divine frivolity" is more an amusing piece of sparring than a serious criticism of philosophy.[90] This leaves three essays in criticism of the critics of orthodoxy—Mr. Bernard Shaw, Mr. H.G. Wells, and Mr. Lowes Dickinson, a statement of what appears to the author the sound theory of drinking in contradistinction to that of Omar as interpreted by Fitzgerald, and a number of miscellaneous essays, in which the influence of a wrong conception of life is

---

88. Shaw's *Quintessence of Ibsenism* was first published in 1891 and is still in print. Shaw has been accused of reading Fabian socialism into Ibsen's plays, hence Cecil's remark about the "Quintessence of Shawism." Cecil may have been as enamored with Ibsen, as Gilbert was critical of him. Shaw believed his book had a major impact on Cecil. Speaking of the heroism many men displayed at the outbreak of World War I, he wrote: "How then could I have disparaged the ardor of Cecil Chesterton, my junior by a generation, whose soul I had saved from Materialism by my Quintessence of Ibsenism?" Bernard Shaw, *Shaw: An Autobiography*, Stanley Weintraub, ed. (New York: Weybright and Talley), 101.

89. Chapter 9. "The Moods of Mr. George Moore" is about George Moore (1852–1933) the Irish novelist rather than George E. Moore, a well-known Cambridge philosopher. Chapter 17, "On the Wit of Whistler" discusses James Whistler (1834–1903), an artist who championed the smug "art for art's sake."

90. In Chapter 16, "On Mr. McCabe and a Divine Frivolity," Chesterton told the writer Joseph McCabe (1867–1955) to lighten up: "To sum up the whole matter very simply, if Mr. McCabe asks me why I import frivolity into a discussion of the nature of man, I answer, because frivolity is a part of the nature of man. If he asks me why I introduce what he calls paradoxes into a philosophical problem, I answer, because all philosophical problems tend to become paradoxical. If he objects to my treating of life riotously, I reply that life is a riot. And I say that the Universe as I see it, at any rate, is very much more like the fireworks at the Crystal Palace than it is like his own philosophy. About the whole cosmos there is a tense and secret festivity—like preparations for Guy Fawkes' day. Eternity is the eve of something. I never look up at the stars without feeling that they are the fires of a schoolboy's rocket, fixed in their everlasting fall."

traced in various developments of modern life and literature "The Yellow Press," "Sandals and Simplicity," "Smart Novelists and the Smart Set," "Slum Novelists and the Slums," "Christmas and the Æsthetes."[91]

What is the essence of Mr. Chesterton's attack on modern thought? Briefly, I think it may be summarized as follows. **The scepticism of the cleverest thinkers has made men doubtful about those axioms which cannot safely be the subject of doubt, and has consequently left their minds derelict on a sea of indecision.** Mr. Shaw doubts the existence of any permanent element in morality, affirming that "the Golden Rule is that there is no Golden Rule."[92] Mr. Wells goes further, and doubts that there is any permanent element in anything—"nothing endures, nothing is precise and certain.... Being, indeed!—there is no being, but a universal becoming of individualities."[93] This sort of scepticism seems to Mr. Chesterton not only anarchic, but reactionary. It destroys all possibility of human effort, for unless our aim is clearly defined beyond possibility of question progress is unmeaning.

> North and south are relative in the sense that I am north of Bournemouth and south of Spitzbergen. But if there be any doubt of the position of the North Pole, there is in equal degree a doubt of whether I am south of Spitzbergen at all. The absolute idea of light may be practically unattainable. We may not be able to procure pure light. We may not be able to get to the North Pole. But because the North Pole is unattainable, it does not follow that it is indefinable. And it is only because the North Pole is not indefinable that we can make a satisfactory map of Brighton and Worthing.

Since in the hands of the philosophers ideas have thus become self-destructive, the common man abandons ideas altogether and puts his trust in phrases like "progress" and "efficiency." Now, progress implies that you are going somewhere, and efficiency that you are doing something, and unless you know where you want to go and what you want to do both words are useless and unmeaning. So at last scepticism lands most men in the worship of material success, with its consequences, the corruption and cowardice of the Press and of politics, the revival of aristocracy, the paralysis of all effort for human improvement. As Mr. Chesterton has put it in his "Introduction to the Book of Job," "we give up the hard task of making good men successful in favour of the much easier task of making out successful men good."[94]

---

91. Cecil did not get all the chapter titles right. Chapter 8, for instance, is "The Mildness of the Yellow Press." He may have used a rough draft, or, like his brother, he may have depended on his memory.

92. This is how Shaw describes Ibsen's plays in *The Quintessence of Ibsenism.*

93. The quote is from Chapter 1 of Wells' *A Modern Utopia* (1905).

94. The actual passage is: "If prosperity is regarded as the reward of virtue it will be regarded as the symptom of virtue. Men will leave off the heavy task of making good men successful. They will adopt the easier task of making out successful men good. This, which has happened throughout modern commerce and journalism, is the ultimate Nemesis of the wicked optimism of the comforters of Job."

Mr. Chesterton vehemently denies that this materialistic success-worship leads even to material success:

> The time of big theories was the time of big results. In the era of sentiment and fine words, at the end of the eighteenth century, men were really robust and effective. The sentimentalists conquered Napoleon. The cynics could not catch De Wet. A hundred years ago our affairs for good or evil were wielded triumphantly by rhetoricians. Now our affairs are hopelessly muddled by strong, silent men.[95]

The revolutionists Mr. Chesterton finds equally shackled by materialism. Some are trusting to "economic forces" and "the materialist conception of history." Others are trusting to science, whose "chief use is to find long words to cover the errors of the rich."[96] Others, again, seek simplicity by living on vegetables and wearing sandals. But simplicity must be sought in the soul. "It does not very much matter whether a man eats a grilled tomato or a plain tomato; it does very much matter whether he eats a plain tomato with a grilled mind.... There is more simplicity in the man who eats caviare on impulse than in the man who eats grape-nuts on principle. And at those who talk to us with interfering eloquence about Jaeger and the pores of the skin, and about Plasmon and the coats of the stomach, at them shall only be hurled the words that are hurled at fops and gluttons, 'Take no thought what ye shall eat, or what ye shall drink, or wherewith ye shall be clothed. For after all these things do the Gentiles seek.

---

95. Gilbert liked this quote (from the introduction to *Heretics*) so much he assigned it to Waterloo Day (June 18) in his 1912 *Chesterton Day by Day*. As the 2002 Inkling edition of *Day by Day* notes: "Christiaan Rudolf De Wet (1854–1922) was the (Dutch) Orange State's commander-in-chief during the Boer War. His brilliant guerrilla tactics and seemingly miraculous escapes made him the hero of the Afrikaners and enraged his British foes. (His exploits are described in his *Three Years War*.)."

96. The last quote is from *Heretics*, Chapter 13, which says: "Science in the modern world has many uses; its chief use, however, is to provide long words to cover the errors of the rich. The word 'kleptomania' is a vulgar example of what I mean. It is on a par with that strange theory, always advanced when a wealthy or prominent person is in the dock, that exposure is more of a punishment for the rich than for the poor. Of course, the very reverse is the truth." In 1922 Chesterton would write about the rich industrialists who were supporting scientific eugenics and birth control:

> He had discovered the divine boomerang; his sin had found him out. The experiment of Individualism—the keeping of the worker half in and half out of work—was far too ingenious not to contain a flaw. It was too delicate a balance to work entirely with the strength of the starved and the vigilance of the benighted. It was too desperate a course to rely wholly on desperation. And as time went on the terrible truth slowly declared itself; the degraded class was really degenerating. It was right and proper enough to use a man as a tool; but the tool, ceaselessly used, was being used up. It was quite reasonable and respectable, of course, to fling a man away like a tool; but when it was flung away in the rain the tool rusted. But the comparison to a tool was insufficient for an awful reason that had already begun to dawn upon the master's mind. If you pick up a hammer, you do not find a whole family of nails clinging to it. If you fling away a chisel by the roadside, it does not litter and leave a lot of little chisels. But the meanest of the tools, Man, had still this strange privilege which God had given him, doubtless by mistake. Despite all improvements in machinery, the most important part of the machinery (the fittings technically described in the trade as "hands") were apparently growing worse. The firm was not only encumbered with one useless servant, but he immediately turned himself into five useless servants." [*Eugenics and Other Evils* (Seattle: Inkling, 2000), 88–89.]

G. K. Chesterton, a Criticism

But seek first the Kingdom of God and His righteousness, and all these things shall be added unto you.'"[97]

So we come back to the necessity for general ideals. What, then, shall be the ideal that man shall follow? Mr. Shaw's Superman is rejected. He is non-human, even anti-human. "Mr. Shaw cannot understand that the thing which is valuable and lovable in our eyes is man—the old beer-drinking, creed-making, fighting, failing, respectable man." Equally unsatisfactory is the more prosaic ideal of Mr. Wells, the production of satisfactory fathers and mothers." This, like the talk about progress, is a mere evasion of the issue. "What is the good of begetting a man until we have settled what is the good of being a man?" But perhaps the most interesting essay in the book is the reply to Mr. Lowes Dickinson, who had boldly put forward the Pagan ideal as superior to the Christian.[98]

Mr. Chesterton's attack on Mr. Lowes Dickinson's Paganism is exceedingly clever debating. But it seems to me that his main argument proves too much, and would, if accepted, destroy the rest of the book. "There is one broad fact about the relations of Christianity and Paganism... that one came after the other. Mr. Lowes Dickinson... suggests that the Pagan ideal will be the ultimate good of man; but, if that is so, we must ask, with more curiosity than he allows for, why it was that man actually found his ultimate good on earth under the stars and threw it away again." And so, at the conclusion of the essay, Mr. Dickinson is accused of "ignoring definite human discoveries in the moral world." "If we do revive and pursue the pagan ideal of a simple and rational self-completion we shall end—where Paganism ended. I do not mean that we shall end in destruction. I mean that we shall end in Christianity."

Now, it is surely obvious that this line of argument is one that can be used against Mr. Chesterton himself with fully equal force. Mr. Chesterton is never tired of telling us that the modern world must be considered as definitely non-Christian. He is never tired of telling us that the Christian ideal is "the ultimate good of man." Why, then, Mr. Dickinson might reply, was it that "man actually found his ultimate good on earth under the stars and threw it away again?" If the absurd theory of uninterrupted progress be valid, then no doubt Christianity must have been an improvement on Paganism, and the Dark Ages must have been an improvement on the Roman Empire, and modern industrialism must be an improvement on feudalism, and modern Rationalism on Catholicism. But if the contrary doctrine, which Mr. Chesterton has so continually proclaimed, be true, then there is no more inherent impossibility in the theory that the change from Paganism and Christianity was a disastrous fall, a submersion of the human

---

97. Chesterton used this quote for March 13 in *Chesterton Day by Day*. The Inkling edition gives more details about Dr. Gustav Jaeger, a sadistic German professor who claimed that wearing wool next to the skin promoted good health, and about Plasmon, a health food made from milk protein.
98. G. Lowes Dickinson (1862–1932) was the author of *Religion: A Criticism and a Forecast* (1905).

spirit in error and sin, than in the theory that the break up of Christian unity and faith was such a fall.[99]

Mr. Chesterton's position is much stronger and more consistent when he undertakes the specific defence of the Christian as against the Pagan ideal. Nothing, I think, could be truer and more vividly expressed than his defence of the Christian virtue of humility—"the psychological discovery that, whereas it had been supposed that the fullest possible enjoyment is to be found in extending our ego to infinity, the truth is that the fullest possible enjoyment is to be found by reducing our ego to zero." Nothing could be more suggestive than his contrast between the Pagan virtues of justice and temperance, which are reasonable and sad, and the Christian virtues of Faith, Hope, and Charity, which are unreasonable and joyous.

But the same fact may be noted in regard to *Heretics,* as we have already noticed in connection with the *Clarion* controversy. Mr. Chesterton criticizes his opponents with much vigour and acumen. But he does not very clearly define, much less defend, his own position. Doubtless that position can be roughly deduced from his criticisms of others, but from one who lays such stress upon the importance of clearly defined doctrines we have a right to expect something more than this negative method of definition. His forthcoming book, to be called *Orthodoxy,* proposes, I understand, to meet the objection. But, so far, almost the only exposition we have of Mr. Chesterton's own system of doctrine is to be found in the wild last chapter of *The Man who was Thursday.*

It could hardly be expected that Mr. Chesterton, whose main reason for accepting Christianity was that it supplied a dogmatic system, would look very favourably on an attempt to make it acceptable to the modern world by stripping it of its dogmas. When the Rev. R.J. Campbell electrified the churches by his preaching of the New Theology, Mr. Chesterton "went for" him with much less restraint and respect than he had exhibited in dealing with the avowedly anti-

---

99. Gilbert believes in neither "unbroken progress" nor the "contrary doctrine"—apparently the ancient pagan (rather than Christian) belief that all history is a slow decline from an golden age. He believes man can progress, as from Paganism to Christianity, or he can regress, as from Christianity to Modernism. What he doubts is that, having come under the influence of Christianity, he can return to genuine Paganism, or as he puts it: "My objection to Mr. Lowes Dickinson and the reassertors of the pagan ideal is, then, this. I accuse them of ignoring definite human discoveries in the moral world, discoveries as definite, though not as material, as the discovery of the circulation of the blood. We cannot go back to an ideal of reason and sanity. For mankind has discovered that reason does not lead to sanity. We cannot go back to an ideal of pride and enjoyment. For mankind has discovered that pride does not lead to enjoyment." Returning to Paganism, Chesterton is suggesting, is as unlikely as returning to a pre-scientific view of blood circulation. And it's in that context that Chesterton closes with a remark that is more a debater's point than an expression of his own belief: "But if we do revive and pursue the pagan ideal of a simple and rational self-completion we shall end—where Paganism ended. I do not mean that we shall end in destruction. I mean that we shall end in Christianity."

Christian polemics of Mr. Blatchford.[100] "Your True Christianity," he wrote in a letter to the *Nation*, "seems to me very like True Free Trade, which dogmatists and coarse fellows call Protection." G.K.C. undoubtedly dealt some shrewd blows at the new religious movement, which indeed sometimes laid itself dangerously open. The attempts of Mr. Campbell and others to minimize and explain away the problem of evil, their rejection of the doctrines of Original Sin and of the Fall, gave a particularly good opportunity for the controversial methods which he had used so effectively against Mr. Blatchford.

But probably his real objection to the New Theology was based upon a deeper ground. The avowed aim of that movement was the reconciliation of Christianity with the modern world. Now, we have seen that, so far from desiring such a reconciliation, it was just his violent reaction against the modern world that had driven Mr. Chesterton into a reconciliation with Christianity. To have convinced G.K.C. that the Christian Faith could be "reconciled with modern thought" would have gone a long way towards convincing him that it was untrue.

I have mentioned *The Man who was Thursday* as containing the only exposition I know of what I may call Mr. Chesterton's constructive theology. It is, of course, a wild book— *A Nightmare*—the author calls it. But there is nothing more characteristic of G.K.C. than that he becomes farcical in proportion as he becomes serious. With the central artistic idea, which is a good one, I deal elsewhere. Here I am concerned with the last chapter only, the chapter in which the symbolism of the book is made clear. Six men, sworn to wage war on the Anarchy of the modern world, have received their commissions from a mysterious hand in a dark room. Their unknown general appears in the story as "Sunday," the Arch-Anarchist, the man they are sworn to fight. At the end of their adventures, when his identity has been discovered, they are summoned to a great festival, and Sunday speaks to them:

> "We will eat and drink later," he said. "Let us remain together a little, we who have loved each other so sadly, and have fought so long. I seem to remember only centuries of heroic war, in which you were always heroes— epic on epic, iliad on iliad, and you always brothers in arms. Whether it was but recently (for time is nothing), or at the beginning of the world, I sent you out to war. I sat in the darkness, where there is not any created thing, and to you I was only a voice commanding valour and an unnatural virtue. You heard the voice in the dark, and you never heard it again. The sun in heaven denied it, the earth and sky denied it, all human wisdom denied it. And when I met you in the daylight I denied it myself."

---

100. It's more likely Chesterton's reaction was similar to a government that takes well-made counterfeit money much more seriously than the play money in children's games. The closer a counterfeit is to the real thing, the more harmful it will be.

There was complete silence in the starlit garden, and then the black-browed Secretary, implacable, turned in his chair towards Sunday, and said in a harsh voice:

"Who and what are you?"

I am the Sabbath," said the other without moving. "I am the peace of God."

The Secretary started up, and stood crushing his costly robe in his hand.

"I know what you mean," he cried, "and it is exactly that that I cannot forgive you. I know you are contentment, optimism, what do they call the thing, an ultimate reconciliation. Well, I am not reconciled. If you were the man in the dark room, why were you also Sunday, an offence to the sunlight? If you were from the first our father and our friend, why were you also our greatest enemy? We wept, we fled in terror, the iron entered into our souls— and you are the peace of God! Oh, I can forgive God His anger, though it destroyed nations; but I cannot forgive Him His peace.'"

Then the others, one by one, take up the complaint. One says, "It seems so silly that you should have been on both sides and fought yourself." And another, "You let me stray a little too near to hell." And yet another, "I wish I knew why I was hurt so much." And Sunday answers, "I have heard your complaints in order. And here, I think, comes another to complain, and we will hear him also."

Enters Gregory, the real Anarchist, and hurls his accusation at the Paladins of Order:

"I know what you are all of you from first to last—you are the people in power! You are the police—the great fat, smiling men in blue and buttons! You are the Law, and you have never been broken. But is there a free soul alive that does not long to break you, only because you have never been broken? We in revolt talk all kind of nonsense doubtless about this crime or that crime of the Government. It is all folly! The only crime of the Government is that it governs. The unpardonable sin of the supreme power is that it is supreme. I do not curse you for being cruel. I do not curse you (though I might) for being kind. I curse you for being safe! You sit in your chairs of stone, and have never come down from them. You are the seven angels of heaven, and you have had no troubles. Oh, I could forgive you everything, you that rule all mankind, if I could feel for once that you had suffered for one hour a real agony such as I—"

Syme sprang to his feet, shaking from head to foot.

"I see everything," he cried, "everything that there is. Why does each thing on the earth war against each other thing? Why does each small thing in the world have to fight against the world itself? Why does a fly have to fight the whole universe? Why does a dandelion have to fight the whole universe? For the same reason that I had to be alone in the dreadful Council of the

88

Days. So that each thing that obeys law may have the glory and isolation of the anarchist. So that each man fighting for order may be as brave and good a man as the dynamiter. So that the real lie of Satan may be flung back in the face of this blasphemer, so that by tears and torture we may earn the right to say to this man, 'You lie!' No agonies can be too great to buy the right to say to this accuser, 'We also have suffered.'"

"It is not true that we have never been broken. We have been broken upon the wheel. It is not true that we have never descended from these thrones. We have descended into hell. We were complaining of unforgettable miseries even at the very moment when this man entered insolently to accuse us of happiness. I repel the slander; we have not been happy. I can answer for every one of the great guards of Law whom he has accused. At least—"

He had turned his eyes so as to see suddenly the great face of Sunday, which wore a strange smile.

"Have you," he cried in a dreadful voice, "have you ever suffered?"

As he gazed the great face grew to an awful size, grew larger than the colossal mask of Memnon, which had made him scream as a child.[101] It grew larger and larger, filling the whole sky; then everything went black. Only in the blackness before it entirely destroyed his brain he seemed to hear a distant voice saying a commonplace text that he had heard somewhere, "Can ye drink of the cup that I drink of?"

I leave this quotation without comment. It is, I think, the best expression of the foothold of faith which G.K.C. has found for himself at the last.

---

101. In Greek mythology, Memnon was the king of Ethopia who, in the *Illiad*, is killed by Achilles. In Chesterton's tale, the child had seen what today's British Museum calls the "Colossal Bust of Ramesses II, the 'Younger Memnon.'" It weighs 7.25 tons. A carved stone body from slightly above the waist, it stands some 8 1/2 feet high (266.8 cm) tall, more than enough to terrify a small child. It has been in the museum since 1818.

Gilbert Chesterton at 31 (about 1905)

6

G.K.C. as Anti-Liberal

Briefly, I think we may summarize Mr. Chesterton's politics by saying that he is a Tory of the seventeenth or early eighteenth century, born out of his due time.

WE have seen that Mr. Chesterton, growing up in an atmosphere of theological Liberalism, has slowly thought himself out of it and become the avowed champion of a strict Catholic orthodoxy. In politics, he has not yet severed himself wholly from the traditions of his youth, but I shall endeavour to suggest that when the process of self-realisation is complete, he will come to see that just as he has become a Catholic in religion he has in effect become a Tory in politics.

The change has, I think, been hidden from Mr. Chesterton's own eyes by reason of the fact that his views on certain problems which especially interested him coincided more or less with the views of a section of the Liberal Party and were diametrically opposed to the opinions fashionable among Conservatives. It may be noted that it is only a comparatively few items in the Liberal programme (and those the items which most Liberals studiously avoid mentioning) which have power to rouse his enthusiasm. In all his many political polemics you will hardly find a word about Free Trade or about Church Disestablishment. You will find no pleas for the reduction of armaments or for a pacific foreign policy. You will find a number of very definite protests against the current Liberal policy in relation to licensing and education. Only two Liberal principles are preached with any decision or emphasis—the principle of Nationality and the principle of Democracy.

Now the identification of Nationalism with Liberalism is an entirely modern and mainly accidental phenomenon. Irish Nationalism, for instance, which especially excites Mr. Chesterton's sympathies, was in past times associated with Toryism (the very name "Tory" means an Irish rebel), with Jacobitism, with what Liberals call "reaction."[102] The Boers again, whatever their claims to

102. Tory comes from from Irish Gaelic *tóraighe*, which literally means a "pursued man." It was applied to an outlaw or guerrilla fighter, particularly during the seventeenth-century wars to determine if Scotland, Ireland and England would be ruled by one king. Jacobitism followed the early Tory movement and was a effort in Scotland and Ireland to restore the Stuart dynasty to the throne. Its supporters opposed the parliamentary removal of the Stuart dynasty and believed that its restoration would allow more religious

admiration, were certainly not Liberals in the ordinary sense of the word. They were a landed squirearchy, proud and tenacious as the slave-owners of Virginia (towards whom Mr. Chesterton is also, I believe, sympathetic), and as untouched by modern ideas in their politics as in their religion. It may also be recalled that for the hundred years at least which intervened between the English and the French Revolutions the Tory party was emphatically the Anti-Imperialist party. Indeed it would not be unreasonable to suggest that the country squire whose point of view was at the back of real Toryism was by his nature an Anti-Imperialist, absorbed in the thought of his own fireside and his own estates and indifferent to everything that did not immediately affect them. On the other hand, the larger ideas of more progressive classes tend to neglect frontiers and local customs, and to become either cosmopolitan or Imperialist.[103] The French Revolutionists drove the steamroller of a highly centralized bureaucracy over the rights and franchises of the provinces with a ruthlessness which no modern Imperialist would dare to imitate, and took Belgium by a cool act of annexation, without the slightest regard for Nationalist sentiment.[104]

Mr. Chesterton's constantly avowed belief in democracy may seem to wed him more deeply to the Liberal creed. But even in this respect the case, when examined, is by no means so clear as it at first appears.

The French Revolution is for Mr. Chesterton the fountain of Liberalism, and he is never tired of boasting himself its child. But both assumptions may be questioned. Modern English Liberalism is a mixed human product, and derived from many sources. In a sense no doubt it is a product of the French Revolution, but only because we are all its products—Tories and Socialists and Anarchists, no less than Liberals and Radicals. Nothing after that astounding cataclysm could be quite the same as it was before it. But Liberalism existed before the Revolution, and many of its most characteristic traits can be traced to movements wholly unconnected with it. The philosophy of the eighteenth century, the tradition of the great Whig houses "that had eaten the Abbey's fruits," as Mr. Chesterton himself puts it, the Puritanism of the middle classes dating from the great struggle with the Stuarts, the economic claims of the

freedom, particularly for Catholics. In that historical sense, as a "Little Englander" and an opponent of large, centralized governments, Chesterton was a Tory and a Jacobite.

103. A book-in-progress, *Chesterton on War*, will explore this aspect of his writings. Chesterton was not a Tory country squire disinterested in anything outside "his own estate." After World War I he strongly supported the new Polish nation. Nor was he a progressive "cosmopolitan or Imperialist." He was a vocal critic of both as well as of pacifism. The best analogy to his nationalism might be to a happily married man generous enough to want to see more happy marriages. A proper love for one's own country, Chesterton believed, teaches us to respect the love others feel for their homelands.

104. Cecil is right. Chesterton was not a Liberal as Liberalism was becoming in his day—the champions of centralized bureaucratic rule. And Chesterton's life-long admiration for the French Revolution, which resulted in a more centralized France and France's Imperialistic wars across Europe and beyond, was strangely inconsistent with his romantic views of people taking the the barricades to defend their rights, as in *The Napoleon of Notting Hill*. Revolutions often pervert the intended goals of their supporters.

new trading interests created by the industrial revolution, the humanitarian and pacificist idealism (characteristically un-Gallic) which Shelley and others popularized in this country—all these have gone to mould modern Liberalism, and the inheritance of each is plainly visible in its features.[105]

The non-identity of English Liberalism with the tradition of the French Revolution can be seen by a very simple test. In the first half of the nineteenth century a party arose in this country which really was imbued with what Frenchmen call "the principles of '89." They were called Chartists. So far from seeing in Liberalism the expression of their ideas, they were as violently Anti-Liberal as the Social Democratic Federation, and much more Anti-Liberal than the Independent Labour Party. Their hostility, it must be remembered, was by no means confined to the old-fashioned Whigs. They denounced Villiers and Bright as vehemently as Palmerston and Russell. They repeatedly broke up Free Trade meetings called by the Anti-Corn Law League. And therein they acted like true successors of the men of '93, for the French Revolutionists were all Protectionists, just as they were Conscriptionists, Unionists, Imperialists, and everything else that the modern Liberal detests.[106]

Mr. Chesterton finds the common foundation of Liberalism and the French Revolution in Democracy. But it may well be questioned whether Democracy is an essential part of Liberalism at all. Lord Macaulay would have justly claimed the title of Liberal; yet he declared that if the working classes ever obtained a preponderance in the State the nation would be ruined. Robert Lowe was a lifelong Liberal; but he looked forward with dread to the enfranchisement, even of the seven-pound householder. It is true that this Liberal opposition to democracy has ceased, but so, it might plausibly be urged, has the Conservative opposition to democracy. No one, Liberal or Tory, now ventures to say that the will of the people ought not to prevail. Even frankly aristocratic institutions like the House of Lords are now defended, as Mr. Chesterton has himself pointed out, on the rather paradoxical ground that the Peers are better interpreters of the will of the people than the Commons.

When we make anything like a careful examination of Mr. Chesterton's theory of democracy we shall find less cause than ever to identify it with the doctrine of Liberalism. Liberals have generally held high the authority of

---

105. The "Abbey's fruits" is from Chesterton's much-quoted poem, "The Secret People" (Appendix A).

106. The Chartists have been called the first working class movement in history. In the 1830s and 1840s they were considered radical and dangerous, but their political success is almost unmatched. Five of their six goals are now regarded as basic to democracy: 1. the vote all men over the age of 21, 2. electoral districts of equal population, 3. secret ballots, 4. no property tests for member of Parliament, 5. pay for members of Parliament, and 6. annual elections. Only the last, which would put the legislature into a permanent and unworkable election mode, has been rejected. George Villiers (1800–1870) and John Bright (1811–1889) supported free trade and opposed Corn Laws that kept the price of grain high, enriching those with land and raising the prices the poor paid for food. Henry Temple, 3rd Viscount Palmerston, (1784–1865) and John Russell (1792–1878) were Prime Ministers during the Chartist period.

Parliaments, even when those Parliaments were in their composition almost entirely oligarchical. Mr. Chesterton, on the other hand, while he professes to "believe very strongly in the mass of the common people," seems always exceedingly sceptical about the value of representative assemblies. He makes it a matter of praise in Dickens that "he realized the thing that Frenchmen and Irishmen understand… the fact that popular government is one thing and representative government another."

His conception of democracy would seem to be satisfied by any system, however undemocratic in seeming, under which the Government was in fact conducted in harmony with the general wishes of the people.[107] Now in all this there is nothing inconsistent with Toryism. That doctrine underlies the whole of Bolingbroke's pamphlet *The Patriot King* perhaps the clearest exposition of the Tory philosophy that has ever appeared in this country—the doctrine that the will of the people can be carried out by other means than those of election and representation.[108]

Another fact which has tended to confirm Mr. Chesterton in the illusion that he is a Liberal is his love of revolutions. He is never tired of asserting the sacred right of insurrection, the necessity of blood and violence for the redemption of our civilization. In the dedicatory poem at the beginning of *The Napoleon of Notting Hill,* he says, after speaking of the confident prophecies of political evolutionists:

Likelier across these flats afar,
These sulky levels, smooth and free,
The drums shall crash the valse of war
And death shall dance with liberty!

Likelier the barricades shall blare
Slaughter below and smoke above,
And death and hate and hell declare
That men have found a thing to love!

And again in criticizing (in the columns of the *Daily News*) Mr. H.G. Wells's statement that Socialism would come slowly, and would not "be announced by a blast of trumpets from Tower Hill," he asks why, if Socialism be really the redemption of mankind, it should not be so announced. "I shall not blame you," he writes, "if you blow trumpets from the Tower or fire guns from the Tower. You have blown trumpets and fired guns for much meaner things."

But here again his doctrine has no necessary connection with Liberalism. He has said quite truly that all revolutions are doctrinal, and that to lose faith in

---

107. The alternative to Chesterton is a system where people elect politicians who ignore their wishes.
108. As noted earlier, Henry St John, Lord Bolingbroke (1678–1751) championed republicanism over monarchy and his writings influenced the American Revolution.

G. K. Chesterton, a Criticism

dogma is to lose faith in revolution. But it is obvious that any doctrine in which a man can believe will serve as the basis of revolution. The Jacobins rebelled for the sake of the Rights of Man, but the Jacobites rebelled as fiercely for the sake of the Divine Right of Kings.[109] The peasants of La Vendée who guarded the passage of the Loire, the gentlemen of Lancashire who rode to Derby With Charles Edward—these also were revolutionaries. These also "had found a thing to love"—and that thing was Toryism.[110]

The one doctrine that is thoroughly and universally characteristic of Liberalism is the doctrine of Progress. The theory that the world is becoming gradually but inevitably better is a dogma common to Macaulay and Dickens, to Lord Rosebery and Mr. Morley, to John Bright and John Burns. It is the real sign manual of Liberalism, and it is the object of Mr. Chesterton's fiercest attacks.

In an article published in the *Independent Review* in 1905 Mr. Chesterton makes this substitution of the idea of Progress for certain defined dogmas the special heresy of the Liberal Imperialists. He wrote:

> When Liberalism met its great debacle there were necessarily two kinds of critics left in the defeated army, with two different plans of campaign, indeed, with two different conceptions of the nature of war. The first formed the coherent and philosophical Liberal Imperialist Party... the other formed the party of which I am a humble member. The first said: "The French Revolution succeeded because it was progressive, because it was the fresh and forward thing at that moment." The second said: "The French Revolution succeeded because it was religious, because it gave a key of principle which cannot grow old." The first said: "The old Liberals won, because they were men of their time." The second said: "They won because they were men of all time; or rather, because the ideas they dealt with are outside time altogether." The first said: "Old Liberal ideas conquered because they were new; but they are new no longer." The second said: "Not so. Old Liberal ideas conquered because they were true. And they are true still."

Now the analysis here given of the attitude of the first party, the Liberal Imperialists, is sound enough; but I cannot help feeling that the second party, of which Mr. Chesterton declares himself "a humble member," consisted exclusively of Mr. Chesterton himself, with the possible addition of Mr. Belloc. The ordinary "Pro-Boer" certainly did not repudiate the doctrine of Progress. He proclaimed it on all occasions—only he called Anti-Imperialism "progressive"

---

109. Despite their similar names, Jacobites are quite different from Jacobins. The first's zeal for resorting the Stuart dynasty and local rule has been described. Jacobins, whose name comes from the French Revolution's Jacobin Club, are political radicals and champions of a powerful central government.

110. In 1792, outraged at how the French Revolution was repressing the Catholic church, the "peasants of La Vendée" (on the west coast of France) rebelled and were murderously crushed. In 1745, Charles Edward (1720–1788) "rode to Derby" in the English Midlands with 6,000 Scotch soldiers in a failed effort to restore the Stuart dynasty. In both cases, these men were "revolutionaries" defending the small, traditional societies they loved, much as in *The Napoleon of Notting Hill*.

and Imperialism "reactionary." Mr. Chesterton's own personal friend, Mr. Masterman, wrote an essay on the decline of the Imperialist movement, and called it "After the Reaction"—a phrase which for Mr. Chesterton and his imaginary "party" would have no meaning.[111] The opponents of Imperialism were just as ready as their opponents to claim a monopoly in "the flowing tide," and they always endeavoured to represent the Imperialist movement as a sort of atavistic reversion to barbarism. The fact is that the doctrine of Progress is common to Liberals of every school; the only difference of opinion is as regards its application.

Mr. Chesterton diverges sharply from Liberalism in that he repudiates altogether this identification of good and bad with progress and reaction. He has a certain vision of a normal human life, and in his view reforms and revolutions must be undertaken not for the purpose of helping mankind on its march to an unattained ideal, but in helping it back to a sanity and health away from which it is constantly tending to fall. This sanity and health (qualified, as, in his view, it always must be qualified, by permanent human imperfection) he finds, for example, in the best period of the Middle Ages, a period which he eulogizes to an extent which must startle and shock the ordinary modern man, especially when coming from a professed Liberal. But he finds the instinct for it still abiding in the great mass of the people. In an article in *The New Age* he wrote of the working classes:

> For the Revolution, if they make it, there will be all the features which they like and I like; the strong sense of English cosiness, the instinct for special festival, the distinction between the dignities of man and woman, responsibility of a man under his roof. If you make the Revolution it will be marked by all the things that democracy detests and I detest; the talk about the inevitable, the love of statistics, the materialist theory of history, the trivialities of Sociology, and the uproarious folly of Eugenics. I know the answer you have; I know the risk I run. Perhaps democracy will never move. Perhaps the English people, if you gave it beer enough, would accept even Eugenics. It is enough for me for the moment to say that I cannot believe it. The poor are so obviously right, I cannot fancy that they will never enforce their rightness against all the prigs of your party and mine...

Now this belief in an ancient tradition abiding in the mass of men may be Democracy, but it is certainly not Liberalism. If it is Democracy it is Tory Democracy. Indeed there is one of Lord Randolph Churchill's speeches about the function of the masses as the guardians of a permanent Conservative tradition, which is almost identical with many passages in Mr. Chesterton's political writings.

---

111. Charles F.G. Masterman (1874–1927) was a liberal journalist and social reformer. His essay, "After the Reaction" can be found in his *In Peril of Change* (New York, B.W. Huebsch, 1905).

It is hardly necessary to point out the discrepancy between Mr. Chesterton's views and those of most Liberals on many minor matters—on the drink question, for example, and on the effectiveness of "undenominational" religious teaching. Mr. Chesterton would doubtless reply that these matters are not of the essence of Liberalism; nay, he would, perhaps, go further, and contend that what may be called the Nonconformist view of such problems is inconsistent with Liberal principles. But he has largely discounted this argument by refusing to accept it in the case of Socialists. In the article quoted above, an article called "Why I am not a Socialist,"[112] he deliberately maintains the position that a propaganda must be judged not merely by the specific doctrine preached, but by the general temper and attitude of the preachers. Certain normal human needs he holds to be inconsistent, not so much with Socialism, but with the visions and ideals of Socialists. "I do not say these things would not occur under Socialism; I say they do not occur to Socialists." Now in such a case it is reasonable to demand one weight and one measure. It would be manifestly unfair that Socialism should be judged by the Socialists unless Liberalism is also to be judged by the Liberals. And surely Mr. Chesterton's human needs which he regards as especially important—drink for instance, and dogma—are wholly left out of the general vision and propaganda of modern Liberalism.

The Napoleon of Notting Hill is Mr. Chesterton's political confession of faith. He has written many serious articles on political questions, but, just as none of his excursions into theological controversy throw so clear a light on his fundamental religious beliefs as the Nightmare of The Man who was Thursday, so none of his political essays sum up his view of politics so completely as this extravagant romance of King Auberon and Adam Wayne. It will be well, therefore, to examine it more closely.

The novel is a prophetic romance of the year 1950 or thereabouts.[113] Men having lost their faith in doctrine, and having come to believe in "a thing called Evolution," have allowed things to drift until a dull oligarchy governs the whole world, its prosaic disillusionment being admirably illustrated by the fact that the despotic King who is at its head is selected like a juryman from an alphabetical rotation list of the governing classes. Unfortunately the lot falls on one Auberon Quinn, a humorist who resolves to use his despotic powers for the purpose of forcing his subjects to assume all the splendour and ritual of feudal times. With this intent he frames the Charter of Cities whereby the various districts of London are provided with Lord High Provosts, flags, city guards with uniforms and halberds, and even with heroic legends conceived by the expansive imagination of King Auberon. The respectable vestrymen who have

---

112. That article, originally published in The New Age on January 4, 1908, is reprinted in Appendix B.

113. Actually it takes place some eighty years after the book's 1904 publication or 1984.

to perform these antics are annoyed, but they are obliged to acquiesce and go sullenly on with their work. The principal task before them at the moment is the construction of a great road from Westbourne Grove to Hammersmith Broadway. But their schemes are suddenly upset by the appearance of a young man named Adam Wayne, to whom the King's joke is a serious thing, a religion. Having become Provost of Notting Hill, he refuses to allow the road to pass through his Free City, and especially objects to a sacrilegious hand being laid upon Pump Street, to which he feels an especially passionate patriotic devotion. Instantly all the forgotten enthusiasms, which men had thought to have vanished from the world for ever when the last Dervishes were exterminated and when the last little Republic in South America was absorbed, flare up and destroy the empire of Modernity. Notting Hill defends itself like Athens, hurls back its enemies, and finally infects the other London districts with its own fiery patriotism and romance. The King's joke has redeemed the world.

With the literary quality of the story I shall deal in another chapter. What concerns us here is its political doctrine, and in this aspect there are several interesting points to be noted.

First of all it is characteristic of Mr. Chesterton that, while most writers who have endeavoured to sketch the future of humanity instinctively conceive it as better than the present, he as instinctively thinks of it as worse.[114] Until men definitely make up their minds to change the world, the world will steadily deteriorate. So far from Progress being the law of life, the law of life is Degeneration. Satan is the Prince of this World.

Then we may observe that the things which Mr. Chesterton selects as the symbols of oppression are the modern things, the progressive things. Buck and Barker, the villains of the piece, are not dull and reactionary landlords or oligarchs obstructing the march of reform. They might quite reasonably be represented as enlightened and public-spirited citizens, intent on a public improvement.

Lastly we may note that the sanctity in defence of which Adam Wayne draws the sword is nothing less than our old friend "the sanctity of private property." No doubt Wayne's enthusiasm for the rights of property is untainted by the sordid desire for gain and power which often prompts such enthusiasm. No doubt also he proves his sincerity by carrying it to lengths from which the most obscurantist member of the Liberty and Property Defence League would shrink.[115] No sane Conservative that I have ever heard of, however much he might denounce

---

114. This was written in 1908, before anti-utopian novels such as *Brave New World* and *1984*. H.G. Wells' writings about the near future (as opposed to the grim distant future of *The Time Machine*) portrayed a world that was "better" in the sense that Wells thought it so. One example is his 1905 *A Modern Utopia*.

115. This league existed from 1882 to the 1920s. Building on Herbert Spencer's ideas and supported by industrialists and large land owners, it opposed trade unions, socialism, and many social reforms.

G. K. Chesterton, a Criticism

the mildest measures of social reform as robbery and confiscation, ever suggested that the State had not the right, after giving full compensation, to take private property for the purposes of a public improvement. Yet Adam Wayne (and apparently Mr. Chesterton also) is willing to deluge Western London with blood rather than admit such a right. Of course, it may be suggested that I am taking the fantastic politics of King Auberon's realm too seriously. But, when all allowance has been made for legitimate exaggeration, the fact remains that the cause for which Adam Wayne was willing to shed oceans of blood was the cause of property.

He is less the Napoleon than the Penrhyn of Notting Hill. No one who had read *The Napoleon of Notting Hill* with reasonable care and intelligence had any right to be surprised when Mr. Chesterton proclaimed himself a opponent of Socialism.[116]

I have already dealt with Mr. Chesterton's attitude towards the idea of Progress, and I need say no more on the subject. But a word may be said with advantage about his hatred of the civic type represented in his tale by Barker and Buck, because that hatred, though it seems to ally him with the cause of democracy, is really, I think, only another sign of his fundamental Toryism.

Mr. Chesterton undoubtedly dislikes the moneyed man, the commercial magnate, the capitalist. This dislike seems to many to imply democracy, but it might equally well imply very old-fashioned Toryism. The alliance of such men with Conservatism is a very recent phenomenon. Down to the middle of the nineteenth century at least they were nearly all Liberals. When commercial interests first began to exercise power in this country that power was always on the Whig or Liberal side. The Tory party from the seventeenth century onwards fought it tooth and nail, and the fight, was continued by the bulk of the party even after their leader Peel had gone over to the commercialists. It was only when Toryism was transformed into Conservatism and lost some of its most characteristic features in the process that it became a possible party for capitalists and traders.

The doctrine of property stated in *The Napoleon of Notting Hill* and elsewhere, is, as I have said, markedly opposed to the modern tendency which we call Collectivism. It is true that Mr. Chesterton does not like the present state of wealth

---

116. What Cecil says is unfair. The conquering Napoleon of history only fits Adam Wayne (who wants to be left alone) in one respect. Both were talented military leaders who changed history (real or fictional). Any tie between Wayne and the wealthy, slate-mining Penrhyn family of Wales is ridiculous, whatever member of the family Cecil meant—the slave-owning, anti-abolitionist Richard Pennant (1737–1808), 1st Baron Penrhyn or (more likely because he's more recent) the paternalistic, strike-breaking George Douglas-Pennant, 2nd Baron Penrhyn (1836–1907). In fact, Notting Hill closes with the trades organized into craft organizations that resemble trade unions for independent craftsmen and small businessmen. It's easy to suspect that on this point, Cecil—who is still a Fabian and a socialist—resents his brother's vision of a future in which people own their own means of production rather than working for a State that owns or regulates everything as paternalistically as the Penrhyn family did their slate mines.

and poverty. As he himself has put it, "No one but Satan or Beelzebub could like the present state of wealth and poverty."[117] But the remedy, in his view, is not to deny property, but to assert it. "It is the negation of property that the Duke of Westminster should own whole streets and squares of London; just as it would be the negation of marriage if he had all living women in one great harem." **Mr. Chesterton would like a state in which each man should own his own land and his own tools, and, I think, he would permit no tools too large or complex for a single man to own and use them.**

Indeed, there is in Mr. Chesterton's later work a tone towards machinery which reminds one sometimes of Ruskin. He seems to see, not merely in the abuse of machinery, not merely in its ownership and exploitation by a limited class, but in the machinery itself a menace to the human soul. He believes, one gathers, that it tends to give men a sense of large knowledge when they have no knowledge, a sense of great power when they have no power.

> And under all this vast illusion of the cosmopolitan planet, with its empires and its Reuter's agency, the real life of man goes on concerned with this tree or that temple, with this harvest or that drinking-song, totally uncomprehended, totally untouched. And it watches from its splendid parochialism, possibly with a smile of amusement, motor-car civilization going its triumphant way, outstripping time, consuming space, seeing all and seeing nothing, roaring on at last to the capture of the solar system, only to find the sun cockney and the stars suburban.[118]

These feelings seem to have begun to affect him very early. In the essay on "The Patriotic Idea" in *England a Nation,* written before his political creed had developed along lines antagonistic to modern Progressivism, we find a passage instinct with dislike and distrust of modern invention:

> There is a decadence possible for our modern civilization, and it is just at this point that my difference from the Imperialists comes in. They think Imperialism (otherwise Cosmopolitanism) is the cure. I think that Imperialism (otherwise Cosmopolitanism) is the disease. I ignore for the moment the question of whether, in the abstract, combinations and centralizations and steamboats and Marconi wires are good things or bad. But to attempt to cure

---

117. This quote and the one that follows are from his January 4, 1908 article, "Why I am not a Socialist," in *The New Age*, p. 189–190, reprinted in Appendix B.

118. Gilbert made these remarks in Chapter 3 of *Heretics* and it's hard to see how the passage in its context says what Cecil claims. The preceding sentences read: "There is nothing large about painting the map red; it is an innocent game for children. It is just as easy to think in continents as to think in cobble-stones. The difficulty comes in when we seek to know the substance of either of them. Rhodes' prophecies about the Boer resistance are an admirable comment on how the 'large ideas' prosper when it is not a question of thinking in continents but of understanding a few two-legged men." The failure did not lie in the news telegraphed out of South Africa by Reuters, it lay with Cecil Rhodes, "a man with singularly small views" like those of a child, a man who could not understand that the Boers would stand and fight for their little farms. Those who live the "real life of man" in "splendid parochialism" are not as deceived as the world-dominating but small-minded builders of empires. It's a marvelous Chestertonian paradox.

the evil of Birmingham and save the soul of Chicago by more combinations and centralizations and more steamboats and more Marconi wires seems to me stark lunacy; it is like a doctor ordering brandy to a man in delirium tremens. It is precisely from these things that we are suffering—from a loose journalism, from a vague geography, from an excitable smattering of everything, from an officious interest in everybody, from a loss of strong national types, of strong religious restraints, of the sense of memory, and the fear of God. We are not suffering from any very painful or dangerous resemblance to the arrogant and cruel zealots who ruled in Sparta or died in the fall of Jerusalem. We are suffering from a resemblance to the mob in decaying Rome.[119]

This attitude is the more curious because you would rather expect to find Mr. Chesterton, with his continual deification of the human will, and his refusal to admit that any obedience is due to Nature from Man, to regard the victories of Man over Nature with approving eyes. He actually did so in the days of *The Wild Knight,* as witness the poems on "King's Cross Station" and "The Lamppost." I think he would do so still if you confined the question to Man's earlier triumphs. The plough, the axe, the ship, the arch, and the sword he would, I am sure, still acclaim enthusiastically as witnesses to the godlike supremacy of Man. But when you bring him face to face with the steam engine and the telephone his tone becomes dubious and even hostile. Even in things mechanical he has become a Tory.[120]

Note again his Tory love of authority and of permanent tradition. This is almost the central idea of *The Man who was Thursday,* where a new police force is organized to fight against Anarchism. It is true that the Anarchy to be combatted [combated] is rather the moral and intellectual Anarchy of modern thought symbolically treated than the ordinary political Anarchy with which we are familiar. But all the same the sympathies of the author are on the side of the

---

119. This is from the third section of Chesterton's "The Spirit of Patriotism," found in *Patriotism*, a Chesterton book now being prepared for publication. Notice that Chesterton clearly says he's making no judgment about whether "steamboats and Marconi wires are good things or bad." The evils of our cities do lie not in them, he says. At worst, they're like giving "brandy to a man in delirium tremens"—they may worsen the illness, but they're not its cause. Our fault lies in our attitudes, and in particular that we are becoming like an easily excited mob in a decaying civilization, a mob lacking a national or religious identity, as well as "the sense of memory, and the fear of God." "Marconi wires" are no more the cause (or solution) of our ills than they were in fourth-century Rome, when they did not exist.

120. Cecil confuses the fact that his brother isn't infatuated with new technology with a Luddite-like hostility toward new tools and technology, which isn't true. In the March 27, 1909 issue of *Illustrated London News*, Gilbert would criticize those who "whisper in a panic-stricken way that Germany is building ironclads of the size of small islands." With remarkable prescience, he argues that the best way to deal with Germany's battleships is to create new weapons and tactics: "If you perceive your enemy plunging on blindly in a particular direction, the real thing to do, if you have any spirit and invention, is to calculate the weakness in his course and advance yourself in some other direction." And that's exactly what happened. In the next war, submarines and torpedo boats, as small as they were, forced Britain and Germany to keep their costly warships in harbor as much as possible. In World War II, the lethality of carrier aircraft would signal the end of the battleship as an effective war weapon.

police. Of course a man need not be a Tory in order not to be an Anarchist. **But the man who instinctively feels the peril of Society to lie in the direction of Anarchy is an instinctive Tory, as the man who instinctively feels its peril to lie in the direction of slavery is an instinctive Liberal. Mr. Chesterton clearly belongs to the former class of mind.**[121]

In the course of the controversy in *The New Age* which raged round the article above referred to, Mr. Chesterton was challenged by both Mr. Wells and Mr. Shaw to "plank down his Utopia." He declined the invitation, but I think that any reasonably intelligent and industrious student of his writings could frame one for him. His ideal state would be very small—perhaps no larger than Notting Hill. Its population would be either peasant farmers owning each his own land or craftsmen working each in his own workshop. They would be devout Catholics, keen patriots, and heavy drinkers.[122] Such a state is clearly not the ideal aimed at by modern Liberals. It is certainly nearer to (though not identical with) the older Tory ideal. It would imply almost necessarily such Tory proposals as Conscription and Protection—not, of course, Imperial Protection, but National or possibly Civic Protection.[123] If Notting Hill is to have a City Wall, why not a City Tariff?

I may mention in passing that my view may find some confirmation in the amusing trialogues which Mr. Chesterton contributed to the *Fortnightly Review,* wherein a Tory, a Socialist, and an Irish Nationalist discussed public affairs month by month. Liberated by the dramatic form from the necessity of pretending to be a Liberal, the author threw himself into the views of the Tory Colonel with unconcealed gusto, and generally gave him (to my way of thinking, at least) the best of the debate. It is notable that no really typical representative of Liberalism was introduced. Mr. Chesterton could not so completely change his skin.

---

121. By this simplistic standard, H.G. Wells, who was constantly trying to organize the planet into a single World State untroubled by the 'anarchy' of nationalism, was the greatest of Tories, while Chesterton, who wanted London filled with rebellious little communities, was a great champion of liberalism. Simple 'this or that' definitions rarely capture the complexity of political systems.

122. That's hardly the case. In *Notting Hill,* little is said about the religion of the characters and, as a drink, sal-volatile (mentioned four times) seems at least as common as beer (mentioned once). Cecil seems to be confusing what Gilbert himself is, with what he would insist others must be. Utopians such as Wells and Shaw may want to remake the world in their image, but Chesterton isn't a utopian.

123. Cecil does not realize his brother is not only not a Tory, he won't become one. Gilbert never seems to have become a protectionist and near the end of *Notting Hill* he delights in a shopkeeper who imports his goods from around the world. During World War I, as the debate over Conscription began to heat up, Gilbert *opposed* the idea with every argument he could muster, only conceding that, "Whether Conscription will help or hinder us in that is a matter for the authorities; and a very difficult matter even for them. If they want it we must give it them, not because they are the best conceivable people who could decide, but because they are the only people who can decide." From *Illustrated London News,* June 12, 1915, page 749 and to be republished in *Chesterton on War.*

I cannot leave Mr. Chesterton's politics without referring to one subject which has been much before the public lately, and upon which he holds strong and what would generally be described as reactionary opinions. I mean the question of the political status of women.

It has been noted by many that *The Napoleon of Notting Hill* does not introduce a single woman from beginning to end. *The Man who was Thursday* does contain a woman, but she is a mere influence, doing nothing herself, but vaguely supposed to be inspiring other people to do things—in a word, the romantically conceived Queen of Love and Beauty. **It would be unfair to call Mr. Chesterton an Anti-Feminist, for his doctrine is rather one of the division of labour between the sexes than of the exaltation of one sex above the other.** But he is certainly a pronounced opponent of the modern movement for the political enfranchisement of women. His statement of the case against it has, at any rate, the virtue of originality, and is worth a moment's thought. Democratic politics, he says, rest on comradeship, that is, on the recognition of a certain affinity with men in the lump. But women have no capacity for comradeship. They can love individuals, but they cannot feel a casual yet genial interest in people generally. "They understand everything," he wrote in the *Illustrated London News*, "except three things—Liberty, Equality, Fraternity."[124] Therefore they are unfitted for politics. I do not propose to argue the question here, or to express my own views on it. But I may remark that it appears to me a tenable criticism that Mr. Chesterton does not sufficiently distinguish between the natural and

---

124. The remark needs a fuller context. In article about holidays and ceremonies, Chesterton wrote:

And I will confess to the dark conviction that keeps my enthusiasm in abeyance on this subject: I mean the conviction that the vast majority of normal women not only do not want Female Suffrage, but actively detest and despise it. Mr. Max Beerbohm, I see, remarked the other day that in his opinion women were unable intellectually to create or achieve. I think it quite a mistake to put it on this intellectual ground; it is a little supercilious, and it is to a great extent untrue. Women are as intellectual as the Devil in their own way. The real difference is not intellectual, but moral. A sister might be sixty times cleverer than her brother, and yet not half so fitted to vote. For voting (which means governing in council) does not presuppose intellect particularly: monkeys do it, for all I know. But it does presuppose camaraderie, a constant habit of dealing with your equals; the habit of the herd—gregariousness. As I said before, Whitman was quite finally accurate when he said that comradeship was the basis of all democracy. And women never have comradeship; never. It is a slander and a lie, undoubtedly, to say that women never have friendships with each other: women can have anything that involves individual devotion. But comradeship is quite a different thing from friendship. You do not find a woman wandering about all day with any five women, whoever they are. You do not find a woman sitting up all night to argue about God or golf with any nine women, whoever they are. Any conversation between five women is personal; also it is always short. Any conversation between five men is impersonal; no one can remember afterwards who said the best things: they were said by the Conversation itself, by the spirit of the whole, by the Community. Women are always in crucial attitudes towards others, attitudes that forbid the equal relation and the equal sentiment. Women are always either protecting or being protected. They are born despots and priests. They understand the most terrible secrets of the human heart; they overlook all our masculine existence with a kind of sacred satire; they have weighed the weakness of the whole world; they understand, I think, nearly everything. There are only three things they do not understand at all: Liberty, Equality, and Fraternity. [From the *Illustrated London News*, May 19, 1906.]

the acquired characteristics of womanhood. It is quite true that few ordinary women are capable of what Mr. Chesterton calls comradeship. But it is also true that where women are leading a type of life approximating to the masculine type—women in the theatrical world, for example—the capacity for it does develop in them. Mr. Chesterton would quite possibly say that such a development was undesirable; but that is not the point. What that development does seem to show is that incapacity for comradeship is rather a result of the present training and life of women than an innate limitation of the sex.

I think also that inconsistency seems to exist between Mr. Chesterton's denial to the woman of the present day of a claim to a public career, and his admiration of women who in past ages carried that claim to the most extreme point. Of no women has he written with more enthusiasm than of Catherine of Siena who held in her hand all the complicated threads of Italian politics, or of Joan of Arc who, dressed in a man's armour, led great armies to victory. Surely it is a rather strange position that a modern woman may not vote for a vestryman while a mediaeval woman might negotiate a treaty or direct a campaign.

Briefly, I think we may summarize Mr. Chesterton's politics by saying that he is a Tory of the seventeenth or early eighteenth century, born out of his due time. In the Cabinet of Bolingbroke he would have found quite a sympathetic atmosphere. He would have found men, by comparison with their opponents at any rate, sympathetic with the national aspirations of the native Irish. He would have found men who disliked Imperialism and foreign complications, and held that our fleets and armies ought to confine their energies to the defence of the actual soil of England. He would have found men who hated plutocracy and the power of riches created by trade, who loved the life of the cornfields and desired a free peasantry. **But, alas! he was born two centuries too late, and by dint of keeping so far behind his time has acquired the reputation of an advanced Radical.**

7

A Teller of Tales

Mr. Chesterton's intellect sees ideas more clearly than persons, yet his temperament leads him to think about ideas as romantically as romanticists think about persons. He wants to give every idea a feather and a sword, and a trumpet to blow and a good ringing voice to speak.

WE have more than once had occasion to remark that the key to nearly all Mr. Chesterton's merits and defects is to be found in the combative and propagandist impulse which is at the back of nearly all his work. He has been throughout not an artist seeking for the most perfect instrument of self-expression, but a soldier seeking the most effective engine of destruction. He tried to preach his crusade in verse; he tried to preach it in prose. In *The Napoleon of Notting Hill* and the tales which have followed it he tried to use for the same purpose the very old method of parable or fable.

It is very necessary that this should be understood, because without it both the intention and the achievement of the stories will be wholly misjudged. They are not novels—I will not say in the ordinary sense, but in any sense based upon a sound critical classification of art-forms. It is not the mere extravagance of the incidents that makes the difference. A story may have a wildly impossible plot, like *The Dynamiter* or *The Wrong Box*, or, for the matter of that, *Wuthering Heights*, and yet be a novel.[125] But all novels, realistic or fantastic or semi-supernatural, have this in common, that they show life as an interplay of human personalities and temperaments. **Mr. Chesterton's tales, on the other hand, show life as an interplay of spiritual forces transcending humanity, of which the human characters are merely the embodiments. They are not novels, but mysteries.**

It is natural Mr. Chesterton's stories should be mysteries—stories in which life is shown as a conflict of spiritual forces—because he really sees life in that way. Indeed, his judgment is often warped by his tendency to see only ideas when others see only persons. Modern politics, for instance, are, at present, almost

---

125. *The Dynamiter* is a 1885 short story collection by Robert Louis Stevenson and Fanny Van De Grift Stevenson. *The Wrong Box* is an 1889 novel by Stevenson and Lloyd Osbourne, his step-son. *Wuthering Heights* (1847) was Emily Brontë's only novel.

wholly personal, being concerned with the contest between two teams of statesmen into whose conflicts principles enter hardly more than they do into the Oxford and Cambridge boat race. Yet for a long while Mr. Chesterton insisted on reading into the struggle between the Outs and the Ins a set battle between rival doctrines of the State. There have been signs of late, since his growing fame has enabled him to see something of politics from the inside, that he has begun to understand the true state of the case. But the effect of this knowledge upon him has not been to make him modify his rigid idealism, but it has rather led him to regard current politics with increasing apathy and distaste.

If indeed he were only an Idealist (I use the word in the Platonic rather than in the current sense) he would probably have been content to express his views directly in the form of essays. But he is a peculiar and rare combination, a Romantic Idealist. Usually the Romantic sees persons much more clearly than ideas; one remembers how Carlyle, the most romantic of historians, exaggerated the importance of personalities in history, and underrated the influence of doctrines. **Mr. Chesterton's intellect sees ideas more clearly than persons, yet his temperament leads him to think about ideas as romantically as romanticists think about persons. He wants to give every idea a feather and a sword, and a trumpet to blow and a good ringing voice to speak. From this eccentric wedding—of Idealism and Romance, is born the Chestertonian novel.**

Without the romance, indeed, Mr. Chesterton's stories would be lost. For he does not possess at all the specific talent of the dramatist-novelist, the power, I mean, of creating characters who talk and act from within. It was the possession of this power in the highest degree of genius that saved Ibsen's symbolic plays from dullness. Ibsen's sense of individual character was so intense that even when he began by conceiving a man as a mere symbol, the living man grew under his hand. He could not help clothing every figure he introduced with a vivid and unmistakable human character, and endowing it with language and action absolutely native and appropriate. Mr. Chesterton never does this—never really attempts it. He never creates figures who talk or act from within, whose quality and dialect is their own and not their author's. Throughout *The Napoleon of Notting Hill*, still more throughout *The Man who was Thursday*, every one is talking in the Chesterton style, even when he is repudiating the Chesterton doctrines. Read the long exposition of Barker of the virtues of the "alphabetical monarchy" which he serves. The opinions are the opinions of Barker, but the voice is the voice of G.K.C. It is not in the least the way in which Barker would talk—Barker, who is supposed to be a dull and decorous official. He would not defend his dull and decorous opinions with such a wealth of paradox. Nor are the speeches of Buck, the "great man of business," in the least like anything that Buck could be conceived as saying. **The only two people who are always themselves, and** who talk and act from within, are Wayne and Auberon, and that is because Wayne and Auberon are the two lobes of Mr. Chesterton's brain.

And yet it remains true that the stories are almost Mr. Chesterton's best, as they are quite his most characteristic work. *The Napoleon of Notting Hill* is, I am inclined to think, quite his best. And this is because the tales, and that tale in particular, though the characters are for the most part but embodied opinions, are so drenched with romance, with colour, movement, humour, and animal spirits and show, moreover, so genuine a gift of pure story-telling, that it is quite impossible for the sternest artistic critic to resist the fascination.

Mr. Chesterton was not mistaken in his vocation when he set out to write stories. He is a born story-teller, which is quite a different thing from being a born novelist. The old trade of story-telling is, as he himself has said, a much older thing than the modern art of fiction. The Oriental who spread his carpet in the marketplace, the medieval bard who sang a ballad at his master's feast, made no appeal to that curiosity about the varieties of the human soul which is increasingly the inspiration of the modern novel. If he touched on human psychology at all he dealt only with those primal passions and desires which are common to all normal men. But, for the interest of his art, he depended simply upon his capacity to tell a good story, and to tell it well. In the last resort, Mr. Chesterton's novels depend for their interest on the same power.

Take *The Napoleon of Notting Hill*. It not only lacks the subtle qualities of fiction. It is not, even of its kind, an artistic whole. There are pages of insanity, pages of horse-play, pages of swash-bucklering slaughter, pages of thoroughly undramatic discussion. But the whole is carried forward by the mere zest of the author for his narrative. From the moment that the story is fairly launched it never flags or stops till it has reached its consummation. From the moment, especially, when the fighting begins, there is never one pause, never one slackening of the tension, never one moment in which to take breath and remember one's common sense.

This is really something of a *tour de force,* because the fighting is avowedly preposterous and farcical. A war between modern suburbs conducted with seventeenth-century halberds is not at first sight a thing that anyone can be expected to take seriously. It is a genuine triumph that, as you read it, you do take it seriously. You forget for the moment everything serious and modern, and agonize, as did King Auberon, with alternate hope and fear over the extravagant fight round the Water Works Tower. When the great and really unexpected climax comes, and Wayne and his few exhausted followers, outnumbered by fifteen or sixteen to one, and clinging desperately to their last refuge on Campden Hill, reduces the vast army of the south to instant submission by threatening to open the reservoir and flood the streets thirty feet deep in water, one is simply too stunned to remember for the moment the absurdity of the London Water Board's property being used for such a purpose. One forgets the exuberant folly of the whole story as men forgot the exuberant folly of King Auberon. Adam Wayne with his "uncanny blue eyes," has hypnotized us as he hypnotized the King and all his subjects.

The best parts of *The Napoleon of Notting Hill* are the battles, and especially the last great battle in Hyde Park, where the Empire of Notting Hill is ultimately overthrown. The last fight of Wayne, when all his followers have fallen around him, is a passage that will bear quoting, for it is a vigorous example of Mr. Chesterton's manner when his blood is up:

> With a shout the West Kensington men closed round Wayne, the great yellow banner flapping over his head.
>
> "Where is your favour now, Provost?" cried the West Kensington leader.
>
> And a laugh went up.
>
> Adam struck at the standard-bearer and brought him reeling forward. As the banner stooped, he grasped the yellow folds and tore off a shred. A halberdier struck him on the shoulder, wounding bloodily.
>
> "Here is one colour!" he cried, pushing the yellow into his belt; "and here!" he cried, pointing to his own blood—"here is the other."
>
> At the same instant the shock of a sudden and heavy halberd laid the King stunned or dead. In the wild visions of vanishing consciousness he saw again something that belonged to an utterly forgotten time, something that he had seen somewhere long ago in a restaurant. He saw, with his swimming eyes, red and yellow, the colours of Nicaragua.
>
> Quin did not see the end. Wilson, wild with joy, sprang again at Adam Wayne, and the great sword of Notting Hill was whirled above once more. Then men ducked instinctively at the rushing noise of the sword coming down out of the sky, and Wilson of Bayswater was smashed and wiped down upon the floor like a fly. Nothing was left of him but a wreck; but the blade that had broken him was broken. In dying he had snapped the great sword and the spell of it; the sword of Wayne was broken at the hilt. One rush of the enemy carried Wayne by force against the tree. They were too close to use halberd or even sword; they were breast to breast, even nostrils to nostrils. But Buck got his dagger free.
>
> "Kill him!" he cried, in a strange stifled voice. "Kill him! Good or bad, he is none of us! Do not be blinded by the face!… God! have we not been blinded all along!" and he drew his arm back for a stab, and seemed to close his eyes.
>
> Wayne did not drop the hand that hung on to the tree-branch. But a mighty heave went over his breast and his whole huge figure, like an earthquake over great hills. And with that convulsion of effort he rent the branch

G. K. Chesterton, a Criticism

out of the tree, with tongues of torn wood; and, swaying it once only, he let the splintered club fall on Buck, breaking his neck. The planner of the Great Road fell face foremost dead, with his dagger in a grip of steel.

Romanticism is in Mr. Chesterton's bones. It leads him not only to worship the good romantic writers—Scott and Dumas[126] and Stevenson—but to devour even bad romantic writers, if no others are available. **He goes about London with his pockets stuffed with sixpenny books and penny magazines, which it would seem incredible that any man of his literary status should look at, merely because there is plenty of blood and combat in them. He is particularly fond of detective stories.** And out of that enthusiasm grew, I fancy, the idea of his latest novel.

Mr. Chesterton is a lover of detective stories. But he is also a mystic and a philosopher. It occurs to him, I should imagine, that it would be rather fun to write a philosophic detective story.

He first played with the idea in a series of short stories called *The Club of Queer Trades*, dealing, as the title implies, with a society, every member of which has to have invented the profession by which he earns his living. One is the founder of an "Adventure and Romance Agency," for surrounding the lives of its subscribers with thrilling and melodramatic incidents. Another was an "Organizer of Repartee," who allowed himself to be scored off publicly by his employers whose epigrams were invented and led up to by their victim. Some of these stories were exceedingly good; one in particular, "The Awful Reason of the Vicar's Visit," showed, not only Mr. Chesterton's usual qualities of energy and humour, but a certain careful artistry which is not so commonly his. But the chief connecting link between the stories with which I am here concerned is the creation of a sort of transcendental Sherlock Holmes, who probes mysteries, not by attention to facts and clues, but by understanding the spiritual atmosphere. Thus, when in the story of the Adventure and Romance Agency a letter is produced, found upon the mysterious assailant of Major Brown, beginning "Dear Mr. Plover—I am annoyed to hear that some delay has occurred in the arrangements re Major Brown. Please see that he is attacked as per arrangement to-morrow," etc. etc., Basil Grant confines himself to remarking, "I don't think it's the sort of letter one criminal would write to another."

> "Facts," murmured Basil, like one mentioning some strange, far-off animals, "how facts obscure the truth. I may be silly—in fact, I'm off my head—but I never could believe in that man—what's his name, in those capital stories?—Sherlock Holmes. Every detail points to something, certainly; but generally to the wrong thing. Facts point in all directions, it seems to me, like the thousands of twigs on a tree. It's only the life of the tree that

---

126. Alexandre Dumas (1802–1870) was a French novelist best known for *The Count of Monte Cristo*.

has unity and goes up—only the green blood that springs, like a fountain, at the stars.'"

But the possibilities of the philosophic detective story were not exhausted with *The Club of Queer Trades*. Why should not the universe itself be the subject of a detective story? After all, the essence of a detective story is that certain facts are known of which the cause and explanation is hidden. And that, when one comes to think of it, is the essence of our knowledge of the universe. *The Man who was Thursday* is a detective story in which the criminal to be hunted and brought to bay is—God.

The idea is a good one. So is the subsidiary idea, the gradual realization that the whole wild story is a dream. By making each chapter just the slightest shade more incredible than the last, Mr. Chesterton gets a really harmonious grada-tion from the comparatively possible scene between the two poets to the pursuit of the flying President, where the atmosphere of a nightmare is very skillfully caught. Also there are good incidental scenes sometimes ending with a really strong and unexpected climax, such as that where Syme and his companions imagine the whole of civilization to have gone over to the side of Anarchy. That chapter, as also the one in which Syme is pursued by the paralytic professor, is an excellent example of Mr. Chesterton's gift of rapid and entertaining story-telling. But there is nothing in the book that one remembers as one remembers the fight round the Water Tower or the scene where Wayne flings his great sword at the feet of King Auberon.

As for the defects in characterization on which I have already commented, they are more conspicuous than ever. Mr. Chesterton evidently intended to dif-ferentiate the characters of the six detectives, but except, perhaps, in the case of Dr. Bull, it is given up almost as soon as it is attempted. When they are supposed to be Anarchists they are distinct and vivid enough, for then their externals only are described, and the author has a quick and picturesque eye for externals. When, however, they all turn out to be detectives, they all at the same moment turn out to be Mr. Chesterton! They do not again become distinct until the last chapter but one, when they describe severally how Sunday (in other words, the Universe) appears to them. And here they are only real because they have ceased to be human beings and become embodied points of view.

As Mr. Chesterton saved *The Napoleon of Notting Hill* by his instinct for Ro-mance and his gift for spirited narration, so he saves *The Man who was Thursday* by his keen sense of fun and his indomitable *joie de vivre*. There are whole chap-ters that are driven forward by mere force of animal spirits. A good example is the scene where Syme, who has been indulging freely in what Mr. Chesterton has called "the traditional drink of our civilization," makes his preparation for challenging the Marquis de Saint Eustache.

"I shall approach. Before taking off his hat, I shall take off my own. I shall say, 'The Marquis de Saint Eustache, I believe.' He will say, 'The celebrated Mr. Syme, I presume.' He will say in the most exquisite French, 'How are you?' I shall reply in the most exquisite cockney, 'Oh, just the Syme—'"

"Oh, shut it!" said the man in spectacles. "Pull yourself together, and chuck away that bit of paper. What are you really going to do?"

"But it was a lovely catechism," said Syme pathetically. "Do let me read it you. It has only forty-three questions and answers, and some of the Marquis's answers are wonderfully witty. I like to be just to my enemy."

"But what's the good of it all?" asked Dr. Bull in exasperation.

"It leads up to my challenge, don't you see?" said Syme, beaming. "When the Marquis has given the thirty-ninth reply, which runs—"

"Has it by any chance occurred to you," asked the Professor, with a ponderous simplicity, "that the Marquis may not say all the forty-three things you have put down for him? In that case, I understand, your own epigrams may appear somewhat more forced."

Syme struck the table with a radiant face.

"Why, how true that is," he said, "and I never thought of it. Sir, you have an intellect beyond the common. You will make a name."

"Oh, you're as drunk as an owl!" said the Doctor.

Then comes the actual challenge

"This man has insulted me!" said Syme, with gestures of explanation.

"Insulted you?" cried the gentleman with the red rosette, "when?"

"Oh, just now," said Syme recklessly. "He insulted my mother."

"Insulted your mother!" exclaimed the gentleman incredulously.

"Well, anyhow," said Syme, conceding a point, "my aunt."

"But how can the Marquis have insulted your aunt just now?" said the second gentleman with some legitimate wonder. "He has been sitting here all the time."

"Ah, it was what he said!" said Syme darkly.

"I said nothing at all," said the Marquis, "except something about the band. I only said that I liked Wagner played well."

"It was an allusion to my family," said Syme firmly. "My aunt played Wagner badly. It was a painful subject. We are always being insulted about it."

"This seems most extraordinary," said the gentleman who was *décoré*, looking doubtfully at the Marquis.

"Oh, I assure you," said Syme earnestly, "the whole of your conversation was simply packed with sinister allusions to my aunt's weaknesses."

"This is nonsense!' said the second gentleman. "I for one have said nothing for half an hour, except that I liked the singing of that girl with black hair."

"Well, there you are again!" said Syme indignantly. "My aunt's was red."

"It seems to me," said the other, "that you are simply seeking a pretext to insult the Marquis."

"By George!" said Syme, facing round and looking at him, "what a clever chap you are!"

The Man who was Thursday is not so good a book as *The Napoleon of Notting Hill*. Yet one feels it was planned to be a better book. It is more lucidly conceived and in some ways more carefully written. It has two coherent artistic ideas which are genuinely good artistic ideas of their kind and admirably suited to Mr. Chesterton's method. Yet, after the former book, it is disappointing. In *The Napoleon of Notting Hill* Mr. Chesterton was wildly irresponsible, yet he produced a masterpiece. In *The Man who was Thursday* he took his art much more seriously. Yet he produced something which by comparison may be described as a failure.

From this it would seem that it would be unwise to urge Mr. Chesterton to write more carefully or to be on his guard against his characteristic faults. The faults are certainly there, but one fears that an attempt to correct them might only lead to the sacrifice of those vital qualities which will keep his stories alive after many more perfectly artistic stories have perished. In imaginative writing, at any rate, Mr. Chesterton is never better than when, as in the best parts of *The Napoleon of Notting Hill*, he gives his romantic and humorous imagination full rein, and lets it carry him by what wild and perilous paths it will.

One cannot leave Mr. Chesterton's imaginative work without noticing that there is one art form which he has left untried. Mr. Bernard Shaw has repeatedly and publicly urged him to try his hand at writing for the stage; but so far he has remained deaf to such entreaties. Except for *The Wild Knight*, a poem written in his early youth, and obviously never intended for representation, he has written nothing which is dramatic even in form.

Personally I regret this abstention on his part, and hope it will not be permanent. It is quite true that his qualities are not those which go to the construction either of the ordinary "well-made" play or of the great drama of human character. But these two do not exhaust the possible types of drama any more than the novels of Miss Braddon and those of Mr. George Meredith (neither of which Mr. Chesterton could write) exhaust the possible types of fiction.[127] In story-writing he has got over the difficulty by inventing a new kind of novel to suit himself. There is no reason why he should not do the same in relation to the stage.

It should encourage Mr. Chesterton that he might bear a part in restoring another popular but despised, and in its present state largely despicable art to fine uses. Just as *The Man who was Thursday* is a sublimated detective story, so I

---

127. Mary Elizabeth Braddon (1837–1915) wrote some 75 novels, including her shocking 1862 *Lady Audley's Secret*. Oscar Wilde said of novelist George Meredith (1828–1909), "Who can define him? His style is chaos illumined by flashes of lightning."

can imagine Mr. Chesterton writing a sublimated musical comedy which would take the world by storm. Musical comedy, with its freedom from necessity of external or psychological realism, and its abundant opportunities for humour, imagination, and romance, would suit him down to the ground. If he could find a composer who suited him as well as Sullivan suited Sir William Gilbert he might do great things.[128]

Failing this, might not we have from Mr. Chesterton some prose phantasy on the lines of *The Napoleon* or *The Man who was Thursday*? The stage gives a specially good opportunity for that direct appeal to the emotions that Mr. Chesterton's romantic method implies, while it almost requires a simplification of psychology which would cover his weaknesses more than written fiction does. He would have to write with his eye on the stage, and that would imply learning a new trade, but his quick power of visualizing his scenes should make such learning easy to him.

Of course he would have to be given a free hand to preach his philosophy. We cannot imagine G.K.C. ceasing to be controversial. His songs in musical comedy, his dialogue in prose drama, like his poems, his essays, and his stories, would be full of fight. **For when he ceases to fight he will cease to be G.K.C. At that moment he may become a classic, but I for one shall no longer read him.**

---

128. Known as Gilbert and Sullivan, Arthur Sullivan (1842–1900), a composer, and William Gilbert (1836–1911), a dramatist, collaborated on comic operas that are still popular today.

Gilbert Chesterton about 1908

8
The Gladiator as Artist

Vitality—that is the key to all that is valuable in Mr. Chesterton's work. As an essayist and critic, his work has a thousand defects, both in substance and form. But it is saved by his vigorous pugnacity, his Donnybrook joie de vivre, his readiness to challenge anybody and everybody to instant combat.

MR. Chesterton has tried his hand upon almost every description of literary work which man can attempt: essays, criticisms, religious controversy, political polemic, biography, fiction, and poetry. **One quality alone is common to all, the fact that whether as critic, as novelist, or as poet, he is incurably and impenitently didactic. In this he is thoroughly consistent with his own doctrine, for no man has ever spoken with more scorn of the doctrine of "Art for Art's Sake."** He has repeatedly denied that for art's sake any great art can be produced. "Just as this repudiation of big words and big visions," he says in *Heretics*, "has brought forth a race of small men in politics, so it has brought forth a race of small men in the arts.... Our new artistic philosophers call for the same moral licence, for a freedom to wreck heaven and earth with their energy; but the upshot of it all is that a mediocrity is Poet Laureate."[129] And again, later in the same book—"In the *fin de siècle* atmosphere every one was crying out that literature should be free from all causes and all ethical creeds. Art was to produce only exquisite workmanship, and it was especially the note of those days to demand brilliant plays and brilliant short stories. And when they got them they got them from a pair of moralists. The best short stories were written by a man trying to preach Imperialism; the best plays were written by a man trying to preach Socialism.[130] All the art of all the artists looked tiny and tedious beside the art which was a by-product of propaganda." Whether Mr. Chesterton's theory in this matter be right or wrong, he has at any rate carried it into practice. His own art is certainly a by-product of propaganda. Beauty and wit, rhetoric and creative energy—these things to him are not ornaments, but weapons.

---

129. At that time England's Poet Laureate was the now long-forgotten Alfred Austin (1835–1913).
130. Rudyard Kipling and Bernard Shaw respectively.

And yet it is a curious fact that it is Mr. Chesterton's artistic qualities, and not his message, which create the unity of his work. Most writers, indeed most artists of all kinds, retain their root point of view all through their lives, while they continually modify their mode of expression. Mr. Chesterton, on the other hand, has, as we have seen, almost wholly outgrown the opinions which were his when he first emerged into notice, but his method of conveying them has hardly varied by a hair's-breadth. Take a passage from *The Defendant* and put it side by side with a passage from *Heretics*, or with his last week's article in the *Daily News* or the *Illustrated*. You will very likely find a considerable change in the opinions expressed; in the mode of expression you will find no change, and even in the technique little improvement. A very able critic, who was also a great admirer of Mr. Chesterton, told me the other day that he considered *The Defendant* still held the field as his best work, and, after carefully rereading it, I am unable to say that it is an untenable view. Different people will prefer different books according to their individual tastes, but it may safely be said that all the artistic qualities which Mr. Chesterton's admirers like in his later work will be found in as full a measure in his first volume as in his last.

Mr. Chesterton is generally regarded as primarily a humorist, and unquestionably his humour is the freshest and most original quality of his work. Humour is probably the most difficult thing in the world to analyse. As Mr. Chesterton himself says of Dickens, "Perfect absurdity is a direct thing, like physical pain or a strong smell." Mr. Chesterton's humour generally consists in the sudden and violent introduction of a grotesque image when it is least expected. In the conception of such images he really, I think, reaches most unmistakably the mark of genius. Such a matter can only be indicated by examples.

In an entirely serious article in the *Daily News,* in defence of what may be called the romantic view of politics, he contrasted "the great rhetoricians who beat Napoleon" with "the strong silent men who could not catch De Wet." I do not know whether the image of those "strong silent men" sends everybody into fits of laughter, as it sends me. As Mr. Chesterton says, "A joke is a direct thing." But, to me, that is almost the most perfect sentence Mr. Chesterton ever wrote. Another example I may give from *Heretics*, a particularly good case, which deserves quoting at length, because it shows how the seriousness and even eloquence of the context can make a grotesque image more wildly and shatteringly funny:

> When Christianity was heavily bombarded in the last century, upon no point was it more persistently and brilliantly attacked than upon that of its alleged enmity to human joy. Shelley and Swinburne and all their armies have passed again and again over the ground, but they have not altered it. They have not set up a single new trophy or ensign for the world's merriment to rally to. They have not given a name or a new occasion to gaiety.

Mr. Swinburne does not hang up his stocking on the eve of the birthday of Victor Hugo. *Mr. William Archer does not sing carols descriptive of the infancy of Ibsen outside people's doors in the snow.*[131]

There is another artistic quality in Mr. Chesterton's work which bears a close analogy to his type of humour, but for which, as yet, criticism has found no name. I can only indicate it by saying that just as he can produce a supremely humorous effect by the sudden introduction of a grotesque image into a serious passage, so he often gets an effect extraordinarily thrilling by the sudden introduction into a passage apparently trivial of a reference to some thing felt by most people to be profoundly solemn and moving. He is particularly fond of using the Bible in this way; indeed, there was never so accomplished a blasphemer as this strenuous defender of the faith. The explanation of this fact may be perhaps that which he gives in *Heretics*. **"Blasphemy depends on belief, and is fading with it. If anyone doubts this let him sit down seriously and try to think blasphemous thoughts about Thor."** Anyhow, Mr. Chesterton's skill in using the Bible in a startling manner is unquestionable. The most striking example of it will be found in the *Dickens*, where he is blaming the novelist for granting to Micawber a prosperous ending:

> But how did it happen, how could it happen that the man who created this Micawber could pension him off at the end of the story, and make him a successful Colonial mayor? Micawber never did succeed, never ought to succeed; his kingdom is not of this world.

There is also a passage in *Heretics* about "the drunkard's liver of the New Testament which is marred for us, which we take in remembrance of him," a passage which has naturally shocked many, but which seems to me profoundly right and exceedingly dramatic.

Many who have been accustomed to think of Mr. Chesterton as a modern and an artistic rebel, a lover of the grotesque in poetry, a romantic and a mystic, must have been surprised in reading his essay on Pope in *Twelve Types* to notice the unstinted praise which he gives to the coldest and most correct of English classical poets. I think the explanation of his admiration for Pope may be found in his liking for those sharp antitheses in which Pope loved to indulge.

And without sneering teach the rest to sneer,

or

---

131. In the 1813 version of his tract, "The Necessity of Atheism," Percy Shelly wrote: "Man would have been too happy, if, limiting himself to the visible objects which interested him, he had employed, to perfect his real sciences, his laws, his morals, his education, one-half the efforts he has put into his researches on the Divinity." Algernon C. Swinburne's "Hymn to Proserpine" (1866) includes the line, "Thou hast conquered, O pale Galilean; the world has grown grey from thy breath." He devoted a poem, "To Victor Hugo," to extravagantly praising the anti-Catholic French writer. The Scottish literary critic, William Archer (1856–1924), introduced the Swedish dramatist Henrik Ibsen to the English speakers.

So obliging that he ne'er obliged[132]

are not much in Mr. Chesterton's poetic style, but they bear some resemblance, in their balance of phrasing and their antithetical use of the same word, as well as in their smoothness and pungency, to the epigrams which are scattered so thickly over his essays. One of the best of these, which achieved the honour of being twice quoted in Parliament, referred to the secret funds of the two great political parties. "Rich men pay into them and are made peers; poor men are paid out of them and are made slaves." It would be difficult to put the state of the case with more biting brevity.

Mr. Chesterton's preoccupation with propaganda has undoubtedly made him a less perfect artist than he might have been. His sense of pure beauty has to an extent been blunted by it. His first object is always to make his point effective, and beauty of expression only comes to him when his theme so inspires him as to make it instinctive. In his style you will sometimes find ugly flaws and careless discords which would be impossible to a man who valued the beauty of words for its own sake. Yet when it suits his mood, he can make his prose sing as nobly as that of any living writer. The "Defence of Rash Vows" is for the most part just such a clever *tour de force* of advocacy as the "Defence of Penny Dreadfuls" which I have already noticed. But in its peroration Mr. Chesterton suddenly catches the note of genuine poetry, and produces a rhetorical passage of which Ruskin need not have been ashamed.[133]

> There are thrilling moments, doubtless, for the spectator, the amateur, and the aesthete; but there is one thrill that is known only to the soldier who fights for his own flag, to the ascetic who starves himself for his own illumination, to the lover who makes finally his own choice. And it is this transfiguring self-discipline that makes the vow a truly sane thing. It must have satisfied even the giant hunger of the soul of a lover or a poet to know that in consequence of some one instant of decision that stange [strange] chain would hang for centuries in the Alps among the silences of stars and snows. **All around us is the city of small sins, abounding in backways and retreats, but surely, sooner or later, the towering flame will rise from the harbour, announcing that the reign of the cowards is over and a man is burning his ships.**[134]

I know nothing better of its kind in contemporary literature than that, unless it be the passage in *The Napoleon of Notting Hill,* where Adam Wayne propounds to the King his remedy for the prosaic flippancy of modern life:

---

132. The quote is from Alexander Pope's "Character of Atticus."

133. John Ruskin (1819–1900) was an influential art and architectural critic.

134. "A Defense of Rash Vows" was reprinted in *The Defendant* (1901). The "strange chain" refers back to earlier in the article where, "One man swore to chain two mountains together, and the great chain hung there, it was said, for ages as a monument of that mystical folly."

"I know," he said, in a strange, almost sleepy voice; "there is truth in what you say, too. It is hard not to laugh at the common names—I only say we should not. I have thought of a remedy; but such thoughts are rather terrible."

"What thoughts?" asked Auberon.

The Provost of Notting Hill seemed to have fallen into a kind of trance; in his eyes was an elvish light.

"I know of a magic wand, but it is a wand that only one or two may rightly use, and only seldom. It is a fairy wand of great fear, stronger than those who use it—often frightful, often wicked to use. But whatever is touched with it is never again wholly common; whatever is touched with it takes a magic from outside the world. If I touch with this fairy wand the railways and the roads of Notting Hill, men will love them, and be afraid of them for ever."

"What the Devil are you talking about?" asked the King.

"It has made mean landscapes magnificent, and hovels outlast cathedrals," went on the madman. "Why should it not make lamp-posts fairer than Greek lamps, and an omnibus ride like a painted ship? The touch of it is the finger of a strange perfection."

"What is your wand?" cried the King impatiently.

"There it is," said Wayne; and pointed to the floor, where his sword lay flat and shining.

Of late years Mr. Chesterton has shown some sign of relaxing of extreme vehemence of his controversial method. Often in his stories, and now and again in his weekly articles in the *Daily News,* he drops the propagandist attitude for a moment, and lets his humour, imagination, and sense of poetry have free play. The result certainly justifies us in believing that Mr. Chesterton has been partly spoiled as an artist by his persistent preoccupation with his gospel. Some of these more irresponsible articles are among the best things he has done. It is true that the humorous ones seem occasionally little more than school-boyish exhibitions of high spirits, delightful to read, but simply impossible to treat critically. I remember an extraordinary article in the *Daily News* about various people who wanted to rebuild St. Paul's Cathedral. I suppose there was some symbolism behind it, but to me it was valuable in virtue of its quite exquisite insanity. One man wanted it built of cubes one on top of the other, each a little smaller than the one below. "If it were built like that it would never fall down." "Does it not occur to you that if it were built like that, we should want it to fall down?" Then there was another (a German) who wanted the top to be larger than the bottom, "like the trees that from the bosom of the great Nature-Mother spring." I am quoting from memory; I would not profane my recollections of that gorgeous piece of absurdity by coldly looking it up. I don't know what it all meant, but it gave me great delight at the time.

As some of these lighter fragments were pure humour, others were pure poetry. And some of them served to show how rich is the imagination, and how really keen the sense of beauty of which Mr. Chesterton only allows himself to give us glimpses in his more responsible work.

That reminds me that I want very much to know why we have not had another volume of poetry from Mr. Chesterton. Since *The Wild Knight* (his first serious publication) he has given us no book of verse. Yet, curiously enough, his verse, judged by the occasional samples contributed to the Press, shows a decided improvement on his earlier efforts which is not noticeable in his prose. His latest essays, as I have said, are not from a technical point of view observably better than those in *The Defendant*; but some of the poetry which has recently appeared from his pen is quite unmistakably better than the best of *The Wild Knight*.

His sense of beauty and of the music of words has developed. Vigorous and original as was much of *The Wild Knight*, there was hardly any beauty in it. His work aimed at strength rather than grace; it startled and thrilled rather than moved and melted. But there is real beauty, and that of a high order, in such lines as these, taken from a fragment of a "Ballad Epic of Alfred," published in the *Daily News*:

> And every English maid that walks
> In good thought apart
> May break the guard of the three Kings
> And know the dear and dreadful things
> I hid within my heart.[135]

Again, there is poetry and music of a kind quite alien from that of *The Wild Knight* in the Christmas poem which he wrote for the *Daily News*, beginning:

> Step softly under snow and rain
> To find the place where men can stay,—
> The way is all so very plain
> That we may lose the way.

And later:

> Step humbly; humble are the skies
> And very lone and fierce the star;
> So very near the manger lies
> That we may travel far.

The best and most original quality of Mr. Chesterton's recent poetry is the skill with which he has learned to blend the poignancy of epigram with the poignancy of poetry. This very poem, after its perfect introduction, goes on:

---

135. Almost identical lines reappear in Book 1 of *The Ballad of the White Horse* (1911), lines 214f, which can be found in *G.K. Chesterton's Early Poetry* (2004).

We have gone round and round the hill
And lost the wood among the trees,
And found long names for every ill,
And served the mad gods, naming still
The Furies, the Eumenides.

The Gods of violence took the veil
Of vision and philosophy;
The Serpent that brought all men bale,
He bites his own accursed tail,
And calls himself Eternity.[136]

But perhaps the most admirable example of this wedding of epigram and poetry will be found in a poem called "The Secret People," which appeared in *The Neolith*. It was on a very characteristic theme, the silence of the English people throughout their history:

Smile at us, pay us, pass us, but do not quite forget,
For we are the people of England, and we have not spoken yet.[137]

In this poem he really contrives, without once dropping out of the key of high poetry, to sum up whole epochs of English history in swift and unforgettable phrases. What, for instance, could more fully describe the state of England after the Wars of the Roses than the line:

And there was only a naked people under a naked Crown.

Or again, how could you more concisely express the change from Tudor to Stuart times than by the phrase:

The name of the King's Servants grew greater than the King.

Then after a spirited description of the great French War, when:

We did and died like lions to keep ourselves in chains,

comes the two powerful verses in which, as it seems to me, Mr. Chesterton touches his high-water mark:

Our patch of glory ended, we never heard guns again.
But the squire seemed struck in the saddle, he was foolish, as if in pain.
He leant on a chattering lawyer, he clutched at a cringing Jew.
He was stricken, may-be after all he was stricken at Waterloo:
Or perhaps the ghosts of the shaven men whose gold was in his house
Came back in shining shapes at last to spoil his last carouse,
Only we see the last sad squires ride slowly towards the sea.

136. These lines are from Chesterton's "The Wise Men." The snake biting its own tail and calling "himself Eternity" refers to Ouroboros, a self-devouring snake symbolic of eternal recurrence. In Chesterton's day the idea was being popularized by Friedrich Nietsche's *Thus Spoke Zarathustra*.
137. "The Secret People" was republished in his 1915 *Poems* and here in Appendix A.

And a new people takes the land. And still it is not we.

They have given us over into the hands of the new unhappy lords,
Lords without anger or honour, who dare not carry their swords.
They fight by shuffling papers; they have dead, bright alien eyes:
They look at our labour and laughter as a tired man looks at flies.
The load of their loveless pity is worse than the ancient wrongs.
Their doors are shut in the evening; and they have no songs.

That last line will serve well to show Mr. Chesterton's increased power over his instrument. Notice the deliberate irregularity of "and they have no songs," compared with the dactylic "worse thăn thĕ ancient wrongs" of the line before, so swiftly suggesting the desolation of the atmosphere described. The same improved technique may be seen in another Christmas poem which appeared in *The Commonwealth*, where two metres were employed alternately to suggest the two sides of the Christian religion:

The happy, silent hill and wood
Are bowed about the Holy Birth,
And for one little hour the Earth
Is lazy with the love of good.
But ready are you and ready am I
When the trumpets blow and the guns go by.
For we are for all men under the Sun,
And they are against us every one.[138]

And so on, through a rattle of eight lines.

It seems rather a pity that, with such rich capabilities almost unexploited, Mr. Chesterton has not found time to get together and publish another volume of verse. Of course it might be urged that the greater advance which he has made in verse than in prose is in part due to his having permitted the soil of his talents in this direction to lie fallow for a season. Perhaps, if he had written verse as unremittingly as he has written essays, his poetic style would have shown as little progress as his prose style. Perhaps, on the other hand, if he had given himself as much rest from essay writing as from poetry, the technique of *Heretics* might have shown as marked an improvement on that of *The Defendant* as the technique of "The Secret People" does on that of *The Wild Knight*. I am willing to leave the question an open one. All the same, I should like to see another volume of verse from his pen, and I would give a good many introductions to various people to get it.

But his gift for serious verse is by no means the only talent which Mr. Chesterton has allowed to lie almost unused so far at any rate as his public utterance goes. He has a rare and genuine gift for the sort of verse of which I gave an

138. This is "The Truce of Christmas," which was placed on Christmas Eve in *Chesterton Day by Day*.

G. K. Chesterton, a Criticism

example in an earlier chapter—the "report" of Mr. Chamberlain's speech.[139] Of this sort of light verse he pours out an enormous amount for the amusement of his personal friends, but hardly any of it has ever got published—indeed, some of the most delightful specimens are much too irresponsibly violent in their personalities for publication.

Mr. Chesterton may almost be said to have invented a new form of light verse, though few specimens of it have seen the light. He has abundant wit and deep-seated humour, and that trick of smooth and easy rhythm which adds so much to the fun of Calverley[140] and of Gilbert. But he adds to these a new and very characteristic touch of his own. He will often end a poem, the bulk of which is simply gorgeous fooling, with a sudden and thrilling note of seriousness. It is difficult to give examples, because nearly all the poems concerned are unpublished, and most of them are unpublishable. But one that has already found its way (though obscurely) into print will give an idea of what I mean. The *Tribune* newspaper, by some odd confusion, described G.K.C. as having been born in 1856. The maligned writer immediately sent the Editor a "ballade" repudiating the suggestion. The first verse ran:

I am not fond of anthropoids as such.
I never went to Mr. Darwin's school.
Old Tyndall's ether, that he liked so much,
Leaves me, I fear, comparatively cool.
I cannot say my heart with hope is full
Because a donkey, by continual kicks,
Turns slowly into something like a mule—
I was not born in 1856.

Then follows another verse in the same vein; and then the third, with its ringing change of tone:

Age of my fathers! Truer at the touch
Than mine! Great age of Dickens, youth and yule!
Had your strong virtues stood without a crutch,
I might have deemed man had no need of rule,
But I was born when petty poets pule,
When madmen used your liberty to mix
Lucre and lust, bestial and beautiful,—
I was not born in 1856.

To summarize Mr. Chesterton's position as a writer we may say that, while he lacks the careful workmanship, the regard for true proportion, the sensitive aesthetic conscience which would make him a great artist, he has enough

139. This is Gilbert's "metrical version of Mr. Chamberlain's election speech," quoted in Chapter 2.
140. Charles S. Calverley (1831–1884) was a brilliant and humourous English poet.

artistry for the work he wants to do, and a little to spare, and this is backed by so prodigious a stock of vital energy, by so much humour, imagination, pugnacity, and sense of romance, that one forgets the slips and defects in the great mass of achievement. Probably, to a Chesterton, at any rate, that achievement would be impossible without those defects. We have seen that he is by no means always at his best when he is writing most carefully. It is when he seems to be writing at post haste, careless of details, carried forward by the stream of his own invention, that his force is greatest. I have already quoted part of the description of the great fight in Hyde Park which closes the career of Adam Wayne. Nowhere does Mr. Chesterton strike more markedly the note of genius. Yet anyone who carefully examines the passage will perceive that it has been written at such breakneck pace, and with so little revision, that Wilson "seemingly smashed like a fly" on page 285, is again "smashed and wiped down on the floor like a fly" on page 287. It is a real tribute to Mr. Chesterton's power that his narrative carries you readily past all such details, and makes you forget everything in the swing and clash of the swords.

Vitality—that is the key to all that is valuable in Mr. Chesterton's work. As an essayist and critic, his work has a thousand defects, both in substance and form. But it is saved by his vigorous pugnacity, his Donnybrook *joie de vivre*, his readiness to challenge anybody and everybody to instant combat. As a story-teller he lacks all the qualities which one would suppose were needful, yet he has the one thing that is really needful. His tales are carried forward on a tide of vital energy, sometimes expressing itself as sheer fun, sometimes as wild romance, but always full of vigour and life. The verse often contains ugly lines which would have been impossible to a careful artist, but there is hardly a poem, even among his bad poems, which is not alive with its own movements.

We must conclude, then, that Mr. Chesterton's success is at least as much due to qualities of character as to qualities of art, to his personality as to his works. It is with a study of his personality, then, that this essay on criticism may fitly conclude.

9

THE PERSONAL EQUATION

*The force that keeps him so continually stirring is clearly a force
that comes from within. It is not ambition or the desire for fame. He
has little or none of either, at any rate in their ordinary sense.*

THERE is probably at present no figure better known in literary circles than
that of G.K. Chesterton. His huge form, half of which, as Mr. Shaw has
said, is usually out of the range of vision, his great flapping hat and romantic
cloak, his walk and his laugh are familiar to every one who knows the world
of Fleet Street and the Strand. Whatever else he may become in the future, he
has certainly become a public personality. There can, therefore, be no harm
in touching upon such of his peculiarities as really throw some light upon his
personality, and thence upon his work.

**Mr. Chesterton carries into his private life that incurable romanticism
which is so marked a feature of all that he has written.** The scenes which he
haunts are not generally regarded as very perilous. Both Battersea and Fleet
Street are, I believe, adequately policed. But Mr. Chesterton insists on traversing
them armed with a sword-stick, and generally carrying a revolver in his pocket.
This is not an affectation; he does not parade it to the world as a self-advertizer
would. He hugs it to himself as did the lantern-bearing boys in Stevenson's delightful essay.[141] He does it because he is really romantic, the essence of romance
being a sense of the unexplored possibilities of life. I believe that in his heart of
hearts G.K.C. hopes that one day some impossible thing will happen to him,
and compel him to use his lethal weapons. At any rate, the sense of having them
to use if he wanted to gladdens his secret heart.

---

141. Robert Louis Stevenson's "The Lantern-bears," describes the joy of a boy free for the summer in "a
certain easterly fisher-village." The climax comes: "Toward the end of September, when school-time was
drawing near and the nights were already black, we would begin to sally from our respective villas, each
equipped with a tin bull's-eye lantern." There was comradeship as boys gathered to talk in the darkness
by the glow of their lanterns, but: "The essence of this bliss was to walk by yourself in the black night; the
slide shut, the top-coat buttoned; not a ray escaping, whether to conduct your footsteps or to make your
glory public: a mere pillar of darkness in the dark; and all the while, deep down in the privacy of your
fool's heart, to know you had a bull's-eye at your belt, and to exult and sing over the knowledge."

Because he has this romantic temperament, this lust for unexplored possibilities, London and all great cities have a fascination for him. To Nature I do not think he has any great devotion. In the dedicatory poem to *The Napoleon of Notting Hill,* he says to Mr. Belloc:

You saw a moon on Sussex downs
A Sussex moon, untravelled still;
I saw a moon that was the town's—
The largest lamp on Campden Hill.

If he sees the country at all he sees it only as a background to human figures. But for his holidays he likes other cities, cities steeped in a different civilization—cities of France, or Belgium, or Italy. About these he has written some of his best light articles. And it is noticeable that these are never about the "sights" of the city, but only about the things seen there. He has, one might almost say, a horror of deliberate sight-seeing. He holds that only when you come upon a historic monument or a great work of art accidentally do you really see it. Moreover, he points out in the *Dickens,* the things peculiar to a country are not the historic things, but the trivial things. "Westminster Abbey is not especially a piece of English architecture. But the hansom cab is a piece of English architecture. The imaginative Englishman will be found all day in a café, the imaginative Frenchman in a hansom cab."

It is the colour and atmosphere of the existing civilization that interests him, and the opportunities which they furnish as a background for human romance. When he has travelled in the North of France it is safe to say that he was thinking less of churches and chateaux than of such wild possibilities of what might happen there, as are recorded in *The Man who was Thursday.*

Another symptom of his romanticism is his love of toy theatres. In a previous chapter I ventured to suggest that Mr. Chesterton might do well to try writing for the stage, but, after all, I fancy the toy-theatre stage is the one which would suit him best. It gives unparalleled opportunities for colour and romance, and subtle psychology is hardly possible within the limit of its conventions. *The Man who was Thursday,* impossible of dramatization for the ordinary stage, might be dramatized on the pasteboard stage of our childhood with remarkable effect. Or why should it not be performed on the lines which "Punch and Judy" has made popular? "Sunday" would make a most impressive doll, and the paralytic professor would strike terror into the infant heart—to say nothing of Dr. Bull and his spectacles.

The growth of Mr. Chesterton's public reputation has made comparatively little difference to his mode of life. Of course his fame has carried him into new circles, and made him acquainted with men of what may roughly be called the governing class, with bishops and cabinet ministers, members of parliament, and men eminent in letters and art. But among these he has, I always fancy, something of the air of a man who has strayed into an environment interesting and even congenial, but at bottom alien to him. His type of life is still the journalistic type. The atmosphere really native to him is still the atmosphere of Fleet Street. And he is never more at his ease, never more amusing, never more wholly himself, than when he is talking to his old brothers of the craft.

It would indeed be a strange thing if anyone with his keen scent for romance did not love Fleet Street. For Fleet Street is a place that really fulfils the true romantic ideal—it is a place where anything may happen. Nowhere else does one meet so many incredible people—people who seem to have stepped straight out of some wild Rabelaisian caricature. Its lies are extravagant beyond the possibilities of ordinary human imagination, yet they are often less extravagant than the truth which they cover. With all its ghastly background of tragedy, it is a paradise for the man who is expecting the unexpected. And such a man is G.K.C.

He has a genuine love for Fleet Street, and he gives the impression of wasting a great deal of time there, as most journalists do, even those who are really working themselves to death.

For hours he will sit over a bumper of burgundy in one of his favourite haunts, especially in a certain wine-bar which from the other side of the main road confronts the Puritanism of the *Daily News,* and pour out torrents of conversation to anyone who happens to be about. He talks, especially in argument, with powerful voice and gesture. He laughs at his own jokes loudly and with quite unaffected enjoyment. He seems at such moments quite unconscious of the flight of time.

G.K.C. gives many people the impression of being a lazy man. His extraordinary lavishness in the taking of cabs has tended to enforce that view. He will take a cab half-way up a street, keep it waiting an hour or so, and then drive half-way down the street again. I know a man who met him in a little bookshop just opposite the Law Courts. A cab was, of course, waiting outside. G.K.C. drove my friend to a neighbouring hostelry about six doors farther down, just opposite St. Clement Danes. There they went in and talked over their wine for three-quarters of an hour, the cab still waiting. The other man naturally thought that the cab was to take G.K.C. back to Battersea. But he was in error. When they got out it appeared that the eminent journalist was only going to the office of the *Illustrated London News,* which is just about another six doors down the Strand. The total distance traversed could not have been more than a hundred and fifty yards. The time occupied was something over an hour. What the cabman charged I do not know, but as, from what I know of Mr. Chesterton, he probably got at least double his proper fare, he presumably did not do badly.

Also he is casual in his methods of work. You will find him writing, usually in penny exercise books, not only in restaurants, tea-shops, and public houses, but in cabs, on the tops of omnibuses, and even walking along the street. He is absent-minded to a degree almost incredible. He himself once announced his intention of writing a series of stories of the Sherlock Holmes type, only for the purpose of illustrating his own inattention to detail. There was to be the "Incident of the Curate's Trousers" and "The Adventure of the Pro-Boer's Corkscrew." But the story I like best myself (which I believe to be strictly true) is that of his calling on a publisher at the hour appointed for a meeting, and placing in the publisher's own hands a letter explaining elaborately why he could not keep the appointment. All this gives a general impression of unbusinesslike slackness.

Yet it is unquestionable that Mr. Chesterton must in fact be one of the hardest workers now living. The amount of writing from his pen which actually gets published is amazing, and it is nothing to the mass that doesn't get published, that could not possibly ever be published that is written solely for his own amusement or that of his personal friends. Every week he has a column article in the *Daily News* and a full-page article in the *Illustrated London News*. A continual stream of prose and verse flows from him into the presses of the other newspapers and reviews. He is indefatigable in writing introductions to everything, from *The Book of Job* to the latest novel of Gorki. His lectures are without number. Indeed, such is his activity that he is ever ready to undertake tasks which cannot possibly add either to his fame or his income. Any humble Nonconformist minister anxious to amuse his P.S.A., any group of Tooley Street tailors who call themselves the Social Democratic League of the Human Race, can draw a lecture from G.K.C. for which many reputable societies would gladly pay more than ten pounds. This may seem to recall the propagandist fervour of Mr. Bernard Shaw in his earlier days. But there is a distinction. Mr. Shaw was a Socialist, a member of a fighting society, trying to help on a practical movement which he really hoped to see succeed. But Mr. Chesterton stands for no one but himself, and, however much he may deny the existence of the inevitable, can hardly seriously hope for the conversion of modern London to Chestertonism through his lectures. He is merely a man expressing his opinions because he enjoys expressing them. He would express them as readily and as well to a man he met in an omnibus.

The force that keeps him so continually stirring is clearly a force that comes from within. It is not ambition or the desire for fame. He has little or none of either, at any rate in their ordinary sense. He is certainly not the sort of man either to be indifferent to other people's opinion of him, or to pretend to be so. Comradeship is a necessity of life to him. He enjoys the sound of his own voice; he laughs openly at his own jokes. But for him the moment's satisfaction is enough. He is, I should say, the last man in the world to be moved powerfully

G. K. Chesterton, a Criticism

by ambition, and most of his activities are the last upon which a really ambitious man would ever enter. It is sheer pugnacity and the zest of self-exposition that keeps him so constantly to the front, and forbids him to allow any opportunity of displaying and defending his ideas to pass unused.

It seems a little curious that at a time when politics are being flooded with men of letters of all types and colours, the most polemic of contemporary writers, and one who can never be persuaded to keep off political topics for more than a hundred lines together, should so far have shown no desire for a political career. I believe that he was once asked to stand for Parliament, and replied that he would stand if he were quite sure he would be defeated. The answer was probably sincere enough. He would keenly enjoy the fun of electioneering, in which he has several times indulged on other people's behalf before now, and would, I should say, be a very popular candidate on the hustings. Whether he would be equally popular with his own party if he got into the House of Commons I do not know. But I doubt if fear of his independence would prevent his being selected. He calls himself a Liberal, and the leaders and organizers of the party are not clever enough to know how much he disagrees with them. If his friend Mr. Belloc could manage it, I do not see why he cannot. No doubt he might find the House a bore at times, and might be tempted, like Mr. Cunninghame Graham, to startle it with a "damn."[142] But, after all, it is a good club, and Mr. Chesterton is very clubable. The drink is excellent, and some of the members are quite intelligent when they are not engaged in performing their legislative functions. Ideas are wanted in politics, and a mild eruption of G.K.C. would do His Majesty's faithful Commons no harm. As for himself, it would only add one more to activities already so numerous as to be past counting.

Mr. Chesterton's extraordinary versatility and copiousness of output is beyond question a danger to his permanent position in literature, if he cares to have one. It is true that, considering the amount he writes, his level of work is remarkably high. But, unless he controls his effervescent desire to write everything that comes into his head, he will never write the best that he might have written. Of course, it is silly to quarrel with a man for his temperament; without that pugnacity and vitality which inevitably results in over-production, G.K.C. would not be G.K.C. But I am not blaming him; I am only pointing out the defects of his qualities. It is quite certain that he could do more than he has done if he could only make up his mind exactly what he wanted to do. Sometimes he seems to want to be a theologian, sometimes a political pamphleteer, sometimes a story-teller, sometimes a critic, sometimes a historian. He has power and vitality enough, I should say, to be any of these things, if he really wills it. But no man

---

142. Robert Cunninghame Graham (1852–1936) was a socialist who sometimes ran as a liberal. Chesterton said he was someone "whom I knew more slightly but always respected profoundly" and an "uncompromising rebel." *The Autobiography of G.K. Chesterton* (New York: Sheed & Ward, 1936), 160.

alive has power and vitality enough to be all of them. It must be remembered that a similar versatility (though accompanied with less interest in practical affairs and a much more careful artistic conscience) has prevented us from ever knowing how great a man Robert Louis Stevenson really was. If Mr. Chesterton seriously wants to leave a permanent name behind, he cannot begin a moment too soon to concentrate on whatever he really thinks he can do best.

But probably he has no such ambition. It would indeed, I fancy, waken in him nothing but Rabelaisian laughter to be told that he ought to crave for the position of a classic or for an immortality of fame. It would be quite out of his character to care for posthumous reputation. In the controversies raging round him he has dealt shrewd blows, blows that will leave their mark. He has fought hard and well, and he will certainly go on fighting till he dies. Whether his words will live (that problem which has tortured so many men of genius) he probably cares nothing. If his name were to be remembered among men at all he would probably prefer the tribute that Heine demanded—the sword of a brave soldier in the Liberation War of Humanity.[143]

I have endeavoured in this book to sketch Mr. Chesterton as he is, to differentiate between what is strong and what is weak in the quality of his work, between what is sound and what is unsound in the doctrines he has preached. I have tried to do this in a sympathetic spirit, but keeping well "this side idolatry." I doubt if any good end would be served by attempting to forecast his career or the fate of his reputation. He would enjoy such a forecast, no doubt, as it would enable him to practise his own game of "Cheat the Prophet." But I have no desire to adopt that character. All I will say is that, if any of his work survives, I think it will be some of his poems, if he can be persuaded to publish the best of them in permanent form, *The Napoleon of Notting Hill*, perhaps, some of the best essays in *The Defendant*, and, I am inclined to think, despite the reservations I made in discussing it, the *Dickens*. *Heretics*, clever and even brilliant as much of it is, I do not think will live. It deals too largely with transitory phenomena and transitory reputations. Kipling, I imagine, our children will read, and probably Bernard Shaw. They will certainly not have forgotten Omar. But I do not imagine that the name of Mr. McCabe will be familiar to them, and one may hope that there will no longer be either vegetarians or yellow pressmen in the happier times to come.[144] Of course, it is not safe to assume that a book will not live because it is journalistic and deals with the passing hour. The comedies of Aristophanes are as crammed with topical allusions and contemporary satire as any modern musical comedy.[145] Yet over two thousand years have failed to age them. Horace

143. This appears to be a remark in a letter Heinrich Heine wrote from Paris on March 30, 1855.
144. These are the heretics in Chesterton's book, including Omar Khayyám (1048 – 1123), author of the *Rubaiyat of Omar Khayyam* and Joseph M. McCabe (1867–1955), a priest who became a critic of religion.
145. Aristophanes (*c.* 446–388 BC) was the father of comic drama. Horace (65–8 BC) was a Roman poet

G. K. Chesterton, a Criticism

again built a monument more enduring than brass out of what were largely in effect *vers de société*. But I do not think that Mr. Chesterton's work has quite the quality that gives to fugitive themes a permanence of its own. If he lives at all it will be by virtue of those parts of his work which deal with things in their nature eternal.

Of course there is another kind of immortality which Mr. Chesterton might conceivably attain. We have seen that the force behind all his work which gives it its value is the force of his personality—that the fascination of that personality often saves him where his technical skill and artistic taste are at fault. Is it possible that the personality divorced from the work might survive—that men might remember his personal idiosyncrasies and the casual sayings dropped in conversation after they had ceased to read a single line that he had written? I need not point out that that has happened with one great figure in English literature. Every one remembers Macaulay's epigram about Dr. Johnson, that he was "regarded in his own time as a classic and in ours as a contemporary." Mr. Chesterton is certainly not regarded as a classic, but will he be a contemporary to our children? Thousands of persons who have never opened "Rasselas" or "The Vanity of Human Wishes" know all about Johnson's habit of counting posts, and his inordinate love of tea. Will Mr. Chesterton's sword-stick and his toy-theatre be remembered by people who have forgotten *Heretics* and *The Napoleon of Notting Hill*? I suppose the answer to that question depends on whether he should have the good fortune to find a Boswell.[146]

I will leave G.K.C. without further speculation as to his destiny.

It may be that the Gulfs will wash him down;
It may be he will touch the Happy Isles.[147]

But, if he does, they will not be less enjoyable for his presence.

---

146. James Boswell (1740–1795) was a friend and biographer of Samuel Johnson.

147. This is a marvelous allusion to Alfred Lord Tennyson's 1842 poem "Ulysses," which adds a postscript to the life of Ulysses in the ancient Greek tales, the *Iliad* and the *Odyssey*. Tiring of life as a king dealing out, "Unequal laws unto a savage race," Ulysses longs to turn his throne over to his son, and "To sail beyond the sunset, and the baths/ Of all the western stars, until I die./ It may be that the gulfs will wash us down;/ It may be we shall touch the Happy Isles,/ And see the great Achilles, whom we knew./ Tho' much is taken, much abides; and tho'/ We are not now that strength which in old days/ Moved earth and heaven, that which we are, we are,—/ One equal temper of heroic hearts,/ Made weak by time and fate, but strong in will/ To strive, to seek, to find, and not to yield."

Gilbert Chesterton in 1909

A

THE SECRET PEOPLE

G.K. Chesterton,

Editor: This poem upset many of Chesterton's critics, leading them to charge that he was claiming to speak for the English people. As you can see, he was doing no such thing. He was suggesting that, for all they have suffered, the people had yet to speak and force their masters—from Norman invaders to modern paper shufflers—to listen. He even leaves open the possibility that they might never speak or act.[148]

Smile at us, pay us, pass us; but do not quite forget,
For we are the people of England, that never has spoken yet.
There is many a fat farmer that drinks less cheerfully,
There is many a free French peasant who is richer and sadder than we.
There are no folk in the whole world so helpless or so wise.
There is hunger in our bellies, there is laughter in our eyes;
You laugh at us and love us, both mugs and eyes are wet:
Only you do not know us. For we have not spoken yet.

The fine French kings came over in a flutter of flags and dames.
We liked their smiles and battles, but we never could say their names.
The blood ran red to Bosworth and the high French lords went down;
There was naught but a naked people under a naked crown.
And the eyes of the King's Servants turned terribly every way,
And the gold of the King's Servants rose higher every day.
They burnt the homes of the shaven men, that had been quaint and kind,
Till there was no bed in a monk's house, nor food that man could find.
The inns of God where no man paid, that were the wall of the weak,
The King's Servants ate them all. And still we did not speak.

And the face of the King's Servants grew greater than the King:
He tricked them, and they trapped him, and stood round him in a ring.
The new grave lords closed round him, that had eaten the abbey's fruits,
And the men of the new religion, with their Bibles in their boots,
We saw their shoulders moving, to menace or discuss,

---

148. This poem was first published in *Neolith*, I (1907), 37.

And some were pure and some were vile; but none took heed of us.
We saw the King as they killed him, and his face was proud and pale;
And a few men talked of freedom, while England talked of ale.

A war that we understood not came over the world and woke
Americans, Frenchmen, Irish; but we knew not the things they spoke.
They talked about rights and nature and peace and the people's reign:
And the squires, our masters, bade us fight; and never scorned us again.
Weak if we be for ever, could none condemn us then;
Men called us serfs and drudges; men knew that we were men.
In foam and flame at Trafalgar, on Albuera plains,
We did and died like lions, to keep ourselves in chains,
We lay in living ruins; firing and fearing not
The strange fierce face of the Frenchman who knew for what he fought,
And the man who seemed to be more than man we strained against and
    broke;
And we broke our own rights with him. And still we never spoke.

Our path of glory ended; we never heard guns again.
But the squire seemed struck in the saddle; he was foolish, as if in pain.
He leaned on a staggering lawyer, he clutched a cringing Jew,
He was stricken; it may be, after all, he was stricken at Waterloo.
Or perhaps the shades of the shaven men, whose spoil is in his house,
Come back in shining shapes at last to spoil his last carouse:
We only know the last sad squires ride slowly towards the sea,
And a new people takes the land: and still it is not we.

They have given us into the hands of the new unhappy lords,
Lords without anger and honour, who dare not carry their swords.
They fight by shuffling papers; they have bright dead alien eyes;
They look at our labour and laughter as a tired man looks at flies.
And the load of their loveless pity is worse than the ancient wrongs,
Their doors are shut in the evenings; and they know no songs.

We hear men speaking for us of new laws strong and sweet,
Yet is there no man speaketh as we speak in the street.
It may be we shall rise the last as Frenchmen rose the first,
Our wrath come after Russia's wrath and our wrath be the worst.
It may be we are meant to mark with our riot and our rest
God's scorn for all men governing. It may be beer is best.
But we are the people of England; and we have not spoken yet.
Smile at us, pay us, pass us. But do not quite forget.

B

WHY I AM NOT A SOCIALIST

G.K. Chesterton,

Now, I wish to say first that Socialistic Idealism does not attract me very much, even as Idealism. The glimpses it gives of our future happiness depress me very much. They do not remind me of any actual human happiness, of any happy day that I have ever myself spent.

Editor: This *New Age* article critical of Socialism is so well-argued it forced H.G. Wells and Bernard Shaw to respond soon after in the same publication. The entire exchange (reprinted here), offers an excellent opportunity to understand what Chesterton believed politically in 1908, and how well he stood up in a debate against two of Socialism's best-known champions. It also illustrates why Chesterton believed that a movement's grand ideals and abstract visions often told more about what it would do in power than any concrete proposals it might be making for solving specific social ills. Ideas matter and we make a serious mistake when we neglect or ignore them.

In his 1936 autobiography, Chesterton noted that, "I myself began with an acceptance of Socialism; simply because it seemed at the time the only alternative to the dismal acceptance of Capitalism." He went on to point out that his brother "took Socialism much more seriously." He was right. Only six weeks earlier Cecil had published an article in *The New Age* which began, "The task which I have set myself is to discuss and meet the principal popular arguments against Socialism. I shall try throughout to state these difficulties as fairly as I can, and I shall then do my best to remove them."[149]

I HAVE been asked to give some exposition of how far and for what reason a man who has not only a faith in democracy, but a great tenderness for revolution, may nevertheless stand outside the movement commonly called Socialism. If I am to do this I must make two prefatory remarks. The first is a short platitude; the second is a rather long personal explanation. But they both have to be stated before we get on to absolute doctrines; which are the most important things in the world.

The terse and necessary truism is the same as that with which Mr. Belloc opened his article in this paper. It is the expression of ordinary human disgust

---

149. This appendix is from G.K. Chesterton, "Why I am not a Socialist," *The New Age*, II:10 (January 4, 1908), 189–190. The autobiographical quote is from *The Autobiography of G.K. Chesterton* (New York: Sheed & Ward, 1936), 229. Cecil's quote is from Cecil Chesterton, "The Problem of Equality" *The New Age*, II:4 (November 21, 1907), 69.

at the industrial system. To say that I do not like the present state of wealth and poverty is merely to say I am not a devil in human form. No one but Satan or Beelzebub could like the present state of wealth and poverty. But the second point is rather more personal and elaborate; and yet I think that it will make things clearer to explain it. Before I come to the actual proposal of collectivism, I want to say something about the atmosphere and implication of those proposals. Before I say anything about Socialism, I should like to say something about Socialists.[150]

I will confess that I attach much more importance to men's theoretical arguments than to their practical proposals. If you will, I attach more importance to what is said than to what is done; what is said generally lasts much longer and has much more influence. I can imagine no change worse for public life than that which some prigs advocate, that debate should be curtailed. A man's arguments show what he is really up to. Until you have heard the defence of a proposal, you do not really know even the proposal. Thus, for instance, if a man says to me, "Taste this temperance drink," I have merely doubt slightly tinged with distaste. But if he says, "Taste it, because your wife would make a charming widow," then I decide. Or, again, suppose a man offers a new gun to the British navy, and ends up his speech with the fine peroration, "And after all, since Frenchmen are our brothers, what matters it whether they win or no," then again I decide.[151] I could decide to have the man shot with his own gun, if I could. In short, I would be openly moved in my choice of an institution, not by its immediate proposals for practice, but very much by its incidental, even its accidental, allusion to ideals. I judge many things by their parentheses.

Now, I wish to say first that Socialistic Idealism does not attract me very much, even as Idealism. The glimpses it gives of our future happiness depress me very much. They do not remind me of any actual human happiness, of any happy day that I have ever myself spent. No doubt there are many Socialists who feel this and there are many who will reply that it has nothing to do with the actual proposal of Socialism. But my point here is that I do admit such allusive elements into my choice. I will take one instance of the kind of thing I mean. Almost all Socialist Utopias make the happiness or at least the altruistic happiness of the future chiefly consist in the pleasure of sharing, as we share a public park or the mustard at a restaurant. This I say is the commonest sentiment in Socialist writing. Socialists are collectivist in their proposals. But they are Communist in their idealism. Now there is a real pleasure in sharing. We have all felt it in the case of nuts off a tree or the National Gallery, or such things.

150. Hilaire Belloc's article, "Thoughts about Modern Thought," appeared in the December 7, 1907 issue of *The New Age*, 108–110.

151. Remember this is 1908 and, while distrust of Germany has been growing rapidly for about a decade, for centuries France has been England's traditional foe, and thus the country whose victory in war— because England had fought with a defective gun—would mean England's defeat.

But it is not the only pleasure nor the only altruistic pleasure, nor (I think) the highest or most human of altruistic pleasures. I greatly prefer the pleasure of giving and receiving. Giving is not the same as sharing: giving is even the opposite of sharing. Sharing is based on the idea that there is no property, or at least no personal property. But giving a thing to another man is as much based on personal property as keeping it to yourself. If after some universal interchange of generosities everyone was wearing someone else's hat, that state of things would still be based upon private property.[152]

Now, I speak quite seriously and sincerely when I say that I for one should greatly prefer that world in which everyone wore someone else's hat to every Socialist Utopia that I have ever read about. It is better than sharing one hat anyhow. Remember we are not talking now about the modern problem and its urgent solution; for the moment we are talking only about the ideal; what we would have if we could get it. **And if I were a poet writing an Utopia, if I were a magician waving a wand, if I were a God making a Planet, I would deliberately make it a world of give and take, rather than a world of sharing.**[153] I do not wish Jones and Brown to share the same cigar box; I do not want it as an ideal; I do not want it as a very remote ideal; I do not want it at all. I want Jones by one mystical and godlike act to give a cigar to Brown, and Brown by another mystical and godlike act to give a cigar to Jones. Thus it seems to me instead of one act of fellowship (of which the memory would slowly fade) we should have a continual play and energy of new acts of fellowship keeping up the circulation of society. Now I have read some tons or square miles of Socialist eloquence in my time, but it is literally true that I have never seen any serious allusion to or clear consciousness of this creative altruism of personal giving. For instance, in the many Utopian pictures of comrades feasting together, I do not remember one that had the note of hospitality, of the difference between host and guest and the difference between one house and another. No one brings up the port that his father laid down; no one is proud of the pears grown in his own garden. In the less non-conformist Utopias there is, indeed, the recognition of traditional human liquor; but I am not speaking of drink, but of that yet nobler thing, "standing drink."

Keep in mind, please, the purpose of this explanation. I do not say that these gifts and hospitalities would not happen in a Collectivist state. I do say that they do not happen in Collectivist's instinctive visions of that state. I do

---

152. In their 'this is what we will do' *proposals*, socialists promised the public that, if they were put in power, large industries (such as steel and rail) would be owned by the government—collectivism. In their more softly spoken 'this what we ought to be doing' *ideals*, they went much further, hinting at the communal ownership of almost everything—Communism. Chesterton is warning that a movement's understated ideals need to be watched more closely than its loudly proclaimed proposals.

153. This is the closest Chesterton comes to "planking down" his Utopia, something both Wells and Shaw will demand from him in their replies (Appendices C and E).

not say these things would not occur under Socialism. I say they do not occur to Socialists. I know quite well that your immediate answer will be, "Oh, but there is nothing in the Socialist proposal to prevent personal gift." That is why I explain thus elaborately that I attach less importance to the proposal than to the spirit in which it is proposed. **When a great revolution is made, it is seldom the fulfilment of its own exact formula; but it is almost always in the image of its own impulse and feeling for life.** Men talk of unfulfilled ideals. But the ideals are fulfilled; because spiritual life is renewed. What is not fulfilled, as a rule, is the business prospectus. Thus the Revolution has not established in France any of the strict constitutions it planned out; but it has established in France the spirit of eighteenth century democracy, with its cool reason, its bourgeois dignity, its well-distributed but very private wealth, its universal minimum of good manners.[154] Just so, if Socialism is established, you may not fulfil your practical proposal. But you will certainly fulfil your ideal vision.[155] And I confess that if you have forgotten these important human matters in the telling of a leisurely tale, I think it very likely that you will forget them in the scurry of a social revolution. **You have left certain human needs out of your books; you may leave them out of your republic.**

Now I happen to hold a view which is almost unknown among Socialists, Anarchists, Liberals, and Conservatives. I believe very strongly in the mass of the common people. I do not mean in their "potentialities," I mean in their faces, in their habits, and their admirable language. Caught in the trap of a terrible industrial machinery, harried by a shameful economic cruelty, surrounded with an ugliness and desolation never endured before among men, stunted by a stupid and provincial religion, or by a more stupid and more provincial irreligion, the poor are still by far the sanest, jolliest, and most reliable part of the community—whether they agree with Socialism as a narrow proposal is difficult to discover. They will vote for Socialists as they will for Tories and Liberals, because they want certain things, or don't want them. But one thing I should

---

154. Some of those who like Chesterton are bothered by his praise for the French Revolution despite the fact that it led to the Great Terror, forced secularization, and the Napoleonic Wars. Here Chesterton briefly describes where he thought it failed and succeeded. It failed to establish written, constitutional protections for human rights like that created by the American Revolution. That was bad, but for Chesterton who, like many Englishmen, anchored rights more in ancient traditions than in modern texts, it did not seem as important as it might for an American. From Chesterton's perspective, however, the Revolution did do something he valued highly. It retained "well-distributed but very private wealth," particularly in France's many small farms, cafes and stores.

155. This is a marvelous illustration of a Chestertonian paradox. Most people believe an ideology will achieve the practical goals it sets, such as reducing the number of hungry people. How can it fail to do something so easily seen and measurable? Their doubts center on whether its more abstract visions of the future will be achieved. Chesterton suggests the opposite is true, that underlying ideals are more likely to happen (or at least be attempted) than the "practical proposals." Stated concretely, Socialism is unlikely to create a collective cigar box from which all may freely take. But it may create a society in which few engage in the "mystical and godlike act" of giving away cigars that Socialists find so repugnant.

affirm as certain, the whole smell and sentiment and general ideal of Socialism they detest and disdain. No part of the community is so specially fixed in those forms and feelings which are opposite to the tone of most Socialists; the privacy of homes, the control of one's own children, the minding of one's own business. I look out of my back windows over the black stretch of Battersea, and I believe I could make up a sort of creed, a catalogue of maxims, which I am certain are believed, and believed strongly, by the overwhelming mass of men and women as far as the eye can reach. For instance, that an Englishman's house is his castle, and that awful proprieties ought to regulate admission to it; that marriage is a real bond, making jealousy and marital revenge at the least highly pardonable; that vegetarianism and all pitting of animal against human rights is a silly fad; that on the other hand to save money to give yourself a fine funeral is not a silly fad, but a symbol of ancestral self-respect; that when giving treats to friends or children one should give them what they like, emphatically not what is good for them; that there is nothing illogical in being furious because Tommy had been coldly caned by a school-mistress and then throwing saucepans at him yourself. All these things they believe; they are the only people who do believe them; and they are absolutely and eternally right. They are the ancient sanities of humanity; the ten commandments of man.

Now I wish to point out to you that if you impose your Socialism on these people, it will in moral actuality be an imposition and nothing else; just as the creation of Manchester industrialism was an imposition and nothing else. You may get them to give a vote for Socialism; so did the Manchester individualists get them to gives votes for Manchester.[156] But they do not believe in the Socialist ideal any more than they ever believed in the Manchester ideal; they are too healthy to believe in either. But while they are healthy, they are also vague, slow, bewildered, and unaccustomed, alas, to civil war. Individualism was imposed on them by a handful of merchants; Socialism will be imposed on them by a handful of decorative artists and Oxford dons and journalists and Countesses on the Spree. Whether, like every other piece of oligarchic humbug in recent history, it is done with a parade of ballot-boxes, interests me very little. **The moral fact is that the democracy definitely dislikes your favourite philosophy, but may accept it like so many others, rather than take the trouble to resist.**

Thinking thus, as I do, Socialism does not hold the field for me as it does for others. My eyes are fixed on another thing altogether, a thing that may move or not; but which, if it does move, will crush Socialism with one hand and landlordism with the other. They will destroy landlordism, not because it is property-,

---

156. "Manchester" refers to a nineteenth-century ideology emphasizing *laissez-faire* and free trade. Chesterton uses it because in many ways it was the direct opposite of Socialism—and yet it attracted many votes. "Manchester individualism" believed the government should regulate private behavior as little as possible. "Manchester industrialism" meant it should do little to regulate business practices.

but because it is the negation of property. **It is the negation of property that the Duke of Westminster should own whole streets and squares of London; just as it would be the negation of marriage if he had all living women in one great harem.** If ever the actual poor move to destroy this evil, they will do it with the object not only of giving every man private property, but very specially private property; they wall probably exaggerate in that direction; for in that direction is the whole humour and poetry of their own lives. For the Revolution, if they make it, there will be all the features which they like and I like; the strong sense of English cosiness, the instinct for special festival, the distinction between the dignities of man and woman, responsibility of a man under his roof. If you make the Revolution it will be marked by all the things that democracy detests and I detest; the talk about the inevitable, the love of statistics, the materialist theory of history, the trivialities of Sociology, and the uproarious folly of Eugenics. I know the answer you have; I know the risk I run. Perhaps democracy will never move. Perhaps the English people, if you gave it beer enough, would accept even Eugenics. It is enough for me for the moment to say that I cannot believe it. The poor are so obviously right, I cannot fancy that they will never enforce their rightness against all the prigs of your party and mine. At any rate that is my answer. **I am not a Socialist, just as I am not a Tory; because I have not lost faith in democracy.**

GILBERT K. CHESTERTON

A CRITICISM

NEW YORK

JOHN LANE COMPANY

MCMIX

C

About Chesterton and Belloc

H.G. Wells

And going back for a moment to that point about a Utopia, I want one from Chesterton. Purely unhelpful criticism isn't enough from a man of his size. It isn't fair for him to go about sitting on other people's Utopias.

Editor: Wells' response to Chesterton came only a week after Chesterton's article. Notice the Chesterton-like feel to the opening paragraph. Knowing Chesterton's talents, Wells will do his best to persuade Chesterton to sit this fight out.[157]

It has been one of the more impossible dreams of my life to be a painted Pagan God and live upon a ceiling. I crown myself becomingly in stars or tendrils or with electric coruscations (as the mood takes me), and wear an easy costume free from complications and appropriate to the climate of those agreeable spaces. The company about me on the clouds varies greatly with the mood of the vision, but always it is in some way, if not always a very obvious way, beautiful. One frequent presence is G.K. Chesterton, a joyous whirl of brushwork, appropriately garmented and crowned. When he is there, I remark, the whole ceiling is by a sort of radiation convivial. We drink limitless old October from handsome flagons, and we argue mightily about Pride (his weak point) and the nature of Deity. A hygienic, attentive, and essentially anaesthetic Eagle checks, in the absence of exercise, any undue enlargement of our Promethean livers . . . Chesterton often—but never by any chance Belloc.[158] Belloc I admire beyond measure, but there is a sort of partisan viciousness about Belloc that bars him from my celestial dreams. He never figures, no, not even in the remotest corner, on my ceiling. And yet the divine artist, by some strange skill that my ignorance of his technique saves me from the presumption of explaining, does indicate exactly where Belloc is. A little quiver of the paint, a faint aura, about the spectacular masses of Chesterton? I am not certain. But no intelligent beholder can look up and miss the remarkable fact that Belloc exists—and that he is away, safely

---

157. This appendix is from: H.G. Wells, "About Chesterton and Belloc," *The New Age*, II:11 (January 11, 1908), 209–210. No text has been edited out. All the dotted ellipses are in the original article.

158. For stealing fire from the Greek gods and giving it to man, Prometheus was chained to a rock, where every day an eagle would come and eat his liver.

away, away in his heaven, which is, of course, the Park Lane Imperialist's hell. There he presides . . .

But in this life I do not meet Chesterton exalted upon clouds, and there is but the mockery of that endless leisure for abstract discussion afforded by my painted entertainments. I live in an urgent and incessant world, which is at its best a wildly beautiful confusion of impressions and at its worst a dingy uproar. It crowds upon us and jostles us, we get our little interludes for thinking and talking between much rough scuffling and laying about us with our fists. **And I cannot afford to be continually bickering with Chesterton and Belloc about forms of expression. There are others for whom I want to save my knuckles. One may be wasteful in peace and leisure, but economies are the soul of conflict.** In many ways we three are closely akin; we diverge not by necessity but accident, because we speak in different dialects and have divergent metaphysics. All that I can I shall persuade to my way of thinking about thought and to the use of words in my loose, expressive manner, but Belloc and Chesterton and I are too grown and set to change our languages now and learn new ones; we are on different roads, and so we must needs shout to one another across intervening abysses. These two say Socialism is a thing they do not want for men, and I say Socialism is above all what I want for men. We shall go on saying that now to the end of our days. But what we do all three want is something very alike. Our different roads are parallel. I aim at a growing collective life, a perpetually enhanced inheritance for our race, through the fullest, freest development of the individual life.[159] What they aim at ultimately I do not understand, but it is manifest that its immediate form is the fullest and freest development of the individual life. We all three hate equally and sympathetically the spectacle of human beings blown up with windy wealth and irresponsible power as cruelly and absurdly as boys blow up frogs; we all three detest the complex causes that dwarf and cripple lives from the moment of birth and starve and debase great masses of mankind. We want as universally as possible the jolly life, men and women warm-blooded and well-aired, acting freely and joyously, gathering life as children gather corn-cockles in corn. We all three want people to have property of a real and personal sort, to have the son, as Chesterton put it, bringing up the port his father laid down, and pride in the pears one has grown in one's own garden. And I agree with Chesterton that giving—giving oneself out of love and fellowship—is the salt of life.

But there I diverge from him, less in spirit I think than in the manner of his expression. There is a base because impersonal way of giving. "Standing drink," which he praises as noble, is just the thing I cannot stand, the ultimate mockery and vulgarisation of that fine act of bringing out the cherished thing saved for the heaven-sent guest. It is a mere commercial transaction, essentially of the

159. The "perpetually enhanced inheritance for our race" included State-directed eugenics.

evil of our time. Think of it! Two temporarily homeless beings agree to drink together, and they turn in and face the public supply of drink (a little vitiated by private commercial necessities) in the public-house. (It is horrible that life should be so wholesale and heartless.) And Jones, with a sudden effusion of manner, thrusts twopence or ninepence (got God knows how) into the economic mysteries and personal delicacy of Brown. I'd as soon a man slipped sixpence down my neck. If Jones has used love and sympathy to detect a certain real thirst and need in Brown and knowledge and power in its assuaging by some specially appropriate fluid, then we have an altogether different matter; but the common business of "standing treat" and giving presents and entertainments is as proud and unspiritual as cock-crowing, as foolish and inhuman as that sorry compendium of mercantile vices, the game of poker, and I am amazed to find Chesterton commend it.

But that is a criticism by the way. Chesterton and Belloc agree with the Socialist that the present world doesn't give at all what they want. They agree that it fails to do so through a wild derangement of our property relations. They are in agreement with the common contemporary man (whose creed is stated, I think, not unfairly, but with the omission of certain important articles by Chesterton), that the derangements of our property relations are to be remedied by concerted action and in part by altered laws. The land and all sorts of great common interests must be, if not owned, then at least controlled, managed, checked, redistributed by the State. Our real difference is only about a little more or a little less owning. I do not see how Belloc and Chesterton can stand for anything but a strong State as against those wild monsters of property, the strong, big private owners. The State must be complex and powerful enough to prevent them.[160] State or plutocrat, there is really no other practical alternative before the world at the present time. Either we have got to let the big financial adventurers, the aggregating capitalist and his Press, in a loose, informal combination, rule the earth, either we have got to stand aside from preventive legislation and leave things to work out on their present lines, or we have to construct a collective organisation sufficiently strong for the protection of the liberties of the some-day-to-be-jolly common man. So far we go in common. If Belloc and Chesterton are not Socialists, they are at any rate not anti-Socialists. If they say they want an organised Christian State (which involves practically seven-tenths of the Socialist desire), then, in the face of our big common enemies, of adventurous capital, of alien Imperialism, base ambition, base intelligence,

---

160. A State powerful enough to crush the rich is more than powerful enough to regiment the poor. Using Wells forced 'either or' argument one could actually argue that unrestricted monopoly Capitalism is far better than Socialism. Socialism's errors include Stalin, Mao and forced labor camps that killed tens of millions. A cold-hearted capitalist may turn a worker out in the cold or terrorize him with factory guards, but he won't do anything that terrible or on that large a scale. He lacks the power of an evil government.

and common prejudice and ignorance, I do not mean to quarrel with them politically, so long as they force no quarrel on me. Their organised Christian State is nearer the organised State I want than our present plutocracy. Our ideals will fight some day, and it will be, I know, a first-rate fight, but to fight now is to let the enemy [w]in. When we have got all we want in common, then and only then can we afford to differ. I have never believed that a Socialist Party could hope to form a Government in this country in my life-time; I believe it less now than ever I did. I don't know if any of my Fabian colleagues entertain so remarkable a hope.[161] But if they do not, then unless their political aim is pure cantankerousness, they must contemplate a working political combination between the Socialist members in Parliament and just that non-capitalist section of the Liberal Party for which Chesterton and Belloc speak. Perpetual opposition is a dishonourable aim in politics; and a man who mingles in political development with no intention of taking on responsible tasks unless he gets all his particular formulae accepted is a pervert, a victim of Irish bad example, and unfit for decent democratic institutions . . .

I digress again, I see, but my drift I hope is clear. Differ as we may, Belloc and Chesterton are with all Socialists in being on the same side of the great political and social cleavage that opens at the present time. We and they are with the interests of the mass of common men as against that growing organisation of great owners who have common interests directly antagonistic to those of the community and State. We Socialists are only secondarily politicians. **Our primary business is not to impose upon, but to ram right into the substance of that object of Chesterton's solicitude, the circle of ideas of the common man, the idea of the State as his own, as a thing he serves and is served by.** We want to add to his sense of property rather than offend it. If I had my way I would do that at the street corners and on the trams, I would take down that alien-looking and often detested inscription "L.C.C.," and put up, "This Tram, this Street, belongs to the People of London."[162] Would Chesterton or Belloc quarrel with that? **Suppose that Chesterton is right, and that there are incurable things in the mind of the common man flatly hostile to our ideals; so much of our ideals will fail. But we are doing our best by our lights, and all we can. What are Chesterton and Belloc doing ? If our ideal is partly right and partly wrong, are they trying to build up a better ideal? Will they state a Utopia and how they propose it shall be managed?** If they lend their weight only to such fine old propositions as that a man wants freedom, that he has a right to do as he likes with his own, and so on, they won't help the common man

---

161. Bernard Shaw, H.G. Wells, Sidney Webb (mentioned later) and Cecil Chesterton belonged to the Fabian Society, which was committed to bringing in Socialism slowly and stealthily.

162. L.C.C. (1889–1965) was the London County Council, ancestor to today's Greater London Authority. Notice how the name has become far more intimidating, the very thing Chesterton feared.

much. All that fine talk, without some further exposition, goes to sustain Mr. Rockefeller's simple human love of property, and the woman and child sweating manufacturer in his fight for the inspector-free home industry.[163] I bought on a bookstall the other day a pamphlet full of misrepresentation and bad argument against Socialism by an Australian Jew, published by the Single-Tax people apparently in a disinterested attempt to free the land from the landowner by the simple expedient of abusing anyone else who wanted to do as much but did not hold Henry George to be God and Lord; and I know Socialists who will protest with tears in their eyes against association with any human being who sings any song but the "Red Flag" and doubts whether Marx had much experience of affairs.[164] Well, there is no reason why Chesterton and Belloc should at their level do the same sort of thing. When we talk on a ceiling or at a dinner-party with any touch of the celestial in its composition, Chesterton and I, Belloc and I, are antagonists with an undying feud, but in the fight against human selfishness and narrowness and for a finer, juster law, we are brothers—at the remotest, half-brothers.

Chesterton isn't a Socialist—agreed! But now, as between us and the Master of Elibank or Sir Hugh Bell or any other Free Trade Liberal capitalist or landlord, which side is he on?[165] You cannot have more than one fight going on in the political arena at the same time, because only one party or group of parties can win.

And going back for a moment to that point about a Utopia, I want one from Chesterton. Purely unhelpful criticism isn't enough from a man of his size. It isn't fair for him to go about sitting on other people's Utopias. I appeal to his sense of fair play. I have done my best to reconcile the conception of a free and generous style of personal living with a social organisation that will save the world from the harsh predominance of dull, persistent, energetic, unscrupulous grabbers tempered only by the vulgar extravagance of their wives and sons. It isn't an adequate reply to say that nobody stood treat there, and that the simple, generous people like to beat their own wives and children on occasion in a loving and intimate manner, and that they won't endure the spirit of Sidney Webb.[166]

---

163. At that time John D. Rockefeller (1839–1937) was perhaps the richest man in the world.

164. Henry George (1839–1897) was an American economist and the author of *Progress and Poverty* (1879). He advocated a single tax on the value of land. The "Red Flag" is linked to worker revolution and communism. Karl Marx (1818–1883) was born into an affluent Prussian family and his on-and-off employment as a journalist never provided him with any "experience of affairs" as a factory worker.

165. Elibank probably refers to Alexander Murray, First Baron Murray of Elibank (1870–1920), a Liberal party politician and at that time the Comptroller of Her Majesty's Household. Sir Thomas Hugh Bell (1844–1931) was a wealthy industrialist and a liberal politican.

166. Sidney Webb (1859–1947) was a prominent Fabian intellectual who became Baron Passfield, a hint that the moral and social gap between plutocrats and Fabians wasn't as great as Wells claims.

WHY I AM NOT A SOCIALIST: G. K. Chesterton.

THE NEW AGE

A WEEKLY REVIEW OF POLITICS, LITERATURE, AND ART
Edited by A. R. Orage.

No. 695 [New Series. Vol. II. No. 10] SATURDAY, JAN. 4, 1908. [Registered at G.P.O. as a Newspaper] ONE PENNY

H. G. WELLS ON CHESTERTON AND BELLOC.

THE NEW AGE

A WEEKLY REVIEW OF POLITICS, LITERATURE, AND ART
Edited by A. R. Orage.

No. 696 [New Series. Vol. II. No. 11] SATURDAY, JAN. 11, 1908. [Registered at G.P.O. as a Newspaper] ONE PENNY

BELLOC & CHESTERTON: by G. BERNARD SHAW.

THE NEW AGE

A WEEKLY REVIEW OF POLITICS, LITERATURE, AND ART
Edited by A. R. Orage.

No. 701 [New Series. Vol. II. No. 16] SATURDAY, FEB. 15, 1908. [Registered at G.P.O. as a Newspaper] ONE PENNY

A REPLY TO G. B. S.: by G. K. CHESTERTON.

THE NEW AGE

A WEEKLY REVIEW OF POLITICS, LITERATURE, AND ART
Edited by A. R. Orage.

No. 703 [New Series. Vol. II. No. 18] SATURDAY, FEB. 29, 1908. [Registered at G.P.O. as a Newspaper] ONE PENNY

D

ON WELLS AND A GLASS OF BEER

G.K. Chesterton

Mr. Belloc expresses fiercely and I express gently a respect for mankind. Mr. Shaw expresses fiercely and Mr. Wells expresses gently, a contempt for mankind.

Editor: Two weeks after Wells' article, Chesterton published a response focusing on Wells' anger at the common custom of treating a friend to a beer, showing his knack for getting at the heart of an issue with a concrete, everyday example.[167]

It is not easy to argue with the most fair-minded man in England, especially when he doesn't want to argue. But there is one point in Mr. Wells' friendly explanation at which his voice rises in anger; it is about the fascinating subject of standing drink. And I really think that if we take this institution as a plain instance or symbol, we can state more clearly where he and I and (incidentally) humanity stand. I say that Jones standing Brown a glass of beer is, as human things go, noble. Mr. Wells says it is ignoble. Moreover, he says that it typifies what is ignoble in our society; "it is a mere commercial transaction; essentially of the evil of our time"; it is therefore akin to the alleged need of Socialism. Very well; let us put that glass of beer in the middle of the table and argue about it.

Before we come to the main point, let me say that I do not believe the modern and scornful theory of Brown and Jones in the pub. Mr. Wells is one of a school of sensitive artists who awoke in the aching void of a world (as he has admirably put it) "full of the ironical silences that follow great controversies":[168] Dickens

---

167. G.K. Chesterton, "On Wells and a Glass of Beer," *The New Age*, II:13 (January 25, 1908), 250.

168. Quoted from Ch. 6, "Schooling," in H.G. Wells' *Mankind in the Making* (1903). Both Chesterton (born in 1874) and Wells (born in 1866) grew up in a world left empty by "great controversies"—such as the publication of Charles Darwin's *The Origin of Species* in 1859—that had ripped apart their parents' generation. The quote comes in a paragraph in which Wells described what he believed was wrong with modern university education.

> In some cases this specialized course may be correlated with a real and present practice, as in the case of the musical, medical, and legal faculties of our universities; it may be correlated with obsolete needs and practices and regardless of modern requirements, as in the case of the student of divinity who takes his orders and comes into a world full of the ironical silences that follow great controversies, nakedly ignorant of geology, biology, psychology, and modern biblical criticism; or it may have no definite relation to special needs, and it may profess to be an upward prolongation of schooling towards a sort of general wisdom and culture, as in the case of the British "Arts" degrees.

was dead; dogmatic democracy was dying. Aristocrats began to "study" the poor, as if they were chimpanzees; and aesthetes began to write slum novels, novels which were pessimistic, not about the empty stomachs of the people, but about the turning of aesthetic stomachs at the very sight of the people. With these dilettantes of disgust and curiosity Mr. Wells is not for a moment to be confused. But he keeps this faint mark of that unsympathetic school, that he is certain that the souls of Brown and Jones in the bar must be as dull and greasy as the bar; that mean streets must have mean emotions. Yet Dickens saw the same men in the same bar; but he was one of them, and he described not what they said but what they meant.

I disbelieve, then, that this ordinary tavern hospitality is lifeless or insincere. If anyone wants to know why I disbelieve it I can tell him. It is because the same aristocrats and aesthetes talked the same supercilious stuff about the class I come from; the comfortable Victorian middle-class; and there (as it happens) I *know* they were wrong. The aesthete attached to the Smart Set always said that because our tables were mahogany our heads were mahogany. The journalistic duchess always said that our Sunday dinners were dull gluttony; or our conventions were cowardice. Now all this I *know* is nonsense. I *know* that in my grandfather's house there was real hospitality in the heavy meals, real goodwill in the pompous birthday speeches. And as the fastidious theory is wildly wrong about the private houses I have lived in, I think it likely that it is also wrong about the public-houses which I visit only occasionally.

This is a point of preliminary sentiment; but before quitting it I may remark that there is in this matter a difference between two kinds of humane feeling. There is the Dickens imagination which is inside certain human habits and sees them as large: and there is the H.G. Wells imagination, (full of astronomical relativity), which is outside them and sees them as small. Both have kindness and sensibility; but the first has the sensibility to accept, the second the sensibility to reject. Mr. Wells hints (quite truly) that Mr. Belloc is fiercer than I. So is Mr. Bernard Shaw fiercer than he. But these religious differences cut across temperament. **Mr. Belloc expresses fiercely and I express gently a respect for mankind. Mr. Shaw expresses fiercely and Mr. Wells expresses gently, a contempt for mankind.**[169]

---

169. A reference to Hilaire Belloc, "Thoughts about Modern Thought," *The New Age*, II:6 (December 7, 1907), 108–110. When forced to recognize that present-day people seem ill-adapted to a Socialist State, Socialists often turned to the evolutionary possibility of a new humanity that was. Belloc's article stimulated numerous responses and one from a Henry M. Bernard the following week: "With his fixed environmental scheme of the divine, Mr. Belloc has to assume that Man's nature also is fixed, an assumption possible only to a theologian whose eyes are not on the facts, but on his dogmatic fancies. The evolutionist fails to see anything at all fixed in human life; he sees nothing but infinite diversity in degree and kind in every department of life's activities, a bewildering maze of infinitesimal differences, so that, no matter how numerous the units are, no two are alike, while no single unit is itself the same

But I willingly admit that there is in "standing treat" as it is now an element of the mean and the mechanical. I admit that the mean and mechanical may justly be called "the evil of our time." Very well. Now I wish to point out to Mr. Wells that he has chosen as the type of the evil of our time one of the evils which Socialism would not and could not cure. There are more of them than you think. There is one evil that Socialism would cure—starvation. There is one argument for Socialism—hunger. It is an argument of huge size and horrible force; and all the theoretic arguments added to it only weaken it. When a man tells me that the state is the organism, not the individual, he only makes me feel sleepy. I know jolly well that England is not an animal in the sense that I am an animal. When a man says, as your correspondent did in answer to Mr. Belloc, that the world will see a new sort of humanity because the world was once dominated by the plesiosaurus, I know he is talking not only bad philosophy but even bad natural history.[170] We are not descended from the plesiosaurus; he came to a head and so have we. When a man says that it is a noble thing in itself that things should be unified, I say it isn't. But the great Socialist fact is this; that (to return to the glass of beer in the middle of the table) there are thirsty people who cannot get it. It does happen that Brown cannot give the beer to Jones because he cannot buy it himself. This is horrible. And most certainly it could be stopped if there

---

for two moments together." In "Replies to Mr. Hilaire Belloc, M.P.," *The New Age* II:7 (December 14, 1907), 129.

170. Plesiosaurus, a large marine reptile from the Jurassic period, was one of the first complete dinosaurs discovered. It excited quite a bit of attention in 1821 when it was found by Mary Anning (1799–1847). Attention continued to focus on it throughout the Victoria era, in part because, since there was nothing like it then living, it demonstrated that at least one major species had gone extinct, leaving no obvious modern offspring. Plesiosaurus and many of its kin thus illustrate extinction rather than evolution. That's why Chesterton can label as "bad natural history" any parallels someone might draw between it and man evolving into a "new sort of humanity." His remarks are in response to a letter critical of Belloc's article from a David Isaacs in the December 14, 1907 issue (p. 129), which said:

Mr. Belloc complains that evolution does not describe a Thing, and he rests firm in his conviction of the finality reached by man. So I can imagine a "dragon of the prime," some Permian lizard, sunning himself on an arid rock, and musing the while: "At last in the saurians perfection is attained, We are the product of time, the heirs of the ages, and after us no higher thing can come!" All this, if you please, oblivious of the fact that he and his kind bore the potentiality of the birds, with all their super-reptilian beauty of form and colour and song.

In a letter in the February 1, 1908 issue (p. 279), Isaacs complained that, "I had no intention of implying that Man has descended from the Plesiosaurus. I wished merely to point out that Man has no more right to assume himself the ultimate outcome of organic evolution than had the Plesiosaurus to make that claim for himself and his kin." But Chesterton wasn't making that claim, merely that one dead end species (his "came to a head" remark) certainly cannot prove that another species would not "come to a head," but instead continue to adapt and improve in a new Socialist environment. Chesterton's argument is actually rendered more powerful because men did not come from reptiles and because evolutionists themselves recognize that a species can fail to adapt. Finally, although Chesterton is not making the point, by keeping virtually everyone alive, no matter how ill-adapted, Socialism would itself turn off the survival mechanism that drives evolutionary improvement. Many Socialists (including Wells and Shaw) would, in fact, support State-directed eugenics out of fears that would happen—that Socialism without eugenics would subsidize a growing and prolific race of the 'unfit.' For more on that, see *The Pivot of Civilization in Historical Perspective* edited by Michael W. Perry (Seattle: Inkling Books, 2001).

were one cask and everyone was allowed one glass and forbidden to give it away. But Mr. Wells would say: "Let him give his glass of beer away, but let him give it spontaneously and sweetly." Now I can see how Socialism might forbid or permit him to give it away. But I cannot see how Socialism could induce him to give it spontaneously and sweetly. How do you propose to permit a custom and yet prevent it from becoming a routine? If you let Jones give beer to Brown, how can you prevent Brown from expecting it from Jones? If the Socialist State permits two reciprocal gifts, how on earth can it prevent their becoming an implied compact? If Brown is pleased to get it, how is "Socialism" to prevent Brown from being cross when he doesn't get it? You will say, very reasonably, that this evil of mean conventions is not one which Socialism proposes to remedy. True; but it is an evil (according to Mr. Wells) which is typical of the essential evil of our time.

It has taken me a long time to get to the point; but this is the point. The most clear-headed of modern Socialists quotes as the typical modern evil something that could not even feebly be attacked by Socialism. If Jones and Brown were both well-paid State servants drinking in a well-managed State restaurant, there would still be no law to prevent Brown cadging for drinks—unless there was a law to prevent Jones giving them. I think, therefore, that in seeking to cure Brown of cadging (so far as possible . . . you know what Brown is), I am increasingly convinced that Mr. Belloc and I are right in seeking what you would call a more mystical and we a more human formula. **Liberalism must come before Socialism—even before Social reform. Brown must be a citizen and have a certain spirit, and all these things shall be added unto him. What influences will give him this spirit? There are many reasonable answers; but one of our answers is—property.**[171]

I will not quote the great examples of the equalisation of property; that triumphant in France or that gradually triumphing in Ireland. But I will quote two phrases from Mr. Wells's own article. First, while he dislikes my glass of beer he approves of my port and my pears. A cheap critic would say that the port and the pears happen to be more expensive; but one cannot be cheap about Mr. Wells. The real truth is this: the port and pears seem generous to him, not because they are associated with a rich class, but because they are associated with the only class in England (alas!) which *owns land*. The hospitality of the poorer man seems paltry, because he is not inviting you to his own house, but to someone else's house. At least that is the only way I can explain Mr. Wells's weakness for the port and contempt for the beer. And I am supported in this view by the other quotation. **He correctly describes the two modern men renting houses they do not own as "two temporarily homeless individuals." Socialism, as I understand it, would make them eternally homeless.**

171. In early 1908 Chesterton was advocating what would later be called Distributism.

G. K. Chesterton, a Criticism

E

BELLOC AND CHESTERTON

G. Bernard Shaw

Wells's challenge to Chesterton is finally irresistible: he must plank down his Utopia against ours. And it must be an intellectually honest and intellectually possible one, and not a great game played by a herd of Chestebellocs.

Editor: Five weeks after Wells, Shaw took up the attack on Chesterton and Belloc with this oddly argued article claiming Chesterton was more French than English. If family heritage made Gilbert French and anti-Socialist, we may ask, why was Gilbert's brother a prominent Fabian along with Shaw? Shaw might be a clever writer of plays, but he is clearly not in Chesterton's league as a thinker or debater.[172]

In this article Shaw challenged whether Chesterton was really English, able to understand the English people, and (at the end) whether he actually believes in democracy. Shaw would have done well to recall some remarks the editors of *The New Age* had published a month earlier.

In the *Daily News* of January 11 Mr. G.K. Chesterton makes an impassioned attack on the prosecution for blasphemy of, Mr. H. Boulter, to which we shall refer later. But perhaps the significant paragraph of Mr. Chesterton's article is his explanation (the clearest he has yet achieved) of his view of Democracy. Readers of his article in *The New Age* of January 4th will be glad of the following extract :

"Now, if there is anyone who thinks that my distinction between public opinion as a whole and the mere triumphant majority is a fallacy or a delusion, I am willing to provide him with what may be called a working test. If you want to know whether a thing is of a mere majority accidentally in power, or whether it is of the people as a people, simply do this. Look at the first man you see in the street, and ask yourself how heavily you would bet that he, a man taken at random, would support the view in question. Do not judge by everybody; judge by anybody. Fix your eye on the man who comes first out of Baker Street Station, and think about him. Bimetallism may have won a wild victory at the polls ; but you would not bet that he is a bimetallist. Liberalism may have swept England like a landslide, but you would not bet that he is a Liberal. Christianity may be unconquerably entrenched and enthroned, it may have its Scriptures in all the schools, Its public prayers in all the Parliaments. But you would not bet a button that that man believes in Christianity. But you would bet sixpence—nay, ninepence—that he believes in wearing clothes. You would bet that he believes in preserving a certain reticence about sex in the presence of girls or children. Of course, he may happen to have a crank on those subjects; as you tour outside Baker Street Station you may strike the millionth man. If you do

---

172. From: G. Bernard Shaw, "Belloc and Chesterton," *The New Age*, II:16 (February 15, 1908), 309–311.

you may treat him as something more than an exception—you may feel as if you had forgotten to take your hat off to the Bearded Lady. He is not a minority: he is a monster. And the only way of keeping this distinction is to keep a deep and vigilant reverence for Anybody."[173]

OUR friend Wells is mistaken. His desire to embrace Chesterton as a vessel of the Goodwill which is making for Socialism is a hopeless one for other reasons than the obvious impossibility of his arms reaching round that colossal figure which dominates Battersea Park. Wells is an Englishman, and cannot understand these foreigners. The pages of *Who's Who* explain the whole misunderstanding. Turn to WELLS, Herbert Geo., and you learn at once that he is every inch an Englishman, a man of Kent, not in the least because he was born in Bromley (a negro might be born in Bromley) but because he does not consider himself the son of his mother, but of his father only; and all his pride of birth is that his father was a famous cricketer. It is nothing to Wells that he is one of the foremost authors of his time: he takes at once the stronger English ground that he is by blood a Kentish cricketer.

Turn we now to CHESTERTON, Gilbert Keith. He is the son of his mother, and his mother's name is Marie Louise Grosjean. Who his father was will never matter to anyone who has once seen G.K. Chesterton, or at least seen as much of him as the limited range of human vision can take in at once. If ever a Grosjean lived and wrote his name on the sky by towering before it, that man is G.K. C. France did not break the mould in which she formed Rabelais. It got to Campden Hill in the year 1874; and it never turned out a more complete Frenchman than it did then.

Let us look up Belloc. The place of his birth is suppressed, probably because it was in some very English place; for Belloc is desperately determined not to be an Englishman, and actually went through a period of military service in the French artillery to repudiate these islands, and establish his right to call himself a Frenchman.[174] There is no nonsense of that kind about Chesterton. No artillery service for him, thank you: he is French enough without that: besides, there is not cover enough for him on a French battlefield: the worst marksman in the Prussian artillery could hit him at six miles with absolute certainty. Belloc's sister is a lady distinguished in letters: she is also in *Who's Who*, which thus betrays the fact that one of their ancestors was Dr. Priestley.[175] Also that Belloc is the son of a French barrister and of Bessie Rayner Parkes. You cannot say that Belloc is wholly French except by personal choice; but still he is not English. Beside

---

173. "Notes of the Week," *The New Age*, II:12 (January 18, 1908), 223. Harry Boulter was a Hyde Park speaker recently jailed for blasphemy, a common law offense in England.

174. Belloc was born in La Celle-Saint-Cloud, west of Paris, but was educated in England.

175. Joseph Priestley (1733–1804) was a scientist with unorthodox religious views.

his friend Grosjean he seems Irish. I suspect him of being Irish. Anyhow, not English, and therefore for ever incomprehensible to Wells.

Before shutting up *Who's Who* turn for a moment to SHAW, George Bernard. He, you will observe, is the child of his own works. Not being a Frenchman like Chesterton, for whom the cult of *ma mère* is *de rigueur,* and not being able to boast of his father's fame as a cricketer, like Wells, he has modestly suppressed his parents—unconsciously; for he never noticed this piece of self-sufficiency before—and states simply that he was born in Dublin. Therefore, also eternally incomprehensible to Wells, but, on the other hand, proof against the wiles of Chesterton and Belloc. I cannot see through Chesterton: there is too much of him for anybody to see through; but he cannot impose on me as he imposes on Wells. Neither can Belloc.

Wells has written in this journal about Chesterton and Belloc without stopping to consider what Chesterton and Belloc is. This sounds like bad grammar; but I know what I am about. Chesterton and Belloc is a conspiracy, and a most dangerous one at that. Not a viciously intended one: quite the contrary. It is a game of make-believe of the sort which all imaginative grown-up children love to play; and, as in all such games, the first point in it is that they shall pretend to be somebody else. Chesterton is to be a roaring jovial Englishman, not taking his pleasures sadly, but piling Falstaff on Magog, and Boythorn on John Bull.[176] Belloc's fancy is much stranger. He is to be a Frenchman, but not a Walkley Frenchman,[177] not any of the varieties of the stage Frenchman, but a French peasant, greedy, narrow, individualistic, ready to fight like a rat in a corner for his scrap of land, and, above all, intensely and superstitiously Roman Catholic. And the two together are to impose on the simple bourgeoisie of England as the Main Forces of European Civilisation.

Now at first sight it would seem that it does not lie with me to rebuke this sort of make-believe. The celebrated G.B.S. is about as real as a pantomime ostrich. But it is less alluring than the Chesterton-Belloc chimera, because as they have four legs to move the thing with, whereas I have only two, they can produce the quadrupedal illusion, which is the popular feature of your pantomime beast. Besides, I have played my game with a conscience. **I have never pretended that G.B.S. was real: I have over and over again taken him to pieces before the audience to shew the trick of him.** And even those who in spite of that

176. Shaw blends fictional characters with mythical. Falstaff is a comic, cowardly knight in three of Shakespeare's plays. Magog and Gog are statues borne in London parades to represent the mythical defenders of the city. In Dicken's *Bleak House,* Lawrence Boythorn is described: "'I went to school with this fellow, Lawrence Boythorn,' said Mr. Jarndyce, tapping the letter as he laid it on the table, 'more than five and forty years ago. He was then the most impetuous boy in the world, and he is now the most impetuous man. He was then the loudest boy in the world, and he is now the loudest man. He was then the heartiest and sturdiest boy in the world, and he is now the heartiest and sturdiest man. He is a tremendous fellow.'" John Bull, stout and beer-loving, represents traditional England.

177. Shaw dedicated *Man and Superman* (1903) to the drama critic Arthur Walkley (1855–1926).

cannot escape from the illusion, regard G.B.S. as a freak. The whole point of the creature is that he is unique, fantastic, unrepresentative, inimitable, impossible, undesirable on any large scale, utterly unlike anybody that ever existed before, hopelessly unnatural, and void of real passion. Clearly such a monster could do no harm, even were his example evil (which it never is).

But the Chesterbelloc is put forward in quite a different way: the Yellow Press way. The Chesterbelloc denounces the Yellow Press, but only because it dislikes yellow and prefers flaming red. The characteristic vice of the Yellow Journalist is that he never says he wants a thing (usually bigger dividends) or that his employer wants it. He always says that the Empire needs it, or that Englishmen are determined to have it, and that those who object to it are public enemies, Jews, Germans, rebels, traitors, Pro-Boers. and what not.[178] Further, he draws an imaginative picture of a person whose honour and national character consist in getting what the Yellow Journalist is after, and says to the poor foolish reader: "That is yourself, my brave fellow-countryman." Now this is precisely what the Chesterbelloc does in its bigger, more imaginative, less sordid way. Chesterton never says, "I, a hybrid Superman, and Grand Transmogrificator of Ideas, desire this, believe that, deny the other." **He always says that the English people desires it; that the dumb democracy which has never yet spoken (save through the mouth of the Chesterbelloc) believes it; or that the principles of liberalism and of the French Revolution repudiate it.** Read his poem in the *Neolith* on the dumb democracy of England: it would be a great poem if it were not such fearful nonsense.[179] Belloc is still more audacious. According to him, the Chesterbelloc is European democracy, is the Catholic Church, is the Life Force, is the very voice of the clay of which Adam was made, and which the Catholic peasant labours. To set yourself against the Chesterbelloc is not merely to be unpatriotic, like setting yourself against the *Daily Mail* or *Express:* it is to set yourself against all the forces. active and latent (especially latent) of humanity. Wells and I, contemplating the Chesterbelloc, recognise at once a very amusing pantomime elephant, the front legs being that very exceptional and unEnglish individual Hilaire Belloc, and the hind legs that extravagant freak of French nature, G.K. Chesterton. To which they both reply "Not at all: what you see is the Zeitgeist." To which we reply bluntly, but conclusively, "Gammon!"[180]

But a pantomime animal with two men in it is a mistake when the two are not very carefully paired. It has never been so successful as the Blondin Donkey, which is worked by one Brother Griffith only, not by the two.[181] Chesterton and

178. Shaw often wrote outrageous nonsense. As he knows quite well, Chesterton opposed the Boer War because he deplored how the war's supporters talked about enlarging the British Empire.

179. Shaw means "dumb" as in speechless. For the poem, see Appendix A.

180. The *Oxford English Dictionary* defines gammon as: "To cheat at play in some particular way."

181. In the 1880s there was a popular Blondkin Donkey act involving two brothers named Griffith who walked a tightrope dressed as a donkey. For such acts, one person was better coordinated than two.

Belloc are so unlike that they get frightfully into one another's way. Their vocation as philosophers requires the most complete detachment: their business as the legs of the Chesterbelloc demands the most complete synchronism. **They are unlike in everything except the specific literary genius and delight in play-acting that is common to them, and that threw them into one another's arms.** Belloc, like most anti-Socialists, is intensely gregarious. He cannot bear isolation or final ethical responsibility: he clings to the Roman Catholic Church: he clung to his French nationality because one nation was not enough for him: he went into the French Army because it gave him a regiment, a company, even a gun to cling to: he was not happy until he got into Parliament; and now his one dread is that he will not get into heaven. He likes to keep his property in his own hand, and his soul in a safe bank. Chesterton has nothing of this in him at all: neither society nor authority nor property nor status are necessary to his happiness: he has never belonged to anything but that anarchic refuge of the art-struck, the Slade School. Belloc, like all men who feel the need of authority, is a bit of a rowdy. He has passed through the Oxford rowdyism of Magdalen and the military rowdyism of the gunner; and he now has the super-rowdyism of the literary genius who has lived adventurously in the world and not in the Savile Club.[182] A proletariat of Bellocs would fight: possibly on the wrong side, like the peasants of La Vendée;[183] but the Government they set up would have to respect them, though it would also have to govern them by martial law. Now Chesterton might be trusted anywhere without a policeman. He might knock at a door and run away—perhaps even lie down across the threshold to trip up the emergent householder; but his crimes would be hyperbolic crimes of imagination and humour, not of malice. He is friendly, easy-going, unaffected, gentle, magnanimous, and genuinely democratic. He can make sacrifices easily: Belloc cannot. The consequence is that in order to co-ordinate the movements of the Chesterbelloc, Chesterton has to make all the intellectual sacrifices that are demanded by Belloc in his dread of going to hell or of having to face, like Peer Gynt, the horrible possibility of becoming extinct.[184] For Belloc's sake Chesterton says he believes literally in the Bible story of the Resurrection. For Belloc's sake he says he is not a Socialist. On a recent occasion I tried to drive him to swallow the Miracle of St. Januarius for Belloc's sake; but at that he struck. He pleaded his belief in the Resurrection story. He pointed out very justly that I believe in lots of things just as miraculous as the Miracle of St. Januarius; but when I remorselessly pressed the fact that he did not believe that the blood of

---

182. The Savile Club was for writers and artists and included Rudyard Kipling and H.G. Wells.

183. Between 1793 and 1796, the devout Catholic peasants of La Vendée in western France opposed the secularizing French Revolution. More than 100,000 died, many of them massacred women and children. Karl Marx used "Vendée" to describe 'reactionary' opposition to communist revolutions.

184. In Henrik Ibsen's 1867 fantasy play, *Peer Gynt*, the main character wanders through life and eventually dies without finding a real purpose for living.

St. Januarius reliquefies miraculously every year, the Credo stuck in his throat like Amen in Macbeth's.[185] He had got down at last to his irreducible minimum of dogmatic incredulity, and could not, even with the mouth of the bottomless pit yawning before Belloc, utter the saving lie. But it is an old saying that when one turns to Rome one does not begin with the miracle of St. Januarius. That comes afterwards. For my part I think that a man who is not a sufficiently good Catholic to be proof against the follies and romancings of Roman Churches, Greek Churches, English Churches, and all such local prayer-wheel-installations, is no Catholic at all. I think a man who is not Christian enough to feel that conjuror's miracles are, on the part of a god, just what cheating at cards is on the part of a man, and that the whole value of the Incarnation nowadays to men of Chesterton's calibre depends on whether, when the Word became Flesh, it played the game instead of cheating, is not a Christian at all. To me no man believes in the Resurrection until he can say: "I am the Resurrection and the Life," and rejoice in and act on that very simple and obvious fact. Without that, belief in the gospel story is like belief in the story of Jack the Giantkiller, which, by the way, has the advantage of not being three different and incompatible stories. I should say, too, that a man who is not Individualist and Liberal enough to be a staunch Protestant, is not an Individualist nor a Liberal at all. That is, in the Chestertonian sense of the words. There is a sense in which you can be a Catholic and burn Jews and Atheists. There is a sense in which you can be a Christian and flog your fellow-creatures or imprison them for twenty years. There is a sense in which you can be a Protestant and have a confessor. But not on the Chestertonian plane. Chestertonesse *oblige*.

Chesterton and Belloc are not the same sort of Christian, not the same sort of Pagan, not the same sort of Liberal, not the same sort of anything intellectual. And that is why the Chesterbelloc is an unnatural beast which must be torn asunder to release the two men who are trying to keep step inside its basket-work. **Wells's challenge to Chesterton is finally irresistible: he must plank down his Utopia against ours. And it must be an intellectually honest and intellectually possible one, and not a great game played by a herd of Chestebellocs.** Nor must it be an orgy of uproarious drunkards—a perpetual carouse of Shakespear[e]s and Ben Jonsons at *The Mermaid*.[186] This may seem rather an uncivil condition to lay down; but it is necessary, for reasons which I will now proceed to state.

185. Saint Januarius, bishop of Benevento, was martyred in 305 AD. On his feast day, September 19, vials of his blood are said to miraculously liquefy. In Shaw's day, critics denied the liquefaction. Today they claim it is a trick done with chemicals. In Shakespeare's Macbeth, Act 2, Scene 2, just after murdering the King, Macbeth tells his wife: "One cried 'God bless us!' and 'Amen' the other; As they had seen me with these hangman's hands. Listening their fear, I could not say 'Amen,' When they did say 'God bless us!'"

186. In the Elizabethan era, *The Mermaid* was a tavern near St. Paul's Cathedral where Shakespeare, Ben Jonson, and others were said to have met in a Friday Street Club for debates. In Appendix G, Gardiner suggests that Chesterton would have been eagerly welcomed by the tavern's illustrious guests.

It is the greatest mistake in the world to suppose that people disapprove of Socialism because they are not convinced by its economic or political arguments. The anti-Socialists all have a secret dread that Socialism will interfere with their darling vices. The lazy man fears that it will make him work. The industrious man fears that it will impose compulsory football or cricket on him. The libertine fears that it will make women less purchaseable; the drunkard, that it will close the public-houses; the miser, that it will abolish money; the sensation lover, that there will be no more crimes, no more executions, no more famines, perhaps even no more fires. Beneath all the clamour against Socialism as likely to lower the standard of conduct lies the dread that it will really screw it up.

Now, Chesterton and Belloc have their failings like other men. They share one failing—almost the only specific trait they have in common except their literary talent. That failing is, I grieve to say, addiction to the pleasures of the table. Vegetarianism and teetotalism are abhorrent to them, as they are to most Frenchmen.[187] The only thing in Wells's earnest and weighty appeal to Chesterton that moved him was an incidental disparagement of the custom of standing drinks and of the theory that the battle of Waterloo was won at the public-house counter.

Now it will be admitted, I think, by all candid Socialists, that the Socialist ideal, as usually presented in Socialist Utopias, is deficient in turkey and sausages. Morris insists on wine and tobacco in *News from No-where;* but nobody in that story has what a vestryman would call a good blow-out.[188] Morris rather insists on slenderness of figure, perhaps for the sake of Burne-Jones (who was *his* Belloc).[189] **As to Wells, his Utopia is dismally starved. There is not even a round of buttered toast in it. The impression produced is that everybody is dieted, and that not a soul in the place can hope for a short life and a merry one.** What this must mean to Chesterton no words of mine can express. Belloc would rather die than face it.

I once met a lady who had a beautiful ideal. Even as Tintoretto chalked up on the wall of his studio "The colour of Titian, and the design of Michael Angelo," this lady wrote on the fly-leaf of her private diary, "The intellect of Chesterton,

---

187. So also for quite a few other nationalities. Shaw seems so obsessed with making Chesterton and Belloc into Frenchmen, that he forgets to display common sense.

188. In William Morris' 1891 utopian novel, *News from No-where*, an outsider is surprised to discover that excellent wine and tobacco are plentiful and free.

"I took it out of her hand to look at it, and while I did so, forgot my caution, and said, "But however am I to pay for such a thing as this?"

Dick laid his hand on my shoulder as I spoke, and turning I met his eyes with a comical expression in them, which warned me against another exhibition of extinct commercial morality; so I reddened and held my tongue, while the girl simply looked at me with the deepest gravity, as if I were a foreigner blundering in my speech, for she clearly didn't understand me a bit.

189. Sir Edward Burne-Jones (1833–1898) was prominent in the Pre-Raphaelite Brotherhood of artists and designers. He met William Morris at Oxford, and they sometimes worked together.

and the figure of Bernard Shaw."[190] I think her bias was rather towards Chesterton, because she concluded, rather superficially, that it is easier to change a man's body than his mind; so instead of sending to me a file of the *Daily News* and a complete set of Chesterton's books to Chesteronise me, she sent to Chesterton—anonymously, and with elaborate precautions against identification—a little book entitled, if I recollect aright, *Checkley's Exercises*.[191] Checkley's idea was that if you went through his exercises, your maximum circumference would occur round your chest, and taper down from that to your toes in a Grecian slenderness of flank. I glanced through *Checkley* and saw that the enterprise was hopeless. His exercises were to be performed without apparatus; and they mostly consisted in getting into attitudes which only a hydraulic press could get Chesterton into, and which no power on earth or in heaven could ever get him out of again. But I, the vegetarian, can do them on my head.

And now I will tear the veil from Chesterton's inmost secret. Chesterton knows about me. I am the living demonstration of the fact that Chesterton's work can be done on a teetotal and vegetarian diet. To Chesterton Socialism means his being dragged before a committee of public health and put on rations from which flesh and alcohol are strictly eliminated. It means compulsory *Checkley* until his waist will pass easily through a hoop for which his chest has served as a mandril. He sees that all his pleas and entreaties will be shattered on Me.[192] When he says, "Look at Charles James Fox: he was the English exponent of the principles of the French Revolution; and he ate and drank more than I do—quite disgracefully, in fact,"[193] they will say, "Yes; but look at Bernard Shaw." When he pleads that a man cannot be brilliant, cannot be paradoxical, cannot shed imagination and humour prodigally over the pages of democratic papers on ginger beer and macaroni, he will get the same inexorable reply "Look at Bernard Shaw: he does not drink even tea or coffee: his austerity shames the very saints themselves; and yet who more brilliant? who more paradoxical? who more delightful as a journalist? And has not he himself assured us that the enormous superiority shown by him in doing everything that you do and writing epoch-making plays to boot, is due solely to the superiority of his diet. So cease your feeble evasions, and proceed to go through Checkley's first exercise at once."

Whoever has studied Chesterton's articles attentively for a few years past will have noticed that though they profess to deal with religion, politics, and literature, they all really come at last to a plea for excess and outrageousness, especially in eating and drinking, and a heartfelt protest against Shavianism,

190. Tintoretto (1518–1594) was the last great painter of the Italian Renaissance. Others translate his inscription as, "Michelangelo's design and Titian's color."

191. This was probably Edwin's Checkley's *A Natural Method of Physical Training. Making Muscle and Reducing Flesh Without Dieting or Apparatus* (London: G.P. Putnam's Sons, 1892).

192. "Me" was capitalized in the original in fitting with the praise Shaw will lovingly lavish on himself.

193. Charles James Fox (1749–1806) was Britain's first Foreign Secretary.

tempered by a terrified admiration of it. Therefore I will now save Chesterton's soul by a confession.

True excess does not make a man fat: it wastes him. Falstaff was not an overworked man: he was an under-worked one. If ever there was a man wasted by excess, I am that man. The Chesterbelloc, ministered to by waiters and drinking wretched narcotics out of bottles, does not know what a real stimulant is. What does it know of my temptations, my backslidings, my orgies? How can it, timidly munching beefsteaks and apple tart, conceive the spirit-struggles of a young man who knew that Bach is good for his soul, and yet turned to Beethoven, and from him fell to Berlioz and Liszt from mere love of excitement, luxury, savagery, and drunkenness? Has Chesterton ever spent his last half-crown on an opera by Meyerbeer or Verdi, and sat down at a crazy pianet to roar it and thrash it through with an execution of a dray-horse and a scanty octave and a half of mongrel baritone voice ? Has he ever lodged underneath a debauchee who was diabolically possessed with the finale of the Seventh Symphony or the *Walkürenritt* whilst decent citizens were quietly drinking themselves to sleep with whiskey—and diluted whiskey at that?[194]

Far from being an abstinent man, I am the worst drunkard of a rather exceptionally drunken family; for they were content with alcohol, whereas I want something so much stronger that I would as soon drink paraffin oil as brandy. Cowards drink alcohol to quiet their craving for real stimulants: I avoid it to keep my palate keen for them. And I am a pitiable example of something much worse than the drink craze: to wit, the work craze. Do not forget Herbert Spencer's autobiography, with its cry of warning against work.[195] I get miserably unhappy if my work is cut off. I get hideous headaches after each month's bout: I make resolutions to break myself of it, never to work after lunch, to do only two hours a day; but in vain: every day brings its opportunity and its temptation: the craving masters me every time; and I dread a holiday as I dread nothing else on earth. Let Chesterton take heart, then: it is he who is the ascetic and I the voluptuary. Socialism is far more likely to force me to eat meat and drink alcohol than to force him to take overdoses of Wagner and Strauss and write plays in his spare time. Let him, I say, throw off this craven obsession with my fancied austerity, and instead of declaring that he is not a Socialist when he clearly does not yet know what he is, accept Wells's challenge, and make up his mind as to how he really wants the world to be arranged under the existing conditions of human nature and physical geography.

---

194. Shaw is certainly indulging himself musically. *Walkürenritt* is the German name for "The Ride of the Valkyries" in Act III of Richard Wagner's 1870 opera *Die Walküre*.

195. Herbert Spencer (1820–1903) was an English philosopher and a leading Social Darwinian.

Wells, like Sidney Webb and myself, is a bit of that totally imaginary Old Victorian England which Chesterton invented in his essay on G.F. Watts.[196] He is intellectually honest. He does not pretend to be the English people, or Democracy, or the indigenous peasant European, or "the folk," or Catholicism, or the Press, or the French Revolution, or any of the other quick changes of the Chesterbelloc.[197] His song is

My name's *not* John Wellington Wells;
And I *don't* deal in magic and spells[198]

He keeps the facts as to WELLS, Herbert Geo. and his difficulties and limitations, and the worse limitations of his much less clever neighbours, honestly and resolutely before you. With wit enough, imagination enough, and humour enough to play with the questions raised by the condition of England quite as amusingly as the Chesterbelloc, he works at it instead, and does what he can to hew out and hammer together some planks of a platform on which a common unliterary man may stand. I also, with a stupendous endowment for folly, have put my cards on the table—even some that are unfit for publication. Webb is far too full of solid administrative proposals to have any time or patience for literary games: when he gets taken that way he puts his witticisms into my printers' proofs, and leaves me to bear the discredit of them and to be told that I should be more serious, like Webb. But, on the whole, we have all three dealt faithfully with the common man.

And now, what has the Chesterbelloc (or either of its two pairs of legs) to say in its defence? But it is from the hind legs that I particularly want to hear; because South Salford will very soon cure Hilaire Forelegs of his fancy for the ideals of the Catholic peasant proprietor. He is up against his problems in Parliament: it is in Battersea Park that a great force is in danger of being wasted.[199]

---

196. In his 1904 *G.F. Watts*, Chesterton would write of his subject:

He has the one great certainty which marks off all the great Victorians from those who have come after them: he may not be certain that he is successful, or certain that he is great, or certain that he is good, or certain that he is capable: but he is certain that he is right. It is of course the very element of confidence which has in our day become least common and least possible. We know we are brilliant and distinguished, but we do not know we are right. We swagger in fantastic artistic costumes; we praise ourselves; we fling epigrams right and left; we have the courage to play the egoist and the courage to play the fool, but we have not the courage to preach.

197. Wells did claim that his opinions were scientific and factual, which is perhaps less honest and more manipulative than claiming they are English or French.

198. Gilbert and Sullivan's 1877 comic opera, *The Sorcerer,* has a song beginning: "My name is John Wellington Wells,/ I'm a dealer in magic and spells,/ In blessings and curses/ And ever-filled purses,/ In prophecies, witches, and knells."

199. Belloc represented Salford South (Greater Manchester) in Parliament from 1906 to 1910. At this time Chesterton was living at Overstrand Mansions in Battersea, a central London borough on the south bank of the Thames not far from the Palace of Westminster. In 1909 he would move to Overroads in Beaconsfield, a suburb northwest of London, where he would live the rest of his life.

F

THE LAST OF THE RATIONALISTS

G.K. Chesterton

We do not "plank down" a Utopia, because Utopia is a thing uninteresting to a thinking man; it assumes that all evils come from outside the citizen and none from inside him.

Editor: Two weeks after Shaw's article was published and seven weeks after that by Wells, Chesterton gave a response to both in *The New Age*.[200] In that article Chesterton explained why they were being attacked when he mentioned that both he and Belloc had recently published criticisms in *The New Age* of the Socialism being promoted by Wells, Shaw and others.

Chesterton's criticism is included in this book as Appendix B. Belloc's criticism, which was entitled "Thoughts about Modern Thought," appeared in December of the previous year, and is probably the article Chesterton suggests "may have been harsh or academic," although, as Chesterton notes, it did have the virtue of keeping to the subject. In that article, Belloc, responding to those who claimed that the "intelligent critics of Socialism" were few, offered this rather telling answer:

The criticism I offer to collectivism is offered by the whole weight and mass of Catholic opinion; in other words, it is the criticism offered by all that is healthy and permanent in the intellectual life of Europe; it is a criticism which has been repeated a hundred times in the French Parliament, and a thousand times in the Irish pulpits throughout the world. The sentiment of property is normal to and necessary to a citizen. Exactly the same thing as makes Catholic opinion as a whole to-day, and Catholic countries in the past, the enemies of the rich, of landlordism, and the rest, exactly the same instinct which in the Middle Ages gave every man capital, forced it on him as it were; exactly the same self-preserving sense as made Catholic societies reject the beastly economies of industrialism in its beginnings; in a word, the moral health which, after a century of industrialism, leaves the Catholic the only healthy soldier in Western Europe, makes him perceive that the divorce of personality from production is inhuman, and of itself just as inhuman when it is effected by collectivism with a charitable object as when it is effected by the present industrial system with an immoral and selfish object.[201]

---

200. This appendix is from G.K. Chesterton, "The Last of the Rationalists: A Reply to Mr. Bernard Shaw," *The New Age*, II:18 (February 29, 1908), 348–349. At this time the two brothers differed greatly. Cecil had published an article *defending* Socialism in the November 21, 1907 issue.

201. Hilaire Belloc, "Thoughts about Modern Thought," *The New Age*, II:6 (December 7, 1907), 108.

IHAVE just seen Bernard Shaw's very jolly article and I hope you will allow me to reply. I have reluctantly come to the conclusion that Belloc and I must be horribly fascinating men. We never suspected it ourselves; but I have been forced to the belief by the discussion in the *New Age*. We offered certain objections to Socialism. We were honoured by being answered, not only by the two most brilliant Socialists alive, but by the two most brilliant writers alive, who both happen to be Socialists. Bernard Shaw and H.G. Wells undertook to reply to us about Socialism. They both forgot to say anything whatever about Socialism, but they insisted on talking (with the utmost humour and luxuriance) about us. The fact can be tested by anyone who cares to look up the file of this paper and compare the articles. My article may have been vague and mystical, but it was about Socialism; Wells's article was about me. Belloc's article may have been harsh or academic, but it was about Socialism; Shaw's article was about Belloc.

The first part of Shaw's article is all about the facts that he has found in *Who's Who*. But as the chief fruit and example of his study of that work is the startling statement that Belloc went to Magdalen, I cannot feel that Shaw's biographies are things to lean one's whole weight upon.[202] Nor is it the question (as Shaw seems to suppose) whether my maternal great grandfather having come from Switzerland unfits me to be a member of this nation. The question is whether Shaw's attitude does not unfit him to be a member of any nation. **What I said about Shaw and his Socialists was quite simple; I said, and I say, that they have no sympathy with the poor. I do not mean that they have no pity for the poor; I know they have Niagaras of pity. But they have no sympathy; they do not feel with ordinary men about ordinary things.**[203] The question is not a question of race, but a question of getting on with men. And I should certainly get on better with Hottentots than Shaw can get on with Irishmen.[204]

In following his admirable career, I have noticed that while Shaw is ready (very rightly) to get excited about anything, he is specially ready to get excited about points of grammar or pronunciation. Therefore I hasten first to quiet his anxiety and to tell him that he is quite right in saying "Shaw and Wells are" while he says "Chesterton and Belloc is." Shaw and Wells are two men of genius. Chesterton and Belloc is mankind. Not mankind as compared with all mankind, not mankind as compared with the people in an omnibus, but as compared with Shaw and Wells, simply mankind. Shaw and Wells, having

---

202. Belloc was educated at Oxford's Balliol College, not Magdalen. A gifted extemporaneous speaker, he became President of Oxford Union, the undergraduate debate society.

203. This may be the passage about the poor: "But one thing I should affirm as certain, the whole smell and sentiment and general ideal of Socialism they detest and disdain. No part of the community is so specially fixed in those forms and feelings which are opposite to the tone of most Socialists; the privacy of homes, the control of one's own children, the minding of one's own business."

204. This demonstrates that Chesterton regarded the differences he saw between nations and races as primarily cultural and something that could be overcome by an amiable "getting on with men."

never seen mankind before in their lives, are naturally alarmed. This monstrous animal, the Chesterbelloc, with its horrible fore legs and its hideous hind legs, may well terrify them; it is Humanity on the move. But Shaw denies this; he suggests that we do not in this matter represent mankind. Very well; the matter is quite easy to prove. It can be proved by simply asking what are the points on which we are actually made game of by modern writers in general and by Shaw and Wells in particular. Of course, every man is both an ordinary man and an extraordinary man. Of course, Belloc and I are ordinary men and also extraordinary men. But we are not derided because of what is extraordinary in us. We are derided because of what is ordinary. Of course, we have peculiarities which are not common to mankind. For instance, I am so fond of the grotesque in art, that I cannot properly appreciate the Greeks. Belloc is so fond of the classic in art that he cannot properly appreciate Browning. These are peculiarities, sometimes lunacies; but we are not mocked about these peculiarities. The only two things which Shaw and Wells and the modern world mock in us, the only two things they notice about us, are two things which are (without any kind of question) common to us and the mass of men. The two best jokes against us, as uttered by the best jester of the age, are also jokes against mankind. The two jokes against us are that we believe in the naturalness of drinking fermented liquor and in the possibility of miracles. We may be right or wrong; but we certainly represent the majority of human beings on those two points: and you only attack us on those two points. It is amusing to note here that Shaw does not read his *New Age* any more carefully than he does his *Who's Who*. He suggests that "the only thing in Wells's earnest and weighty appeal to Chesterton that moved him was an incidental disparagement of the custom of standing drinks." The fact is, of course, that the only thing in Chesterton's earnest and weighty appeal to the world in general that moved Wells was an incidental admission of the custom of standing drinks. If Shaw will go and read Wells's article (it is well worth his trouble) he will find that standing drink was the only point on which I quarrelled with Wells, for the simple reason that it was the only point on which he quarrelled with me. He wrote a whole article packed with all my own opinions; but broke out with considerable violence on this special point. This distinction is important, because it is not Belloc and I who make beer important. It is Shaw and Wells who entertain the wild idea of so ordinary a thing being questionable. Shaw turns our claim for the common human drink into some nasty ideas about "excess"; and then, being evidently unable to boast of having drunk with another man in his life, goes off (I speak with reverence and affection) into some rubbish about a piano. **But Belloc and I are not maintaining that beer is a divine glory, but that it is a normal habit and natural right; as normal as meat, and much more normal than soap.** We do not get excited on beer. It is Shaw who gets excited on beer. And it really seems a pity to get drunk on beer when you have not even drunk it.

It is proved, then, that on the first fact which Shaw sees as odd about us we are not odd but ordinary: it is proved that we are mankind or (as Shaw would put it) we is mankind. The same exactly is true about the other thing that Shaw thinks odd: the belief in the supernatural. The first and most important fact is that the experience of mankind is on the side of miracles, and men like Shaw can only get out of it by despising mankind and saying that men are filthy and superstitious. There are, no doubt, other and minor facts, notably the fact that I believe in the possibility of miracles, and I can tell Shaw why I believe in it: but Shaw cannot tell me why he disbelieves in it: I know, because I asked him. He has accepted the impossibility of miracles, of course, as a part of the positivist philosophy in which we were all brought up; but some of us have thought our way out of it. He has not. He still clings to his old mental habits of the Hall of Science, of which the great tenet was that all men were rising against religion except the men who weren't, and they didn't count. Now of this old-fashioned materialism to which Shaw clings (I like the word "clings"; Shaw uses it of Belloc, and it seems to call up Belloc's habit and figure so vividly before one)—of this old creed to which Shaw clings, there was one main method and principle. It was this; that the true Freethinker must contradict Christianity, even if he contradicted himself. That wretched creed must be accused of all evils, even if they were inconsistent evils. Thus the old Atheists abused Christianity for being meek and Quakerish, while they also abused it for being bloody and imperialistic. The two sins of the Christian were first that he would not fight, and second that he was always fighting. Similarly, Christianity was attacked, first for concealing the kindness of Nature and then for concealing the unkindness of Nature. This extraordinary religion was first the black spot on a white world and then the white spot on a black world.

Now Shaw is submissive to his old Hall of Science traditions. Shaw will make an attack on Christianity even if it is also an attack on Shaw. Here is a perfectly plain case. Shaw has been telling us ten times a week that what we want is not reason but life, that the lust to live, to live even for oneself, to live infinitely, is glorious. Exactly: but the moment you mention life beyond the grave, Shaw's mind drops forty feet to the level of the Hall of Science, and he begins to say that it is mean and cowardly to wish to live for ever. This is manifest nonsense. It cannot be noble to desire life and mean to desire everlasting life. Shaw has meekly tied himself in this mental knot in obedience to the old materialist tradition to which he clings; he has sacrificed his own Life-Force to the ghost of Bradlaugh.[205] It is exactly the same with this point of miracles. The plain fact is that Shaw does not know what the Catholic doctrine of Miracles is; but he has

---

205. Almost forgotten now, Charles Bradlaugh (1833–1891) was once famous as an atheist.

(to his eternal glory) almost discovered it for himself. He has toiled and panted in the train of the Catholic doctrine of Miracles; and whenever he picked up a piece of it, he was hugely and legitimately proud. **The Catholic doctrine of Miracles is this. That the highest power in the universe is not (as the Materialists, say) Law: the highest power in the universe is Will, the will of God which is Good Will. Akin to this, though much weaker, is the will of man.** There is also in the universe another element of routine and rule; but Will, being the higher, can overpower law, the lower. Therefore, though law says that the blood of St. Januarius must be dry, Will might say that it shall be wet. Now for the last five years Shaw has been preaching this doctrine of the transforming power of will. But it will give him a great shock when he discovers that it is only the Christian doctrine of Miracles: then, very likely, he will drop it like a hot potato. As it is, he takes refuge in a poor sample of the Hall of Science: the comparison between miracles and cheating at cards. Of course, the comparison will not bear even an instant's intellectual examination. Cheating at cards is only wrong because a game exists on a contract that certain rules will be observed; rules that can be written down. Where is the contract between us and Nature that she will not show us new wonders? or if Nature is bound by rules, will Shaw be so obliging as to write them down? If Shaw's comparison proved anything it would prove that it was wicked to do conjuring tricks with cards. But I do Shaw a wrong in taking this part of him seriously at all; this is not Shaw, but Bradlaugh. I only remark that we are all going back, consciously or unconsciously, to the faith of Christendom, and that I am sorry for those who, like Shaw, will only discover where they are going when they have got there.

And, finally, let me recall you to the unwelcome subject of Socialism. Perhaps you have wondered why Beer has been so prominent in this discussion. Obviously Beer is not important, except to teetotallers. **The reason is that the proposed abolition of personal property has its only practical parallel in teetotalism, the abolition of normal drink. Drink and property have both swelled in our world into abominations.** But there are some like Shaw who want to abolish drink; and there are some, like Belloc and me, who only want to abolish drunkards and teetotallers. Similarly there are some, like Shaw, who want to abolish property, and there are some, like Belloc and me, who want to abolish the wealthy and the unemployed. **We do not "plank down" a Utopia, because Utopia is a thing uninteresting to a thinking man; it assumes that all evils come from outside the citizen and none from inside him.** But we do "plank down" these much more practical statements: (1) that a man will not be humanly happy unless he owns something in the sense that he can play the fool with it; (2) that this can only be achieved by setting steadily to work to distribute property, not to concentrate it; (3) that history proves that property can be so redistributed and remain so distributed, while history has no record of successful Collectivism outside monasteries. That is what we say, and you may call it right or wrong. But so far you have not called it anything: you have confined yourselves to charming essays on our two charming personalities.

In thinking [thanking] you, Mr. Editor, for your characteristic chivalry in affording me so much space, may I point out a misprint in a recent issue ? You make Mr. Shaw say, in describing certain wild gymnastic attitudes, that he can do them "on his head," which is absurd. If you consult his MS., you will see that he said he could do them "in his head," a far more characteristic phrase and one much more in accord with the physical and mental facts.[206]

---

206. Chesterton could have only known this if he had seen a copy of the article's manuscript, most probably because Shaw had sent him a copy.

G

GILBERT K. CHESTERTON

A.G. Gardiner

Editor: This delightful description of Chesterton, written by his editor at the *Daily News,* was published the same year as Cecil's biography. In Chesterton's day Fleet Street was home to many London newspapers. Most moved elsewhere in the 1980s, making today's Fleet Street the dull haunt of legal and financial firms.[207]

WALKING down Fleet Street some day you may meet a form whose vastness blots out the heavens. Great waves of hair surge from under the soft, wide-brimmed hat. A cloak that might be a legacy from Porthos floats about his colossal frame.[208] He pauses in the midst of the pavement to read the book in his hand, and a cascade of laughter descending from the head notes to the middle voice gushes out on the listening air. He looks up, adjusts his pince-nez, observes that he is not in a cab, remembers that he ought to be in a cab, turns and hails a cab. The vehicle sinks down under the unusual burden and rolls heavily away. It carries Gilbert Keith Chesterton.

Mr. Chesterton is the most conspicuous figure in the landscape of literary London. He is like a visitor out of some fairy tale, a legend in the flesh, a survival of the childhood of the world. Most of us are the creatures of our time, thinking its thoughts, wearing its clothes, rejoicing in its chains. If we try to escape from the temporal tyranny, it is through the gate of revolt that we go. Some take to asceticism or to some fantastic foppery of the moment. Some invent Utopias, lunch on nuts and proteid at Eustace Miles', and flaunt red ties defiantly in the face of men and angels.[209] The world is bond, but they are free. But in all this they are still the children of our time, fleeting and self-conscious. Mr. Chesterton's extravagances have none of this quality. **He is not a rebel. He is a wayfarer from the ages, stopping at the inn of life, warming himself at the fire and making the rafters ring with his jolly laughter.**

---

207. From: A.G. Gardiner, *Prophets, Priests and Kings* (London: Alston Rivers, 1908), 322–332.

208. Porthos is a large man who loves wine, food and song in three Alexandre Dumas' novels.

209. In E.M. Forster's *Howard's End* (1910), Eustance Miles Restaurant is described:

> She smiled at such incongruities. "Next time," she said to Mr. Wilcox, "you shall come to lunch with me at Mr. Eustace Miles's." "With pleasure." "No, you'd hate it," she said, pushing her glass towards him for some more cider. "It's all proteids and body-buildings, and people come up to you and beg your pardon, but you have such a beautiful aura."

Time and place are accidents: he is elemental and primitive. He is not of our time, but of all times. One imagines him wrestling with the giant Skrymir and drinking deep draughts from the horn of Thor, or exchanging jests with Falstaff at the Boar's Head in Eastcheap, or joining in the intellectual revels at the *Mermaid Tavern*, or meeting Johnson foot to foot and dealing blow for mighty blow.[210] With Rabelais he rioted, and Don Quixote and Sancho were his "vera brithers." One seems to see him coming down from the twilight of fable, through the centuries, calling wherever there is good company, and welcome wherever he calls, for he brings no cult of the time or pedantry of the schools with him.

He has the freshness and directness of the child's vision. In a very real sense indeed he has never left the golden age—never come out into the light of common day, where the tone is grey and things have lost their imagery. He lives in a world of romance, peopled with giants and gay with the light laughter of fairies. The visible universe is full of magic and mystery. The trees are giants waving their arms in the air. The great globe is a vast caravanserai carrying us all on a magnificent adventure through space. He moves in an atmosphere of enchantment, and may stumble upon a romance at the next street corner. Beauty in distress may call to him from some hollow secrecy; some tyrannous giant may straddle like Apollyon across the path as he turns into Carmelite Street.[211] It is well that he has his swordstick with him, for one never knows what may turn up in this incredible world. Memory goeth not back to a time when a sword was not his constant companion. It used to be a wooden sword, with which went a wooden helmet glowing with the pigments of Apollo. Those were the days when the horn of Roland echoed again through Roncesvalles, and Lancelot pricked forth to the joust, and

> Ever the scaly shape of monstrous sin
> At last lay vanquished, fold on writhing fold.[212]

---

210. This is impressive, fun-loving company. In Nordic mythology, Skyrmir is the giant form that Utgartha-Loki, King of Utgard, assumed to deceive Thor. Elsewhere, Thor is challenged to drain a horn whose other end draws water from the sea itself. John Falstaff, who ate prodigiously at the *Boar's Head*, is a large man in three of Shakespeare's plays. During the Elizabethan era, the *Mermaid Tavern* is said to have hosted lively debates between William Shakespeare, Ben Johnson and others. Samuel Johnson (1709–1784) was a talented writer who authored the first proper English dictionary. François Rabelais (*c*. 1494–1553) was a brilliant and funny French writer. Don Quixote and Sancho are in characters in *Don Quixote*, a humorous tale of chivalry and knighthood by Miguel de Cervantes (1547–1616).

211. "The Valley of Humiliation" in John Bunyan's *Pilgrim's Progress* has Christian, fleeing the City of Destruction, encounter Apollyon, prince of that city, who blocks the "King's highway, the way of holiness." Then Apollyon straddled quite over the whole breadth of the way, and said, 'I am void of fear in this matter: prepare thyself to die; for I swear by my infernal den, that thou shalt go no further; here will I spill thy soul.'" After a half-day of fierce fighting, Christian drives Apollyon away with his sword.

212. *The Song of Roland* (Fr. *La Chanson de Roland*) is the oldest major literary work in French and the story of a brave French knight named Roland. Facing a far larger foe in the 778 A.D. Battle of Roncevalles Pass in northern Spain, Roland refuses to use his horn to summon aid until the battle is lost and those coming to his aid can do no more than avenge his death. The corresponding figure in English history is Sir Lancelot of King Alfred's Knights of the Round Table. The two lines of poetry may refer to Lancelot.

Ah, *le bon temps où j'étais—jeune.* But he still carries with him the glamour of the morning; his cheek still blanches at Charlemagne's "What a marching life is mine!"[213] I burst in on him one afternoon and found him engaged in a furious attack on a row of fat books, around which his sword flashed like the sword of Sergeant Troy around the figure of Bathsheba Everdene.[214] His eye blazed, his cheek paled, and beads of perspiration—no uncommon thing—stood out on his brow. It was a terrific combat, and it was fortunate that the foe were not, as in the leading case of Don Quixote, disguised in wine-skins, for that would have involved lamentable bloodshed. As it was, the books wore an aspect of insolent calm. One could almost see the contemptuous curl upon the lip, the haughty assurance of victory. I own it was hard to bear.

Adventure is an affair of the soul, not of circumstance. Thoreau, by his pond at Walden, or paddling up the Concord, had more adventures than Stanley had on the Congo, more adventures than Stanley could have.[215] That was why he

In an article in his 1912 *Miscellany of Men,* based on articles published earlier in the *Daily News,* Chesterton gave an unusual name to the noble spirit of Roland and Lancelot, calling it "The Thing," and linking it to Christianity and local self-government. (In 1929 he would publish *The Thing: Why I am a Catholic.)* A biblical illustration of "The Thing" is the descent of the Holy Spirit "like the blowing of a violent wind" at Pentecost in Acts 2. Chesterton used a mighty wind to introduce change in his 1912 novel, *Manalive.*

> The wind awoke last night with so noble a violence that it was like the war in heaven; and I thought for a moment that the Thing had broken free. For wind never seems like empty air. Wind always sounds full and physical, like the big body of something; and I fancied that the Thing itself was walking gigantic along the great roads between the forests of beech.

> Let me explain. The vitality and recurrent victory of Christendom have been due to the power of the Thing to break out from time to time from its enveloping words and symbols. Without this power all civilisations tend to perish under a load of language and ritual....

> Now, it never was supposed in any natural theory of self-government that the ordinary man in my neighbourhood need answer fantastic questions like these. He is a citizen of South Bucks, not an editor of *Notes and Queries.* He would be, I seriously believe, the best judge of whether farmsteads or factory chimneys should adorn his own sky-line, of whether stupid squires or clever usurers should govern his own village. But these are precisely the things which the oligarchs will not allow him to touch with his finger. Instead, they allow him an Imperial destiny and divine mission to alter, under their guidance, all the things that he knows nothing about. The name of self-government is noisy everywhere: the Thing is throttled.

> The wind sang and split the sky like thunder all the night through; in scraps of sleep it filled my dreams with the divine discordances of martyrdom and revolt; I heard the horn of Roland and the drums of Napoleon and all the tongues of terror with which the Thing has gone forth: the spirit of our race alive. But when I came down in the morning only a branch or two was broken off the tree in my garden; and none of the great country houses in the neighbourhood were blown down, as would have happened if the Thing had really been abroad.

213. As a military leader, Charlemagne (742/747–814) marched over much of Western and Central Europe, establishing his empire and making him the spiritual father of a common European culture. The Battle of Roncevalles Pass in which Roland died was his greatest defeat.

214. Thomas Hardy's *Far from the Maddening Crowd* (1874) has its heroine, Bathsheba Everdene, romantically involved with three very different men: Sergeant Troy (handsome but unreliable), Farmer Boldwood (honourable but middle-aged) and Gabriel Oak (worthy and patient).

215. Henry Thoreau's 1854 *Walden* describes a life lived simply next to Walden Pond in well-civilized Massachusetts. That hardly compares with the adventures of Henry Stanley (1841–1904), a journalist who searched Africa for David Livingstone (1813–1873) a Scottish medical missionary. But some argue that Stanley's well-financed, 200-porter expedition was hardly an adventure.

refused to come to Europe. He knew he could see as many wonders from his own backyard as he could though he sought for them in the islands of the farthest seas. "Why, who makes much of miracles?" says Whitman.

> As to me, I know of nothing else but miracles…
> To me every hour of the light and dark is a miracle.[216]

Miracles and adventures are the stuff of Mr. Chesterton's everyday life. He goes out on to the Sussex downs with his coloured chalks—in the cavernous mysteries of his pockets there is always a box of pastels, though "the mark of the mint," in his own phrase, may be unaccountably absent—and discovers he has no white chalk with which to complete his picture. His foot stumbles against a mound, and lo! he is standing on a mountain of chalk, and he shouts with joy at the miracle, for the world has never lost its freshness and wonder to him. It is as though he discovers it anew each day, and stands exultant at the revelation.

> It is a splendid pageant that passes unceasingly before him—
> New and yet old
> As the foundations of the heavens and earth.

Familiarity has not robbed it of its magic. He sees it as the child sees its first rainbow or the lightning flashing from the thunder-cloud. Most of us, before we reach maturity, find life stale and unprofitable—

> a twice-told tale
> Vexing the dull ears of a drowsy man.[217]

We are like the *blasé* policeman I met when I was waiting for a 'bus at Finchley one Bank Holiday. "A lot of people abroad to-day?" I said interrogatively. "Yes," he said, "thahsands." "Where do most of them go this way?" "Oh, to Barnet. Though what they see in Barnet I can't make out. I never see nothin' in Barnet." "Perhaps they like to see the green fields and hear the birds," I said. "Well, perhaps," he replied, in the tone of one who tolerated follies which he was too enlightened to share. "There'll be more at the Exhibition, I suppose?" I said, hoping to turn his mind to the contemplation of a more cheerful subject. "The Exhibition! Well, I was down there on duty the day it was opened, and I never see such a poor show. Oh yes, the gardens; they're all right, but you can see gardens anywhere." Despairingly I mentioned Hampstead as a merry place on Bank Holiday. "Well, I never see nothin' in 'Ampstead myself. I dunno what the people go for. And there's the Garden City there, and crowds and crowds a-going to look at it. Well, what is there in it? That's what I asts. What-is-there-in-it? I never see nothin' in it."

---

216. Gardiner quotes lines from the opening and close of Walt Whitman's "Miracles" in *Leaves of Grass*.

217. From Shakespeare's *King John*, Act III, Scene 4: "There's nothing in this word can make me joy:/ Life's as tedious as a twice-told tale/ Vexing the dull ear of a drowsy man;/ And bitter shame hath spoil'd the sweet world's taste,/ That it yields nought but shame and bitterness."

The world of culture shares the policeman's physical ennui in a spiritual sense. It sees "nothing in it." We succeed in deadening the fresh intensity of the impression, and burying the miracle under the dust of the common day—veiling it under names and formulas. "This green, flowery, rock-built earth, the trees, the mountains, rivers, many-sounding seas;—that great deep sea of azure that swims overhead; the winds sweeping through it; the black cloud fashioning itself together, now pouring out fire, now hail and rain; what *is* it? Ay, what? At bottom, we do not yet know; we can never know at all. It is not by our superior insight that we escape the difficulty; it is by our superior levity, our inattention, our *want* of insight. It is by not thinking that we cease to wonder at it.... This world, after all our science and sciences, is still a miracle; wonderful, inscrutable, magical and more, to whomsoever will *think* of it." It is this elemental faculty of wonder, of which Carlyle speaks, that distinguishes Mr. Chesterton from his contemporaries, and gives him kinship at once with the seers and the children.[218] He is anathema to the erudite and the exact; but he sees life in the large, with the eyes of the first man on the day of creation. As he says, in inscribing a book of Caldecott's pictures[219] to a little friend of mine—

This is the sort of book we like
(For you and I are very small),
With pictures stuck in anyhow,
And hardly any words at all.

. . .

You will not understand a word
Of all the words, including mine;
Never you trouble; you can see,
And all directness is divine—

Stand up and keep your childishness:
Read all the pedants' screeds and strictures;
But don't believe in anything
That can't be told in coloured pictures.

Life to him is a book of coloured pictures that he sees without external comment or exegesis. He sees it, as it were, at first hand, and shouts out his vision at the top of his voice. Hence the audacity that is so trying to the formalist who is governed by custom and authority. Hence the rain of paradoxes that he showers

218. In Chapter 10 of his *Sartor Resartus,* Thomas Caryle wrote: "The man who cannot wonder, who does not habitually wonder (and worship), were he President of innumerable Royal Societies, and carried the whole *Mecanique Celeste* and *Hegel's Philosophy,* and the epitome of all Laboratories and Observatories with their results, in his single head,—is but a Pair of Spectacles behind which there is no Eye. Let those who have Eyes look through him, then he may be useful."
219. Randolph Caldecott (1846–1886) was a Victorian era story illustrator much loved by children and the artist for whom the Caldecott Medal is named.

down. It is often suggested that these paradoxes are a conscious trick to attract attention—that Mr. Chesterton stands on his head, as it were, to gather a crowd. I can conceive him standing on his head in Fleet Street in sheer joy at the sight of St Paul's, but not in vanity, or with a view to a collection. The truth is that his paradox is his own comment on the coloured picture.

There are some men who hoard life as a miser hoards his gold—map it out with frugal care and vast prescience, spend to-day in taking thought for to-morrow. Mr. Chesterton spends life like a prodigal. Economy has no place in his spacious vocabulary. "Economy," he might say, with Anthony Hope's Mr. Carter, "is going without something you do want in case you should some day want something which you probably won't want."[220] Mr. Chesterton lives the unconsidered, untrammelled life. He simply rambles along without a thought of where he is going. If he likes the look of a road he turns down it, careless of where it may lead to. "He is announced to lecture at Bradford to-night," said a speaker, explaining his absence from a dinner. "Probably he will turn up at Edinburgh." **He will wear no harness, learn no lessons, observe no rules. He is himself, Chesterton—not consciously or rebelliously, but unconsciously, like a natural element.** St Paul's School never had a more brilliant nor a less sedulous scholar. He did not win prizes, but he read more books, drew more pictures, wrote more poetry than any boy that ever played at going to school. His house was littered with books, filled with verses and grotesque drawings. All attempts to break him into routine failed. He tried the Slade School, and once even sat on a stool in an office. Think of it! G.K.C. in front of a ledger, adding up figures with romantic results—figures that turned into knights in armour, broke into song, and, added together, produced paradoxes unknown to arithmetic! He saw the absurdity of it all. "A man must follow his vocation," he said with Falstaff, and his vocation is to have none.

And so he rambles along, engaged in an endless disputation, punctuated with gusts of Rabelaisian laughter, and leaving behind a litter of fragments. You may track him by the blotting-pads he decorates with his riotous fancies, and may come up with him in the midst of a group of children, for whom he is drawing hilarious pictures, or to whom he is revealing the wonders of his toy theatre, the chief child of his fancy and invention, or whom he is instructing in the darkly

---

220. Anthony Hope (1863–1933) was a London novelist best known for his *Prisoner of Zenda* (1894). A short story called "An Uncounted Hour" his *Dolly Dialogues* (1894) opens this way:

"Do you know," pursued Lady Mickleham, "that the Dowager says I'm extravagant. She thinks dogs ought not to be fed on *pate de foie gras*." "Your extravagance," I observed, "is probably due to your having been brought up on a moderate income. I have felt the effect myself." "Of course," said Dolly, "we are hit by the agricultural depression." "The Carters also," I murmured, "are landed gentry." "After all, I don't see much point in economy, do you, Mr. Carter?" "Economy," I remarked, putting my hands in my pockets, "is going without something you do want in case you should, some day, want something which you probably won't want." "Isn't that clever?" asked Dolly in an apprehensive tone. "Oh, dear, no," I answered reassuringly. "Anybody can do that—if they care to try, you know."

mysterious game of "Guyping," which will fill the day with laughter. "Well," said the aunt to the little boy who had been to tea with Mr. Chesterton,—"well, Frank, I suppose you have had a very instructive afternoon?" "I don't know what that means," said Frank, "but, oh!" with enthusiasm, "you should see Mr. Chesterton catch buns with his mouth." **If you cannot find him, and Fleet Street looks lonely and forsaken, then be sure he has been spirited away to some solitary place by his wife, the keeper of his business conscience, to finish a book for which some publisher is angrily clamouring. For "No clamour, no book," is his maxim.**

Mr. Chesterton's natural foil in these days is Mr. Bernard Shaw. Mr. Shaw is the type of revolt. The flesh we eat, the wine we drink, the clothes we wear, the laws we obey, the religion we affect—all are an abomination to him. He would raze the whole fabric to the ground, and build all anew upon an ordered and symmetrical plan. Mr. Chesterton has none of this impatience with the external garment of society. He enjoys disorder and loves the haphazard. With Rossetti he might say, "What is it to me whether the earth goes round the sun or the sun round the earth?"[221] It is not the human intellect that interests him, but the human heart and the great comedy of life. He opposes ancient sympathies to modern antipathies. It follows that Mr. Shaw's weapon is wit, sharp-edged as the east wind, and that Mr. Chesterton's weapon is humour that buffets you like a gale from the west.

No man was ever more careless of his reputation. He is indifferent whether from his abundant mine he shovels out diamonds or dirt. You may take it or leave it, as you like. He cares not, and bears no malice. It is all a blithe improvisation, done in sheer ebullience of spirit and having no relation to conscious literature. He is like a child shouting with glee at the sight of the flowers and the sunshine, and chalking on every vacant hoarding he passes with a jolly rapture of invention and no thought beyond.

But there is one thing, and one only, about which he is serious, and that is his own seriousness. You may laugh with him and at him and about him. When, at a certain dinner, one of the speakers said that his chivalry was so splendid that he had been known to rise in a tramcar and "offer his seat to three ladies," it was his laugh that sounded high above all the rest. But if you would wound him, do not laugh at his specific gravity: doubt his spiritual gravity. Doubt his passion for justice and liberty and patriotism—most of all, his patriotism. **For he is, above all, the lover of Little England and the foe of the Imperialist, whose love of country is "not what a mystic means by the love of God, but what a child might mean by the love of jam."** "My country, right or wrong!" he cries. "Why, it is a thing no patriot could say. It is like saying, 'My mother, drunk or sober.' No doubt, if a decent man's mother took to drink, he would share her

221. This is probably Dante Gabriel Rossetti (1828–1882), a gifted poet and artist.

troubles to the last; but to talk as if he would be in a state of gay indifference as to whether his mother took to drink or not is certainly not the language of men who know the great mystery.... We fall back upon gross and frivolous things for our patriotism.... Our schoolboys are left to live and die in the infantile type of patriotism which they learnt from a box of tin soldiers.... We have made our public schools the strongest wall against a whisper of the honour of England.... What have we done and where have we wandered, we that have produced sages who could have spoken with Socrates, and poets who could walk with Dante, that we should talk as if we had never done anything more intelligent than found colonies and kick niggers? We are the children of light, and it is we that sit in darkness. If we are judged, it will not be for the merely intellectual transgression of failing to appreciate other nations, but for the supreme spiritual transgression of failing to appreciate ourselves."[222]

But sincere though he is, he loves the argument for its own sake. He is indifferent to the text. You may tap any subject you like: he will find it a theme on which to hang all the mystery of time and eternity. For the ordinary material cares of life he has no taste, almost no consciousness. He never knows the time of a train, has only a hazy notion of where he will dine, and the doings of to-morrow are as profound a mystery as the contents of his pocket. He dwells outside these things in the realm of ideas. Johnson said that when he and Savage walked one night round St James' Square for want of a lodging, they were not at all depressed by their situation, but, in high spirits and brimful of patriotism, traversed the square for several hours, inveighed against the minister, and "resolved that they would *stand by their country*."[223] That is Mr. Chesterton's way. But he would not walk round St James' Square. He would, in Johnson's circumstances, ride round and round in a cab—even if he had to borrow the fare off the cabman. He is free from the tyranny of things. Though he lived in a tub he would be rich beyond the dreams of avarice, for he would still have the universe for his intellectual inheritance.

I sometimes think that one moonlight night, when he is tired of Fleet Street, he will scale the walls of the Tower and clothe himself in a suit of giant mail, with shield and sword to match. He will come forth with vizor up and mount the battle-steed that champs its bit outside. And the clatter of his hoofs will ring through the quiet of the city night as he thunders through St Paul's Churchyard and down Ludgate Hill and out on to the Great North Road. And then once more will be heard the cry of "St George for Merry England!" and there will be the clash of swords in the greenwood and brave deeds done on the King's highway.

222. These quotes are almost identical to that in "A Defense of Patriotism" at the end of Chesterton's 1901 *The Defendant*, but Gardiner may be quoting from the original article in *The Speaker*.
223. Quoted from James Boswell's 1791 classic biography, *Boswell's Life of Johnson*.

INDEX

A

Adam 9
Addington, Henry 25
Agnoticism 71
Alcohol. See Drinking
Alighieri, Dante 32
"Alliance, An" 37
Anglo-Boer War. See Boer War
Animal rights 139
Archer, William 117
Aristophanes 130
Arnold, Matthew 28
Art 25, 115; Gilbert on art school 33; Gilbert studies 33; loathing for decadent 33
Asquith, Herbert H. 25
Atheism 116
"Ave Maria" 32
Aylesford Review, The 9

B

Balfour, Arthur J. 21, 25
"Ballad Epic of Alfred" 120
"Ballad of God-Makers, The" 41
Ballad of the White Horse, The (1911) 120
Battersea 139, 152, 160
Bax, E. Belfort 29
Bedford Chapel 30
Beecham, Sir Thomas 18
Beer. See Drinking
Beerbohm, Max 47
Belgium 92, 126
Bell, Hugh 145
Belloc, Hilaire 7, 64, 126, 129, 135, 136, 143, 148, 150, 162; Cecil's courage 23; Emmanuel Burden (1904) 33; H. G. Wells on 141; influence on Cecil 12; Jews 12; Parkes, Bessie Rayner (mother) 152; Party System, The 15, 22; Shaw on 152
Blasphemy 117
Blatchford, Robert 63, 68, 75
Blondin Donkey 154
Boar's Head 168
Bodley Head G. K. Chesterton, The 8
Boer War 42, 46, 49, 65, 68
Bolingbroke, Henry St John 16, 94, 104
Bookman, The 35

Boythorn, Lawrence 153
Braddon, Elizabeth 112
Bradlaugh, Charles 164
Brogan, Dennis 15
Brontë, Charlotte 56, 57
Brooke, Rev. Stopford A. 30
Browning, Elizabeth Barrett 56
Browning, Robert 35, 52
Bryon, Lord 7, 56
Bunyan, John 168
Burke, Edmund 55, 58
Burne-Jones, Edward C. 58, 157

C

Caine, Hall 47
Caldecott, Randolph 171
Calverley, Charles S. 123
Campbell, Rev. R. J. 66, 68, 86
Capitalism 99
Carlyle, Thomas 34, 56, 66, 106, 171
Catholicism 50, 64, 91, 154, 164
Cecil Chesterton (1975 biography) 11, 18
Cecil, Lord Robert 15
Cervantes, Miguel de 168
Chamberlain, Joseph 50, 123
Charlemagne 169
Charles Dickens (1906) 55, 56, 59, 117, 126, 130
Chartist 93
Checkley, Edward 158
Chesterbelloc 154, 163
Chesterton, Cecil; as a writer 14; becomes Catholic 12, 21; Belloc's influence 12; biography of 6, 18; birth and childhood 19; courage of 23; death from nephritis 13; Distributivism 12; Fabian membership 20, 135; Fabian Society 12; Gladstonian Ghosts 14; History of the United States, A (1919) 15; Israel a Nation 17; Jews 12; joins Church of England 12; Macaulay admired 15; Marconi Scandal 18, 22; Meyer, Rev. F. B. 16; Morrison, Steinie defended 17; mother 14; Party and People 14; Party System, The 15, 22; Perils of Peace, The (1916) 15; Prussian Hath Said in his Heart, The (1914) 15; role of eloquence 20; role of Thomas Huxley in conversion

17; socialism as slavery 21; solution to *The Mystery of Edwin Drood* 17; *Story of Nell Gwyn, The* 15; Syme, John defended 17; Unitarian upbringing 12; World War I 13

Chesterton, Edward (father) 27, 29

Chesterton, Edward (great-grandfather) 27

Chesterton, Francis Blogg (Gilbert's wife) 64

Chesterton, G. K.; 1914 illness *11*; 1923 becomes Catholic 12; absent-minded 128; anti-Imperialism of 25, 42; appeal to ordinary people 46, 94, 96, 121; arguments with Cecil 19; art for art's sake 25, 115; artistic limitations 123; becomes well-known 39; biography of Cecil 6; birth 29; Catholicism 64; childhood 28; Christianity 64, 69, 73, 87, 116, 122; Conservatism 37; devil, discovery of 66; didactic 115; digressions 56; Distributivist after Cecil 12; early poetry 32; fame, lack of interest 128; family politics liberal 29; family theology undogmatic 29; fascination with London 126; humour 116; Jewish question 12; joins Church of England 12; journalism entered 35; journalist personality 127; liberalism 37; life as coloured pictures 171; literary skills as weapons 26; love of cities with different cultures 126; marriage 64; Nationalism 43; no clamour, no book 173; patriotism 43, 64; poetry 120, 122; progressivism rejected 37, 65, 95; propagandist & preacher 25; relation to mother 14; romantic idealist 106; romanticism 125; romantic taste 35; sacrificed academic support 7; scientific temper, lack of 62; Scottish roots 27; story-teller not novelist 107; St Paul's School 30; studies art 33; Swiss roots 27; Tory Socialism 36; Unitarian upbringing 12; war, not adverse to 43; Whitman's influence 36; worst essay 57; writing style 128

Chesterton, Marie Louise (mother) 14, 29, 152

Chesterton, Mrs. Cecil 14

Chesterton on War 92

Christian Herald 50

Christianity 64, 69, 73, 85, 87, 116, 122, 143, 164

Christmas poem 120, 122

Clarion, The 37, 63, 68, 75

Club of Queer Trades, The (1905) 7, 80, 109

Collectivism 137. *See* Socialism

Commonwealth, The 80, 122

Corelli, Marie 55

Cosmopolitanism 44

Crimes of England, The (1915) 15

D

Daily Chronicle 49

Daily News 33, 49, 51, 53, 55, 56, 82, 94, 116, 119, 120, 128, 167

Dante Alighieri 174

Danton, Georges 19, 32, 127

Darwin, Charles 65, 123

Davidson, John 39

Debater, The 32

"Defence of Patriotism, A" 44, 174

"Defence of Penny Dreadfuls" 47, 118

"Defence of Rash Vows" 118

Defendant, The (1901) 36, 41, 44, 47, 48, 63, 66, 116, 120, 122, 130, 174

Democracy 93, 94, 96, 135, 140, 154, 160

Determinism 70, 80

De Wet, Rudolf 84, 116

"Diabolist, The" 33

Dickens, Charles 35, 60, 61, 81, 95, 116, 123, 147

Dickinson, Lowes 85

Didactic 115

Dinosaur 149

Distributism 12, 14, 21; GKC joins 12

Douglas, James 39

Drinking 50, 82, 84, 97, 102, 110, 129, 141, 142, 147, 149, 157, 163, 165, 168, 173

Dumas, Alexandre 109

"Dunciad" 55

E

"Earth's Shame, The" 36, 40

Eastern philosophy 70

"Ecclesiastes" 36, 40

Elibank, Baron 145

Emmanuel Burden (1904) 7, 33

England a Nation (1904) 100

Eugenics 140

Eustace Miles (restaurant) 167

Everdene, Bathsheba 169

Everlasting Man, The (1925) 11

Evil 34, 66, 71

Evolution 65, 66, 97

Eye-Witness, The 12, 22

F

Fabianism 36, 44, 144
Falstaff 153, 159, 168, 172
Father Brown stories 8
Feminism 103
Fleet Street 14, 53, 125, 127, 167, 172, 173, 174
Forster, E. M. 167
Fortnightly Review 102
Fox, Charles 19, 25, 158
France 45, 71, 92, 126, 136, 138, 150, 152
Francis of Assisi 64
Free Will 71, 80
French Revolution 56, 92, 93, 138, 154, 158

G

Gardiner, A. G.; describes GKC 6, 167; *Prophets, Priests and Kings* 6, 167
George, Henry 145
George, Lloyd 12
Germany 13, 101, 136
G. F. Watts 58
Gilbert, William 113, 123
G. K.'s Weekly 6
Gladstone, Herbert 36
Gladstonian Ghosts 14
Graham, Cunninghame 129
Grant, Basil 7
Grindea, Miron 9
Guyping (game) 173

H

Hall of Science 164
Heine, Heinrich 130
Henley, William E. 43
Heretics 41, 49, 50, 66, 76, 81, 86, 115, 116, 117, 122, 130
History of the United States, A (1919) 15
Home Rule 36
Hope, Anthony 172
Horace 130
Hugo, Victor 117
Humility 86
Humour 116
Huxley, Thomas H. 67
Hyndman, Henry M. 29

I

Ibsen, Henrik 79, 106, 117, 155

Idea of a Patriot King, The (1738) 16
Illustrated London News 103, 127, 128
Imperialism 25, 42, 44, 95, 173
Independent Review 95
Individualism 79, 139
Intellectuals 28
Ireland 36, 43, 91, 150
Isaacs, Godfrey 13, 22
Isaacs, Sir Rufus 12
Islam 70
Italy 56, 126

J

Jack the Giantkiller 156
Jacobins 95
Jacobites 91, 95
JDC. *See* Junior Debating Club
Jefferson, Thomas 23
Jews 12, 28, 121, 145, 156
Job introduction to 83
John Bull 153
Johnson, Samuel 131, 168
Jonson, Ben 156
Junior Debating Club (JDC) 31, 36

K

Kavanagh, P. J. 8
Khayyám, Omar 130
"King's Cross Station" 75, 101
Kipling, Rudyard 25, 42, 49, 76, 78, 130

L

"Lamp-post, The" 101
Landlordism 98, 139, 161
La Vendée 155
L. C. C.. *See* London County Council
Leaves of Grass 35, 40
Le Queux, William 55
Liberalism 37, 91, 92, 138, 144, 150
Light, value of 77
Like Black Swans 9
Little England 173
London County Council 144

M

Macaulay, Lord Thomas 15, 35, 54, 65, 93, 95, 131
Macbeth 156
Macdonald, Edward 14
Mackey, Aidan 6, 15
Magog 153

Manchester School *139*
Man over nature *101*
Man Who Was Thursday, The (1907) *31, 36, 80, 86, 87, 97, 101, 103, 106, 110, 112, 126*
Marconi Scandal (1911–1913) *12, 18, 22*
Marson, Rev. Charles *69*
Martin Chuzzlewit 61
Marx, Karl *145*
Massie, Alan *8*
Massingham, Henry W. *49*
Mastermind, Charles *96*
Maupassant, Guy de *50*
McCabe, Joseph *16, 82, 130*
McNabb, Fr. Vincent *18*
Meredith, George *39, 54, 112*
Mermaid Tavern *156, 168*
Meyer, Rev. F. B. *16*
Michael Angelo *157*
Middle Ages *77, 96*
Milton, John *68*
Miracle *155, 163, 164, 170*
Modernity *76, 83*
Moore, George *47, 82*
Morley, John *52*
Morrison, Steinie *17*
Morris, William *56, 157*
Murray, Lord *13*
My Dear Time's Waste 9
Mystery of Edwin Drood, The 17
Mysticism *70*

N

Napoleon *56, 65, 84, 116, 121*
Napoleon of Notting Hill, The (1904) *26, 66, 80, 92, 94, 97, 105, 106, 110, 112, 118, 124, 126, 130*
Nation 87
Nationalism *43, 91*
Nature worship *71*
"Negative Spirit, The" *81*
Neolith, The 121, 154
New Age, The 6, 12, 13, 96, 102, 135, 161
New Jerusalem, The (1920) *12*
Newman, John H. *21, 55*
News from No-where 157
New Theology *30, 68, 86*
New Witness, The 12, 22
No clamour, no book *173*
Novels as mysteries *105*

O

O'Donnel, Frank Hugh *12*
Orange, A. R. *12*
Original Sin *73, 81, 87*
Orthodoxy (1908) *73, 86*
Oxford Fabian Society *36*
Oxford University *155, 162*

P

Paganism *85*
Pantheism *71*
Paradox *26, 48, 70, 138*
Parliament *94*
Party and People (1910) *14*
Party System (1911) *15*
Patriotic Idea, The 44, 100
Patriotism *43, 64, 79, 173*
Patriot's Club *44*
Penny dreadfuls *47, 72, 109*
People of England *8, 133, 138, 139*
Perils of Peace, The (1916) *15*
Picture of Tuesday, A 35
Plesiosaurus *149*
Poetry *120, 122*
Pope, Alexander *55, 56, 117*
Pound, Ezra *8*
Priestley, Joseph *152*
Progress *37, 65, 95, 98, 99*
Prohibition. *See* Drinking
Propagandist impulse. *See* Pugnacity
Property *14, 16, 21, 22, 48, 93, 98, 99, 137, 139, 142, 145, 150, 155, 161, 165*
Prophets, Priests and Kings 6
Prussian Hath Said in his Heart, The (1914) *15*
Pugnacity *46, 105, 113, 118, 124, 128*

Q

Quarto, The 35
Quixote, Don *168*

R

Rabelais, François *127, 130, 152, 168, 172*
Relativism *83*
Resurrection *156*
Return of Don Quixote, The (1927) *11*
Revolution *30, 45, 56, 57, 63, 79, 84, 92, 94, 96, 135, 138, 140, 145*
Robert Browning (1903) *7, 53, 56, 59, 61*
Rockefeller, John D. *145*

Roland *168*
Romantic Idealist *106*
Romanticism *125*
Rossetti, Dante Gabriel *173*
Rousseau, Jean-Jacque *23*
Ruskin, John *100, 118*
Rutherford, Mark *67*

S

Samuel, Herbert *13*
Santayana, George *61*
Science *75, 84*
Scott, Sir Walter *35, 56, 57, 109*
"Secret People, The" *121, 133*
Sewell, Brocard *6, 9, 11*
Sewell, Michael. *See* Sewell, Brocard
Shakespeare, William *35, 81, 156, 170*
Shaw, Bernard *6, 18, 29, 44, 49, 76, 79, 82,
    85, 102, 125, 128, 130, 135, 148, 153, 161,
    173*
Shelley, Percy B. *57, 65, 116*
Skrymir *168*
Slade School *155, 172*
Socialism *37, 79, 94, 97, 135, 149, 150, 152,
    157, 161, 165*; attack on middle class *28*;
    H. G. Wells on *142*
Socialistic Idealism *136*
Socrates *174*
"Song of Labour, A" *35*
Song of Roland, The 168
South African War. *See* Boer War
South Salford *160*
*Speaker, The 35, 41, 46, 48, 50, 53, 56, 64,
    66, 174*
Spenser, Herbert *159*
Spiritual conflict *105*
Star 39
Stevenson, Robert Louis *42, 46, 56, 109,
    125, 130*
"St. Francis Xavier" (poem) *31*
St. Januarius *155, 165*
Story of Nell Gwyn, The (1911) *15*
St. Paul's School *30*
Sullivan, Arthur *113*
Swineburne, Algernon C. *32, 35, 116*
Syme, John *17*

T

Technology *101*
Teetotalism *157, 165*

Tennyson, Alfred Lord *35, 54, 65, 68*
Theatre, toy *126*
Thoreau, Henry *169*
Titterton, W. R. *14*
Tolstoy, Leo *43, 50, 56, 57*
Tory *91, 95, 96, 101, 104, 138, 140*
Tribune 123
Trinity, tangled *71*
Twelve Types (1902) *50, 56, 57, 64, 66, 117*

U

Utopia *136, 137, 145, 156, 165*

V

Vegetarianism *157*
Victorian Era *27, 35, 66, 148, 149, 160, 171*
Vitality. *See* Pugnacity

W

Walker, F. W. *31*
Walkley, Arthur *153*
Wars of the Roses *121*
Watts, George F. *58, 160*
Webb, Sidney *145, 160*
Wells, H. G. *6, 29, 83, 94, 102, 135, 141, 147,
    152, 156, 161*
White, William Hale *67*
Whitman, Walt *35, 40, 46, 81, 170*
Who's Who 152, 153, 162, 163
Wilde, Oscar *48*
Wild, Ernest *13*
*Wild Knight and Other Poems, The 36, 39, 50,
    63, 66, 75, 101, 112, 120*
Wilson, Colin *9*
"World Lover" *36*

Y

Yeats, W. B. *58*